LIBERTY ROAD

Liberty Road

*Black Middle-Class Suburbs and the Battle
Between Civil Rights and Neoliberalism*

Gregory Smithsimon

NEW YORK UNIVERSITY PRESS
New York

NEW YORK UNIVERSITY PRESS
New York
www.nyupress.org

References to Internet websites (URLs) were accurate at the time of writing. Neither the author nor New York University Press is responsible for URLs that may have expired or changed since the manuscript was prepared.

Library of Congress Cataloging-in-Publication Data
Names: Smithsimon, Gregory, author.
Title: Liberty road : Black middle-class suburbs and the battle between civil rights and neoliberalism / Gregory Smithsimon.
Description: New York : New York University Prerss, [2021] | Includes bibliographical references and index.
Identifiers: LCCN 2021013304 | ISBN 9781479845118 (hardback) | ISBN 9781479861491 (paperback) | ISBN 9781479831975 (ebook) | ISBN 9781479860692 (ebook other)
Subjects: LCSH: African Americans—Maryland—Randallstown. | African American neighborhoods—Maryland—Randallstown. | Discrimination in housing—Maryland—Randallstown. | Randallstown (Md.)—Social conditions. | Randallstown (Md.)—Race relations.
Classification: LCC HN80.R36 S65 2021 | DDC 305.896/073075271—dc23
LC record available at https://lccn.loc.gov/2021013304

New York University Press books are printed on acid-free paper, and their binding materials are chosen for strength and durability. We strive to use environmentally responsible suppliers and materials to the greatest extent possible in publishing our books.

Manufactured in the United States of America

10 9 8 7 6 5 4 3 2 1

Also available as an ebook

CONTENTS

Introduction

Arriving on Liberty Road

The day lawyer George McMechen moved into a stately brick rowhouse on McCulloh Street, stones began flying through the windows. Someone pitched a brick through the rooftop skylight that smashed down through the building to the ground floor.[1]

McMechen was a rising African American attorney in Baltimore. His landlord, W. Ashbie Hawkins, was also his law partner. It was May 1911. The violence directed at the home of McMechen, his wife Ana, and their children expressed white neighbors' rage that McMechen had crossed Eutaw Street, which whites had hoped to maintain as an impenetrable barrier to Black residents. In 1910 Baltimore was home to about eighty thousand African Americans, the second largest Black population in the country after New Orleans.[2]

McMechen's move to McCulloh Street triggered more than neighborhood violence. White residents and civic leaders mobilized and instituted a form of segregation more far-reaching than anything introduced since the Civil War. Under a hastily drawn city ordinance, every single block in the city would be identified as majority white or Black.[3] No Blacks could move into white blocks, nor whites into Black blocks. Anyone who did would be subject to criminal charges. Baltimore's "liberal" mayor claimed the legislation was in everyone's best interests. Garrett Power, a legal historian who has studied the segregation legislation, has aptly called the new ordinance "Apartheid Baltimore Style."[4] The legislation was soon adopted by cities including Richmond, Norfolk, and Roanoke, Virginia; Asheville, North Carolina; Atlanta; Birmingham; St. Louis; and Louisville.

Twenty people were charged with violating segregation.[5] Even to contemporaries, unpacking the implications of the legislation quickly led to the kinds of absurd situations inherent in segregation laws. A Black Methodist minister wrote to the mayor because he lived in a church

George W. McMechen, a Negro Lawyer, Whose Occupancy of the House 1,834 McCulloh Street, Caused the Segregation Ordinance.

Figure 0.1. When George W. McMechen crossed the color line in 1910, Baltimore sought to impose block-by-block segregation citywide.
Source: *New York Times*, December 25, 1910.

parsonage on an otherwise white block. When he eventually moved to another church on the orders of his bishop, was it then illegal for the church to assign another Black minister to live in the parsonage next to the church? (The major's representative curtly responded that Black ministers should use their skills living among their own kind.) On a block that had a one-person white majority, a family moved out to have their house renovated. When they left they created a Black-majority block and so could not legally move back into their own home.

More pressing than the absurdities of the legislation were the serious hardships it was sure to impose on Black residents. The Black population was growing rapidly and the neighborhoods in which African American residents were restricted were already overcrowded, but the law provided no way for the community to grow geographically, ensuring that it would become only more and more densely packed. Meanwhile, the mayor of Baltimore was already pursuing some of the earliest slum clearance policies (having copied seizure laws he learned about while visiting London). When dilapidated buildings in Black neighborhoods were razed, overcrowding in the remaining Black-designated blocks grew only more severe.

The mayor of Baltimore justified the 1911 apartheid legislation by arguing that "our problem here in Baltimore is different than any other city in the country" because the city had neither the degree of terror with which segregation was enforced in the Deep South nor the overwhelmingly white population of northern cities. Contrary to the mayor's claim, Baltimore's location actually made it more *like* every city in the country. It had both the large Black population and the entrenched white culture of racial segregation that would characterize desegregation battles for the next century. The city captures northern and southern threads of the country's racial history, lying south of the Mason-Dixon Line but outside the Confederacy. Frederick Douglass had been enslaved in Baltimore, and the city was later the birthplace of NAACP lawyer and Supreme Court justice Thurgood Marshall and sociologist of the Black middle class E. Franklin Frazier. For more than a century, Baltimore has been central to struggles for liberty and desegregation.

McMechen and Hawkins could not have doubted that moving to McCulloh Street transgressed a racial boundary staunchly defended by whites. However Hawkins was not simply a landlord but a social justice lawyer.[6] Hawkins "had been prominent in every major campaign on behalf of racial justice in Baltimore since the 1890s" and was a founding member of the Baltimore chapter of the NAACP.[7] Hawkins took on the appeals of several clients who had been convicted of violating the segregation ordinance. He successfully brought court challenges against the constitutionality of three successive versions of Baltimore's apartheid legislation.[8] Challenging these residential segregation ordinances in Baltimore energized the newly formed NAACP, which covered the

Baltimore segregation ordinance in the first issue of its publication *The Crisis*.[9] (Baltimore's NAACP branch was the second to be formed in the nation, the year after McMechen moved to McCulloh Street.) By 1916 Hawkins was the head of the Baltimore branch of the NAACP.[10] He later served as the chapter's legal counsel.[11]

For McMechen overturning the law was a partial victory. The violence had forced his family out of the McCulloh Street house, and he was able to move back only five years later. By that time the wall of segregation had been reconstructed: white Baltimoreans had developed a series of unofficial, backroom agreements to exclude Blacks from white areas, and McCulloh Street was quickly resegregated as an all-Black block. Hawkins and McMechen's successes were real but modest, hampered by the strength of official government opposition and organized obstruction by white citizens.

From City to Suburb

McMechen's move was part of a century-long process in which African Americans on the west side of Baltimore moved from the center of the city outward to the northwest. Inheritors of Hawkins and McMechen's legacy continued to push African American access along an arterial road that begins as Liberty Heights Avenue and, as it nears the suburban boundary, becomes Liberty Road. Block by block, much as Hawkins and McMechen had, Black Baltimoreans gained access to housing all the way to the city line in Northwest Baltimore. This book picks up the epic story of desegregation as it crosses that boundary and enters the suburbs in the late twentieth and twenty-first centuries. As in Hawkins and McMechen's era, the landscape of contemporary African American suburbs has been shaped by a contest between people seeking to open access to housing—who continue to be driven by simultaneously practical and principled reasons—and efforts to reverse those gains. In recent decades that opposition has been part of a conservative, neoliberal shift that threatens not just the homes but the larger economic and social gains Black families have made in their move out to the suburbs.

Liberty Road understands contemporary African American suburbs as the conflict between two opposing meanings of liberty—as civil rights progress or conservative neoliberal retrenchment. That conflict is most evident in twenty-first-century, middle-class, African American suburbs like Liberty Road, where civil rights and gains have been most successfully secured but where they exist in unresolved contradiction with the conservatism of the neoliberal age. The fundamental opposition of these two forces shapes the future of Liberty Road, as well as the norms, goals, and politics of the people who live there.

Although it has borne the name since it was a nineteenth-century turnpike, Liberty Road has the ring of a symbolic pseudonym an ethnographer might choose to represent the journey of the African American community toward prosperity, beginning in the inner-city Black ghetto and delivering some members to a promised land of safe neighborhoods, high-quality housing, good incomes, and successful, hardworking families. That said, if the end of Liberty is the end point of the civil rights movement thus far, then Liberty Road is just as much a cause for alarm and dismay. While whites didn't leave en masse as they had in the past, they did stop buying houses in the area. Newly arrived parents became dissatisfied with some of the area schools, corporations invested more money in nearby white neighborhoods, African Americans remained the most frequent victims of home mortgage manipulations, and the stress of trying to hold together a middle-class life amid twenty-first-century uncertainty took its toll on residents' health. Despite new half-million-dollar homes with cathedral ceilings and new cars in the driveways, many of the central demands of the civil rights movement remained blatantly unfulfilled. Liberty Road poses one of the persistent questions for African Americans regarding activism and progress: what has been gained in accumulating moderate, pragmatic, measured gains without radical, more fundamental changes?

Adding another layer to the metaphor, "liberty" has a second, colder meaning, as a rallying cry embraced by conservatives and neoliberals. In that context, liberty is not a collective accomplishment but a denial of responsibility for the larger good: the libertarian freedom from government regulations, affirmative action, or fair housing rules. In that context, liberty is the freedom to disregard one's neighbor and the liberty of capital to pursue profits in hyperactive, unregulated ways. This deceptive formulation of liberty has been especially damaging to African Americans through its economic policies that decimated unions, outsourced stable jobs, unraveled the social safety net, defunded government programs, and rolled back affirmative action programs. But the ideological power of neoliberalism is just as significant. As political scientist Michael C. Dawson has argued, African American identity is based on perceived common group interest that crosses individual and class interests; neoliberalism denies any basis to such commonality.[12] This conservative agenda (which has counterintuitively been given the name neoliberalism) has been framed by critics as a class war. *Liberty Road* makes clear that neoliberalism was just as much a racial reaction. For several decades, the neoliberal definition of liberty has been ascendant, its impact focused on African American communities like Liberty Road.

To unravel the meaning of suburban liberty and its limitations, this book studies the growth of African American suburbs outside Baltimore. Sixty years after Hawkins and McMechen crossed Eutaw Street, it was not clear how much might have changed in Baltimore and its suburbs. African Americans had moved into more city neighborhoods but remained segregated from whites. As late as 1970, the barrier keeping Black Baltimore City from white Baltimore County, which surrounded it, seemed impenetrable. Louis Diggs, a longtime county resident who moved one block outside of a tiny, hundred-year-old rural African American enclave, had his car windows shot out and a cross burned on his church's lawn. Herbert Lindsey, newly arrived to teach at a historically Black college, couldn't find any landlord willing to rent him an apartment in the county. He was told he'd have to wait "a long time" and should look in another county. The reverend and state delegate Emmett Burns, who knew the racism of the Deep South firsthand from growing up in Mississippi when Medgar Evers and Emmett Till were murdered, called the suburban county "a plantation."

But local civil rights activists seized the momentum of the landmark Fair Housing Act, just passed in 1968, and pushed into the suburbs. Harnessing the interests of Black realtors, a liberal white mortgage lender, and the desire of upwardly mobile Black families for the suburban lifestyle of quiet neighborhoods, quality schools, single-family homes, backyard barbeques, and shopping malls, African Americans challenged segregation and developed unique strategies to desegregate all-white suburbs. A decade after Herbert Lindsay tried unsuccessfully to rent an apartment, the suburbs along Liberty Road were home to over twenty-four thousand African Americans. While in McMechen's day—or even as late as the 1950s—whites departed almost immediately when African Americans moved in, Blacks and whites both continued to live in the housing developments along Liberty Road for several decades. By the start of the twenty-first century, that suburban corridor was home to almost as many African Americans as had lived in all of Baltimore City when George McMechen's move across Eutaw Street began African Americans' northwesterly migration out of the center city along the Liberty Heights corridor. Liberty Road was 80 percent African American, yet long had a higher median household income than the county, the state, or the nation.[13] In some ways the expansive, varied suburban community that stretched right up to the rural boundary of the metro area represented the high-water mark of the midcentury civil rights movement.

For almost a century, urban sociology has examined racial inequality in the context of low-income urban ghettos. This study offers a new view of racial discrimination by examining a middle-class African American suburb. Based on ethnographic observations, fifty interviews, and archival research, *Liberty Road* explains how African Americans were able to break the color barrier and what conflicts shape the community today.[14] Unlike earlier sociological accounts of blockbusting that focused on predatory white realtors and saw African Americans as dupes or victims, this research identifies how residents, activists, and local professionals opened the suburbs to African Americans who had been rigidly excluded. African American suburbanization is a nationwide sea change, but one that is developing unevenly; this study identifies the conditions and efforts that allowed African Americans to move into the suburbs outside Baltimore; Black people in so many other cities were not able to enter the suburbs. In examining community battles against the expansion of bus lines or for the arrival of Walmart, *Liberty Road* demonstrates that suburban space and middle-class status reposition residents' views on classic community issues of economic development, growth, and class status. One key difference in this suburb is the failure of government to respond to predations that threaten the entire community, like the foreclosure and subprime mortgage crisis. This research proposes a new model to understand how racial inequality persists in communities that are not economically desperate. Despite ongoing challenges such as these, however, African American suburbanites build strong communities (of long resident tenure and stable home values) in the face of racially discriminatory business practices, threats to their middle-class position, and strained relationships with both suburban whites and poor, urban Blacks. Residents in these suburbs demonstrate that race remains as real as ever, but that struggles against racial inequality are taking new forms as they move into the new suburban landscape.

Nineteenth-century Black life was almost entirely rural. The twentieth-century Black experience was preeminently urban. Twenty-first-century Black America is suburban. From 1960 to 1991, the African American middle class doubled in size. Today, over half of African Americans in the hundred largest metropolitan areas live in suburbs, not cities.[15] The American experience today is centered in the suburbs. Our understanding of racial inequality needs to be updated to recognize that reality.

The story of George McMechen and the city's apartheid legislation one hundred years ago highlights how stories of residential racial transition must be told differently than they have been—from the perspective of the African American families who moved. Accounts must acknowledge the role of Black activism, while still recognizing that pioneers' expansion of Black neighborhoods is motivated by pressing personal needs (for better housing, schools, and communities), not just political goals. Economic realities that confound African American efforts to improve their housing have persisted. The results of residents' and activists' efforts were qualified successes, and pioneers' moves should be judged by the sum of what they did accomplish and improve, rather than dismissed as failures for not achieving integration or true equality. Developing a perspective on contemporary suburban racial transition from the story of McMechen's move to McCulloh Street ultimately leads us to be skeptical of what one scholar called "the righteous rhetoric of reform."[16] The mayor who imposed apartheid on Baltimore was a liberal reformer who promised the segregation scheme was the best arrangement for whites and Blacks. Studying racial transition in the contemporary suburbs discredits liberal accounts that paint such transitions as the nefarious doings of greedy real estate speculators rather than efforts of activists and residents. While an ecological impression of neighborhood change might imagine that Black neighborhoods "grew" naturally, instead African Americans had to *move* themselves and their families, and do so against considerable opposition.

Certainly, the context of discrimination had changed since neighbors threw rocks through McMechen's windows and forced his family to move out. In the earlier case, laws required segregation; by the time African Americans reached the suburbs, laws prohibited it. Residents maintained stable middle-class communities, quality schools, and attractive houses on quiet residential streets. Like African Americans in cities, African American suburbanites still faced challenges that residents in white neighborhoods did not. But Black suburbanites had resources few urban Black communities could access. As middle-class residents, they had social status—which needed to be defended but could also be translated into political capital. They expected to be listened to, and expected county government to be responsive to middle-class taxpayers' demands—whether by promoting economic investment, implementing school improvements, enforcing community standards through zoning regulations, or regulating real estate development.

African American suburbanites' relationship to African Americans still living and struggling in the city, and to white suburbanites who no longer moved to Liberty Road, became more delicate, as residents adopted some of the defensiveness of white suburbanites toward "people from the city," but could harbor few illusions about white people from the suburbs either.

African American suburban residents, shaped by their class position, social resources, and suburban location, challenge and re-form the conventional narratives of Black neighborhoods, sometimes dramatically improving outcomes for this Black community. In other cases, age-old racial conflicts erupt in different ways, and residents deploy the resources of middle-class suburbs to protect their families and communities. The suburban century in Black America requires a new understanding of both the manifestation of racism in the suburban landscape and the new—although sometimes troubling—ways middle-class residents confront challenges.

Liberty Road: Moving to the Suburbs

Baltimore offers one of the clearest examples of the mid-twentieth-century African American suburbanization that took place in many US cities. The area along Liberty Road is known as Randallstown (though it, like all places in suburban Baltimore County, is an informal place name, not an actual incorporated town). Liberty Road runs through a suburban stretch of neighborhoods of single-family homes, schools surrounded by vast sports fields, shopping malls, garden apartments, supermarkets, small businesses, and new big-box stores. Today the area along Liberty Road is home to 82,000 African Americans.[17] The median income of African Americans living along Liberty Road was $70,864 in 2018, higher by 11 percent than the median for the United States.[18] In the 1980s Randallstown had been a largely Jewish area with a significant African American population. By the start of this study it was majority–African American. In some cities immigrants make up a substantial portion of African American neighborhoods, but during the time of this study the substantial majority of residents were US-born.[19]

I grew up near Randallstown. I performed in musical productions at Randallstown High School, went to parties at houses in Randallstown, played sports against Randallstown teams. I also knew the neighboring, predominantly white communities like Owings Mills and Reisterstown, where I grew up. For this project I interviewed several people I had known long before, particularly teachers who I knew had experience teaching in a variety schools that had had different racial compositions. Knowing some of the looping subdivision roads was often more help than a GPS in getting to interviews, and saying that I had "grown up nearby" was a regular part of my introduction in the hopes that local credentials would help open doors.

I wanted to go to Randallstown to take a new look at racial inequality, paying attention to three things: people, class, and space. I wanted to consider how residents had actively created their communities, how race worked in middle-class settings, and how the landscape of the suburbs reshaped race, a subject researchers knew mostly from studying urban settings.

First, to move beyond chronicling racial inequality and implicit comparisons between a specific Black community and an imagined white ideal, *Liberty Road* considers African Americans as active agents seeking to achieve their own goals. Studying what people had to accomplish to cross the suburban color line in this community identifies the sorts of factors that likely helped residents in some cities to create Black suburbs (as in Baltimore, Chicago, Washington, and Atlanta), while other cities still lack them (such as Philadelphia and Boston). This study of neighborhood change also goes beyond the conventional account of "blockbusting." In that narrative, African Americans played only the role of boogeyman, as white realtors moved Blacks in to scare white residents out of neighborhoods, then charged other Blacks exploitative rates for the newly vacant homes. Historically, the story of racial transition has been told from the perspective of whites resisting that change, and even academic accounts have focused on the tragic loss of community at the hands of manipulative real estate agents. African Americans realtors, home buyers, and their allies tell a very different story of how they improved their housing options (while still caught in a racially restrictive market) by moving into suburban neighborhoods. Residents were initially able to meet an important goal—decent housing—even though they often fell short of the hopes of many sympathetic white observers, for whom stable integration was the yardstick of success.[20]

Second, *Liberty Road* measures African American progress as the gains of civil rights activism versus neoliberalism. Civil rights activists won the gains enjoyed in African American suburbs today, from good jobs to more affordable housing to antidiscrimination legislation. But all of those accomplishments are attacked by neoliberalism. The conservative agenda pursued by presidents from Ronald Regan to George W. Bush, neoliberalism married anti-Black backlash with regressive economic policies and particularly hurt African American communities, decimating unionized jobs and government civil service positions that secured the middle class, slashing financial regulations that could have constrained speculation in the home mortgage market, reducing government services, and opposing affirmative action.

Third, this project integrates class and space into the study of race. Sociology has focused on comparisons between Black and white. But African Americans have always been aware of the importance of class-based differences between the middle class and others. Scholars have wondered if growing class differences will reduce the significance of race.[21] *Liberty Road* considers a middle-class African American community both in terms of its relationship to the larger, whiter world and in terms of how its class position and spatial location shape its relationship to the larger Black world. At the intersection of space, class, and race, African American middle-class suburbs occupy an intermediate point, in which their political issues remain distinct from those of their white counterparts, but different as well from African Americans who do not share the suburban landscape.

This study takes urban sociology's growing interest in the role of physical space in social conflicts and improves its application to issues of race.[22] Racial inequality manifests itself differently in suburban settings, and suburbanites use their own set of spatially defined tools to either promote or combat racial segregation. The book's examination of how the suburban landscape reshapes racial inequality builds on a growing recognition in the social sciences of how physical space shapes social conflicts.

Seeing race in its interaction with middle-class status and suburban space identifies new patterns of inequality. Rather than the story of precipitous decline first told in accounts of blockbusting and ghettoization, this project finds that the suburbs experience change analogous to what evolutionary biologist Stephen Jay Gould described as *punctuated equilibrium*. Decades of stable incomes, well-maintained houses, and decent (if uneven) schools may be disrupted by the shock of the foreclosure crisis that has been focused on Black communities, by recession, or by other catastrophes. Because the comparative calm of the suburbs is periodically interrupted by dangerous threats to residents' stability and livelihoods, middle-class African Americans can experience long periods of relative promise even while the damage of American racial inequality lurks.

Construction of the American Suburb

Researchers studying the suburbs have produced a notable number of classic works; given the centrality of suburbs to the twentieth-century American experience, writers have had to articulate the multiple cultural meanings of the suburbs and tie that symbolism to an explanation of the physical production of space. Critically, academic attention to the suburbs was never as color blind as the suburbs themselves were reputed to be. Kenneth Jackson's *Crabgrass Frontier* is a sweeping survey of the history of the American suburb and its construction on a national scale, chronicling its long development as a residential form to demonstrate its obvious yet perplexing importance to American society. While his tone avoids the easy criticisms of suburbs, eventually Jackson cannot help but ask of suburbs, "How is it that a rich, powerful, and technologically sophisticated country can tolerate such inefficiency, such poverty, and such contrasts? Why have we neglected our cities and concentrated so much of our energy, our creativity, and our vitality in the suburbs?"[23] He concludes that the American suburbs required a cultural ideal, a material reality, and a racial chasm: "Clearly, no single answer can be held accountable for such an important phenomenon, but I will argue that there were two necessary conditions for American residential deconcentration—the suburban ideal and population growth—and two fundamental causes—racial prejudice and cheap housing."[24] In the book that initiated historians' work on postwar US suburbs, race is a fundamental component.

Baxandall and Ewen's *Picture Windows* follows the trail of the symbolic meanings of the suburbs in the American psyche.[25] In popular culture, the suburbs have represented an idyll but, dialectically, a retreat from the urban, imagined as dangerous, disorganized, immigrant, and nonwhite. The percentage of the US population living in suburbs long ago passed the halfway mark. But partisans of city living can point out that suburbs today are outside the city only in the legal sense of lying beyond often arbitrary city boundaries. Suburbs play many of the same general roles as cities' residential neighborhoods, commercial centers, and peripheral business districts (albeit at lower densities and typically with more inadequate public transportation). In step with the growing popularity of the suburbs, critics have targeted the suburbs. More recently suburbs have been disparaged as un-environmental consumers of fossil fuels. In the second half of the twentieth century anti-suburban critics could complain that they were boring and more homogenous than the democratic, diverse, and riotous city—that there was nothing to do. Paradoxically, in the first decades of the growth of the postwar suburb cultural critics worried that there was *too much* to do in the suburbs; they demanded a frantic if implicitly mindless level of social activity as conformist suburbanites dutifully if unimaginatively went from PTA meetings to Lions Club events to Tupperware parties to church gatherings to neighborhood card parties. Sociologist Herbert Gans moved into Levittown, New Jersey, to separate truth from fiction. (Levittown is one of three eponymous towns built by the early suburban proponent William Levitt, who did as much as anyone to turn building the American home into an assembly-line process. The predictable result was homes that were initially homogeneous, but they were an impressive achievement in terms of price and amenities for an ascendant working-class America, right down to the television included in the sale price.) Gans's characteristically clear-eyed and uncompromising book *Levittowners* is unambiguous and generous toward residents: they were neither bored nor harried conformists but city residents who wanted some of the conveniences the suburb provided; if elite critics didn't like housing that was made affordable to the mass market, that was neither surprising nor of any importance.[26]

While Gans defended the housing choices of everyday people, his work, in its detailed examination of working-class, lower-middle, and upper-middle-class residents, did document inherent tensions and shortcomings within the suburbs. Working-class and upper-middle-class residents wanted different things from their schools (a football team that could beat the neighboring town versus French classes, for instance). More importantly, although Gans defended the suburbs, his residents voiced dissatisfaction: the women were stranded when the men left for work in the only car, and they felt cut off from their own mothers, friends, and family back in the city, which was now a lengthy drive or a costly long-distance call away. Members of ethnic groups left behind the cultural institutions that would still have been meaningful to them, poorer residents could find few people they felt comfortable with, richer residents sought more of their own kind, and kids, beyond toddlers, were dissatisfied as well. Critically, all three Levittowns (in New Jersey, Pennsylvania, and New York) were officially for whites only. Gans's Levittown eventually became a rare pioneer in racial integration, but William Levitt wove racism into the origins of Levittown, a name that became synonymous with suburbs. "We can solve a housing problem, or we can try to solve a racial problem. But we can't combine the two," Levitt claimed in explaining why he refused to sell to Blacks—or to Jews, despite being Jewish himself. (As Richard Rothstein pointed out in his book on segregation, government-endorsed financial standards *required* Levitt to segregate his housing developments in order to be considered stable enough to get financing for the project.)[27]

The suburbs' inextricable entanglement of race-class exclusion and physical form continued even as the racial and ethnic diversity of the suburbs grew. Setha Low, in her book *Behind the Gates*, penetrated the gated communities that had hardened the defenses of growing numbers of US suburbs from Long Island to San Antonio.[28] Within them she found clear evidence of the contradictory function of gated communities: living behind the gates was supposed to be all about safety, but residents felt increasingly insecure. The more the gates were built to protect them from some unspecified outside threat, the more residents worried that the barriers were insufficient and that a predator might enter. Children growing up in a gated community in the Southwest had unvarnished prejudices against Mexicans that left groups of teenagers unwilling to travel downtown for a fireworks display. Parents worried that although they now lived behind gates, the passage of home contractors and delivery men through the gates meant the very classes and strangers they were trying to escape could still enter. Critically, Low found that the exclusive attitudes that the built form of suburban gated communities both reflected and fostered were expressed not only along the predictable hierarchical lines of power and status—elites looking down at the lower class, or whites toward people of color. Lower-middle-class gated communities provided more working-class residents with their own chance to worry about the other outside, just as Latino residents of a gated community could worry about the Latinos beyond the gates. At least in the more extreme case of the gated community, the link between space and exclusivity was clear, and as the demographic groups who had access to such physical spaces increased, so did their embrace of exclusive attitudes. How groups like African Americans, who were once the target of suburban exclusion, adapt and employ the spatial strategies of the suburbs constitutes a central question of this book.

Civil Rights and Neoliberalism

Understanding the importance, in African American suburbs, of neoliberalism and the civil rights movement expands our understanding of the breadth of each of those opposing forces.

Writers have largely limited their use of "neoliberalism" to considerations of political economy, but I argue that the term makes sense only if it is understood as fundamentally racial. Marxist geographer and social theorist David Harvey laid out the economic aspects of neoliberalism. In the postwar period, democratic institutions and policies like labor unions, labor laws, and accords between labor and management brought widespread union membership, high minimum wages, job and income security, unemployment insurance, and welfare benefits. Harvey defines neoliberalism as the response, beginning around 1975, of business owners and conservative politicians to re-secure the power of their class against these gains.[29] Elites were motivated by falling rates of profit for their businesses to reassert greater economic and political power over people who had made democratic and economic gains.[30] Neoliberalism selectively implemented deregulation and privatization and expanded the role of financial markets in ways that benefited elites and hurt working people.[31] Wages fell, economic and social insecurity mounted, and market speculation upset what stability middle- and working-class people had established. (It is worth noting that while in the United States "liberals" are Democrats and use government to defend individuals' rights and freedoms, in the rest of the world a "liberal" is a conservative and defends rights and freedoms *from* government meddling. "Neoliberals" are thus "new conservatives" who defend the rights and privileges of private property against social welfare efforts to reduce inequality.)

Harvey argued that neoliberalism is less a consistent philosophy than a class war of the corporate wealthy against working people. While neoliberalism's defenders claimed that it was intended to reinvigorate a stagnant economy, Harvey pointed out that neoliberalism's "actual record in stimulating economic growth is dismal."[32] Neoliberalism's main accomplishment has been not to create more wealth but to create conditions of widespread powerlessness in order to redistribute the existing wealth upward.

Yet calling neoliberalism class warfare defines the term too narrowly and fails to comprehend its racial quality. James Baldwin criticized Marxist analysis of inequality as insufficient in its scope, noting that for Black Americans "humiliation did not apply merely to working days, or workers."[33] Baldwin and other Black intellectuals like W. E. B. Du Bois, Richard Wright, and C. L. R. James were concerned with Marxism not because it was too radical (as it appeared to some white commentators) but because, being primarily a diagnosis and prescription for economic oppression, it was not thoroughly radical and critical *enough*. As Cedric Robinson made clear in *Black Marxism*, even the most radical criticisms of capitalism could sound insufficient in the context of struggles for racial justice because they failed to illuminate the struggle against racism.[34] In this vein, *Liberty Road* expands our understanding of what neoliberalism is by showing that it is inextricably a racial and economic program.

Neoliberalism is not only class warfare but just as centrally a reaction against the gains of civil rights activists and people of color.[35] More than Harvey's narrowly economistic conception, neoliberalism is what theorists Michael Omi and Howard Winant call a "racial project"—an ideological initiative to mobilize racist explanations, justifications, and narratives that serve efforts to redistribute political, cultural, and economic resources along racial (and class) lines.[36] Neoliberalism sought not only to take back gains from the working class but to undo progress that had been made by African Americans and other people of color as well.

Scholars are only beginning to recognize that neoliberalism is a racial project just as much as an economic one. Loïc Wacquant argues that conceptualizing neoliberalism as merely "market rule" is "thin and incomplete."[37] It is in Wacquant's description of this more expansive social meaning of neoliberalism that we see the first hints of how race is intertwined with neoliberalism.[38] Wacquant examines neoliberal regimes' emphasis on crime fighting, criminal predation, and a more punitive prison system (even in the face of historically low crime rates). He points out that by "elevating criminal safety . . . to the frontline of government priorities, state officials have condensed the diffuse class anxiety and simmering ethnic resentment generated by the unraveling of the Fordist-Keynesian compact [the labor gains that preceded neoliberalism] and channeled them toward the (dark-skinned) street criminal."[39]

With the "racialization of state policy" described by Oliver and Shapiro, neoliberal racial scapegoating facilitated the implementation of neoliberal economic assaults and racialized policy.[40] And as neoliberals attacked policies that sought to provide quality education, health care, and housing to all, leaving households to rely on their own private resources, the Black-white wealth gap Oliver and Shapiro identified served to further increase the difficulties African Americans faced in obtaining middle-class stability.

As a few critics have recognized, the role of racial reaction in the neoliberal agenda is more than opportunistic scapegoating; it is a core objective. Cultural critic Lisa Duggan's identification of the core components of neoliberalism recognized its integration of attacks on unions and New Deal programs with "attacks on downwardly redistributive social movements, especially the Civil Rights and Black power movements, but including feminism, lesbian and gay liberation, and countercultural mobilizations. . . . The politics of race, both overt and covert, have been particularly central to the entire project [of neoliberalism]."[41] In her book Duggan focuses on neoliberalism's assaults against gender and sexuality movements, but her definition makes clear that critics of neoliberalism should expect its multifront assault by now: "The goal of raising corporate profits has never been pursued separately from the rearticulation of hierarchies of race, gender, and sexuality."[42]

In the United States, elites' neoliberal agenda was driven by both a class-based agenda to take back the gains of the working class from the postwar era of relative labor strength and an effort to challenge the gains made by the African American civil rights movement. In this way, the Republican Party's embrace of the revanchist neoliberal agenda fit neatly with their "Southern Strategy," which was based on fanning white resentment of African Americans in the post–civil rights era.[43] Neoliberal retrenchment was even more palatable to a backlash electorate if attacks on working people doubled as attacks on African Americans (as did cuts to welfare, unemployment, and, recently and less explicitly, civil service wages and unions) and if the impact of neoliberalism's destructive power was focused disproportionately on the comparatively isolated and politically less powerful African American electorate.[44] Studies of places close to Liberty Road suggested that politicians could gain widespread support among whites for neoliberal policy initiatives if they implicitly targeted them against African Americans. Christopher Niedt found politicians could cultivate support among whites in working-class, postindustrial Baltimore County for a neoliberal-style business-government program of gentrification by suggesting gentrification could keep "people from the city" from coming into their white enclave.[45] As David Theo Goldberg ultimately concluded, "Race is a key structuring technology . . . of neoliberalism."[46]

Despite neoliberalism's central role in the past thirty years, the term is more common in academic discussions than in popular debates. White liberals may describe neoliberal policies as conservative or Republican, but doing so misses the bipartisan implementation of neoliberalism. In a similar vein, African Americans never fully enjoyed the benefits of postwar prosperity that preceded neoliberalism and thus may posit little difference between earlier and more recent efforts to repress and exploit. But political progressives' articulation of these developments as neoliberalism identifies a strategic shift in the politics of reaction, points to the sea change in liberal as well as conservative politics in the era, and ties US economic uncertainty and regressive social policies to similar reversals elsewhere. Just as important, a neoliberal framework helps understand political changes occurring within African American suburban communities. The four years of the Trump administration in many ways distilled the neoliberal backlash that was covered in theoretical justification to unadorned backlash. That version dispensed with neoliberal elements like free trade but doubled down on racial revanchism as when Trump weakened federal regulations against segregation and housing discrimination for the explicit preservation of white suburban enclaves.[47]

The neoliberal era changed the very meaning of the suburbs for people like the residents of Randallstown. There is a profound difference between reaching middle-class status in a community like those along Liberty Road under neoliberalism as opposed to the preceding regime. The mid-twentieth-century US suburb developed in a context of relatively secure lifetime employment, growing real wages, security against economic crises, and moderated business cycles. There are substantial challenges to maintaining middle-class status under a neoliberal regime of insecure work, no job security, frequent and severe economic crises, and an ideology of personal responsibility that challenges any expectation of social support in hard times and blames those who lose jobs, wealth, or security for their woes. African Americans experienced an absolute decline in income between 1973 and 1993.[48] The real estate collapse dramatically widened the racial wealth gap.[49] The fundamental and widespread social insecurity of neoliberalism proves to have profound impacts on communities like Randallstown.

What Is the Middle Class?

In the United States, "middle class" is a claim of political and economic enfranchisement more than a description of a specific income bracket. Politicians regularly make promises to the middle class—about tax cuts, homeownership, or making college affordable—irrespective of what economic stratum the policies will most benefit. In political discourse the middle class is valorized, as Bill Clinton defined it, as people who "work hard and play by the rules."[50] In the popular imagination the middle class contains several ideals. The first concept goes back to the American dream. The meaning of that phrase is now mostly forgotten. But when historian James Truslow Adams coined the term in 1931, he focused less on material abundance than on the idea that each person advanced on the basis of their own hard work and abilities rather than the inherited nobility or castes preponderant in so many societies.[51] The second element of the middle class is investment in American capitalism. As suburban builder William Levitt himself said, "No man who owns his own house and lot can be a communist. He has too much to do."[52] In the Cold War and the twentieth-century contest between capital and labor, middle-class identification and homeownership was an ideological strategy that deterred Americans from seeing their best chance at economic stability coming from identifying as workers, leftists, or union members. In the United States this Cold War middle-class identity was racialized as white: the identity of white middle class tied the loyalties of tens of millions of Americans to white elites, not the working class or nonwhite Americans. Finally, being middle class represented stability: middle-class Americans, the promise went, could work and expect that their economic situation would be secure and that their children could anticipate at least a similar level of economic security. A steady job (or two) in the imagined middle-class household brought homeownership, a car, the necessities of life, perhaps a vacation, and education for the children.

Because of the power of the middle class's image in America and its deceptive claim to universal inclusion, its actual boundaries generally elude us. Most importantly, the middle class is not the majority, and *the middle class is not in the middle.* As Michael Zweig, an economist who has conducted the most extensive contemporary study on the meaning of class in America, notes, "The usual talk of a mass middle class with some rich and poor at the fringes around it is deeply misleading and contributes to . . . central problems in American politics."[53] Zweig, looking at the kinds of jobs Americans have and the power they have (or lack) at those jobs, concludes that the United States remains a working-class nation, where approximately two-thirds of the country is working class, about one-third is middle class, and 2 percent are elites.[54]

Zweig's percentages hold up whether class is defined by occupation, income, education, or other measures. All three of those are used to define class in different moments, Karyn Lacy and others have pointed out.[55] Lacy, working independently from Zweig, found it does not make intuitive sense to define middle class at the middle: the median household income, which in 2018 was $62,000, could be earned by a couple each earning $15 an hour, and without enough money to afford the material elements of an American middle-class lifestyle. Lacy defined the middle class not as those at the 50th percentile but as those above, in the 60th to 85th percentile of the nation's income distribution.

Lacy's definition makes sense. A middle-class family should be able to afford the average priced home. By a traditional real estate measure, a household can afford a home three times their income, which is the bottom of Lacy's distribution. Furthermore, I would argue that it makes sense to distinguish households in the top 10 percent of the income distribution as something other than middle class. I apply these measures to current income and housing data. The median home price in the United States in 2018 was $222,800.[56] A third of that is about $75,000. The top 10 percent of households bring home $175,000. Thus the middle class, defined only by income, would have household incomes of $75,000 to $175,000. By that quantitative measure, 28 percent of the United States is middle class, as are nearly 20 percent of African American households.[57] The percentages are slightly smaller than Zweig's and slightly larger than Lacy's but comparable and compatible with both of their work. These data show that the Black middle class is smaller—racial inequality remains real and measurable—but significant and substantial.

Income is only one way to define the middle class and is by no means identical to class position. Others use wealth, occupation status, culture, and education level. This study concerns itself with the community, not individuals. Randallstown fits the cultural ideal of a conventional middle-class suburb (at least in every way except race, to the extent that in the United States middle class is coded as white). Almost all of Randallstown's houses were built between the 1960s and today. Most are single-family homes. The place is *autocentric*—people rely almost entirely on automobiles to get around. Schools are surrounded by expansive sports fields, shopping malls by giant parking lots, and homes by green lawns and driveways. Randallstown as a community is middle class, even though, as in every community, not all of its residents are middle class.

Civil Rights Activism and the Black Middle Class

The role of the Black middle class in civil rights activism is at once contentious and understudied. Authors and activists have at times argued that middle-class African Americans pushed the movement forward, held it back, or were irrelevant to it. This book does not compare the contributions of professionals and the bourgeoisie to the much larger Black working class but rather examines, at the micro level, the role the middle class played.

In the period of Randallstown's greatest growth, civil rights activism occurred at four different levels. First there was the work of national organizations whose successes set the context for what occurred in middle-class suburbs nationwide. Then there were local organizations, including the Baltimore County chapter of the NAACP, Baltimore groups like BLEWS (the political and linguistic merger of "Blacks" and "Jews"), and local homeowner associations. Third, I include the daily professional activities of many middle-class African Americans. To be a Black real estate agent often meant expanding access for Black home seekers or obtaining mortgages for them. Finally, middle-class suburbanites had sufficient resources that in some cases even their individual, seemingly private choices had political and social import in the aggregate.

Choosing to buy a home across the color line, seeking a mortgage, and moving to the suburbs all contributed to larger, community-level movements that pushed open the options available to African Americans.

Regarding the role of the Black middle class in the civil rights movements, some historians have emphasized the necessity of a mass Black base for such groups, others have noted their middle-class leadership, and still others have criticized the class biases of that same leadership. For instance, some of the best work in this area, such as Aldon Morris's *Origins of the Civil Rights Movement*, has demonstrated the fundamental association of civil rights organizations to an organized *mass* base of African Americans.[58] Others have noted the role of Black professionals, particularly ministers, in filling the leadership of such organizations, either to quietly salute those leaders or to criticize that leadership. Malcolm X was one of the most vocal critics of the bourgeois bias of mainstream civil rights organizations, of course, criticizing "integration-mad Negroes," the self-appointed "local Negro 'leader,'" and the NAACP and the other "big six" civil rights organizations that organized the March on Washington to call for integration, which Malcolm derided for its "weakening, lulling and deluding effects."[59] Integration, he argued, was promoted by bourgeois Black leaders and offered nothing for most Black Americans: "Only a few thousands of Negroes, relatively a very tiny number, are taking any part in 'integration,'" he argued.[60] In contrast to the integrationist political program promoted by the professional Black middle class ("these fancy, bourgeois Negroes"), Malcolm argued, "the black masses prefer the company of their own kind."[61]

Malcolm may have been the most prominent critic of the role of the Black bourgeoisie in civil rights groups.[62] But he was part of a long-standing discussion about the political role of the Black middle class. E. Franklin Frazier's indictment of the Black middle class is probably the most extensive and scathing. In *Black Bourgeoisie*, Frazier excoriated two strands of the Black bourgeoisie. Both the inherited, light-skinned bourgeoisie built around pedigree, and the new economic middle class of professional corporate employees lived, according to Frazier, in a world of "make believe." They imagined that proper markers of membership in upper-class Black society (skin color, lineage, fraternity and sorority affiliations) could distinguish them from the Black masses.[63] Frazier's book, published in 1957, drew implicit conclusions about the role of the

Black middle class in racial uplift and progress. While Bart Landry argued that Frazier was convinced that Black progress lay in the integration of the Black middle class into the larger society, *Black Bourgeoisie* is more often read as an argument that the bourgeoisie had segregated themselves into a pleasant irrelevance and that the Black masses were the agents of history.[64]

Others observers have noted the friction between the more radical desires of the people and the more cautious approach of the middle class. Historian Kimberly Phillips, for instance, noted that in the early civil rights movement, boycotts and other actions undertaken by working-class Blacks were often short-circuited or moderated by the bourgeois leadership in the Black community. In contrast, she found that groups run by and for working-class people could undertake more directly confrontational tactics than groups run by professionals whose positions required that they not overly antagonize the white community. In such accounts, the middle class was hardly in the vanguard.[65]

The role of the Black middle class has varied. As Karen Miller suggested, at some moments Black elites could promote their class interests before those of poor and working-class residents, and at others achieve important gains with broader benefits.[66] Darlene Clark Hine has demonstrated how Black professionals played an early and important role in the civil rights movement. Some of the earliest breaks in the segregationist wall were chiseled by Black professionals, such as African American nurses and doctors who pushed to be allowed to treat soldiers during the Second World War.[67] Middle-class activists employed both parallelism (the creation of separate Black organizations) and integrationism (the demand that Black professionals gain access to segregated institutions on an equal footing with whites). In accounts such as these, the Black middle class, while smaller than the mass-based organizations, made significant inroads to racial equality.

The role of African American suburbanization has been as contested as the role of the Black middle class more generally. On one hand, observers like William Julius Wilson have worried that the departure of the Black middle class from urban ghettoes increased the concentration of poverty, removed middle-class resources, and isolated poor people from middle class role models.[68] Others celebrated the suburbanization of the Black middle class as a collective statement of upward mobility and success. Still others, like Michael C. Dawson, asked whether upward mobility would break Black middle-class professionals' long-standing perception of group interests as dominant "in shaping African American . . . political choice and public opinion."[69]

There is no single resolution to the question of the impact of suburbanization on the African American community. Just as Hine, Miller, and Phillips showed that the middle class played a range of roles, both pioneering and moderating, in the civil rights movements, so suburbanization plays a multifaceted role. The community along Liberty Road has undertaken campaigns that at times have carried gains for the broader Black community and at other times have pursued objectives oriented only toward their own immediate needs. On occasions the suburbs have been at the front lines politically just as they literally occupy the forward edge of the growth of the African American community. But what power Liberty Road holds comes not only from their own class-based resources but from being at the edge of a larger African American community (that is predominantly not middle class). Developing independence while avoiding isolation shapes residents' responses to political opportunities and obstacles.

Civil Rights and Neoliberalism Enmeshed in Physical and Social Space

Understanding the suburbs as the intersection of civil rights activism and neoliberalism makes sense of changing realities in post–civil rights America. I approach this task by synthesizing work on central concerns of sociology—race, class, and space—and by building on researchers' growing interest in African American suburbs.

Urban sociology, my own field, has paid growing attention to the role of space for how it organizes social interactions and operates as an institution that reproduces power relations.[70] Early Chicago School researchers studied the effect of space in their influential community studies and conceived of a spatial ecology of the city. Later researchers were put off by ecologists' normative and deterministic approach to neighborhoods and space.[71] But as Thomas Gieryn recognized in 2000, sociologists have developed a renewed interest in space.[72] Urban sociologists in particular have increasingly considered the ways that space gives durability to structural categories and inequality, arranges face-to-face interactions, and embodies cultural norms, identities, and memories.[73] The interest in space grew out of work by Marxist geographers, starting with interpretations of the work of Henri Lefebvre by geographers David Harvey, Edward Soja, and others.[74] Mike Davis is probably the best known example of an author who married attention to urban space with opposition to capitalism.[75] Thus as this new attention to space was integrated into sociology and other fields, it was embraced earliest by Marxists.

But the development of the sociology of space through a European Marxist tradition has meant that studies of space have tended to look in detail at the depredations of capital and the deleterious effects of economic discrimination while giving less central attention to categories of inequality such as race. A significant example in this vein is the book *Place Matters*, which makes a strong case for the importance of the spatial manifestation of inequality. The authors make place-based recommendations for equity like leveling the playing field between cities' tax bases and deconcentrating poverty.[76] But they pay little attention to ghettoes, racially segregated schools, or other places where space interacts with race more than class. Instead, the authors hew to an argument, long rehashed in some circles, about the primacy of class *over* race.[77] The insights provided by a spatial perspective cannot be monopolized by class-based studies. As is evident along Liberty Road, the study of the social role of space provides valuable analytic leverage in understanding racial as well as economic inequality.

While work on space still must better address race, studies of the suburbs are beginning to more fully consider the complexities of race. This has begun on two fronts. First, Andrew Wiese and others have rewritten histories of the suburbs, arguing that they always included working-class people and people of color and were never as uniformly white or middle class as popular conceptions of them were.[78] Second, ethnographers have slowly begun to add, beside ethnographic studies of poor, urban Black ghettoes, new studies of working-class, middle-class, and, just recently, suburban Black communities. Alexandra Murphy's work in Pittsburgh is one of the most recent examples of this much-needed development.[79] Mary Pattillo's pathbreaking and evocatively named book *Black Picket Fences* looks at the unique challenges for African Americans maintaining a stable community. The neighborhood, which she calls Groveland, has many single-family houses and families raising children. Pattillo's work is presented as an ethnography of the Black middle class in a suburban setting.[80] But as Karyn Lacy and others have argued, the community is more accurately described as working class and is located inside the city of Chicago, not in the suburbs. Unlike in contemporary US suburbs, over half of the houses were built before the 1950s. The residents faced problems that were more characteristically urban than suburban: the loss of industrial jobs, the dangerous lure of drugs and drug money in the less well-off communities nearby, the prospect of young people "thrilled" or "consumed" by the "ghetto trance" of hip-hop style and gangster posturing. Even if most residents were working class, Groveland confronted some of the same problems that nearby urban low-income communities face. These issues overlap with those found in suburban settings but manifest themselves differently inside Chicago, in a community whose history of proximity to the larger South Side African American community links it to urban Black experiences more than suburban ones. Furthermore, Groveland could not employ the key strategy employed by suburban communities of putting physical distance and municipal boundaries between themselves and urban poverty.

Pattillo identifies the effects neoliberalism has had on Groveland. Most dramatically, the deindustrialization of the US economy meant employers moved many of the stable, unionized, industrial jobs that financed the first generation of Black Groveland residents' home purchases to lower-wage locations. While unemployment remained low in Groveland, younger generations were more tenuously connected to the labor force than their parents and continued to live in Groveland only because they had inherited houses there. In contrast, deindustrialization had a less visible impact on Randallstown, Maryland, because while Groveland went from 6 percent Black in 1960 to 80 percent Black in 1970, Randallstown was still virtually all white in 1970. The loss of those jobs devastated already-established Groveland. But by the time Randallstown became predominantly Black, the industrial jobs that had sustained the Black working class in Baltimore were largely gone. The only people who could move out to Randallstown had found other sources of stable middle-income jobs. Instead, neoliberalism had other effects on Randallstown, as deregulation, reduced government services, and downward pressure even on middle-class wages in the white-collar and service sectors, all characteristic of neoliberalism, slowly made their mark.

Nonetheless, Pattillo's book was the most high-profile work in some time that studied an African American community outside of ghettoes of concentrated poverty. Periodic studies of the Black working class have, like Pattillo's, sought to expand the ethnographic representation of African Americans beyond the ghetto but, like work by Steven Gregory, Bruce Haynes, and Shirley Ann Wilson Moore, have most often focused on working-class communities in urban areas.[81]

Most recently, the attention to race in the suburbs initiated by revisionist historians was brought to sociology with Karyn Lacy's study of middle- and upper-middle-class suburbs outside of Washington, DC.[82] In that setting, Lacy could identify the identity-constructing strategies African American parents used with their children in several income- and race-segregated suburbs. Lacy's work provided valuable insights into the influence of class and suburban location on African American identity, self-presentation, and cultural reproduction, while simultaneously hinting at the range of topics yet to be explored across that terrain.

Each of these ethnographies of African American communities make valuable contributions through their integrated attention to race and class, especially to the class divisions among African Americans. Further insights into those divisions have been provided through unconventional research and extended reflections on class distinctions among African Americans by writers like Lawrence Otis Graham and John Langston Gwaltney.[83]

Social science literature on African American communities needs to include the middle class because if studies overwhelmingly examine low-income ghettoes, researchers risk exoticizing and pathologizing the very communities they wish to exonerate and explicate. As historian Robin D. G. Kelley has most astutely observed, social scientists (urban ethnographers in particular) have "contributed to the construction of the ghetto as a reservoir of pathologies and bad cultural values."[84] Kelley examined how social science has shaped the public discourse on the Black urban poor through studies that focused almost exclusively on antisocial or criminal behavior, generalized too rapidly, amplified researchers' preexisting stereotypes about authentic Blackness, and framed policy debates in unproductive terms of cultures of poverty and dysfunction. Such work was directed more toward a white readership than a multiracial one.

Those shortcomings notwithstanding, there remains a great deal of value in the ghetto ethnographies Kelley critiques. The best of them, including classics like Elliot Liebow's *Tally's Corner* and Carol Stack's *All My Kin* and contemporary work like Sudhir Venkatesh's *American Project*, compassionately portray individual African Americans, complex social communities, and the relentless daily challenges posed by widespread, racialized poverty. Among its other contributions to policy, work in that tradition presents a well-researched and more realistic portrait of Black lives to white readers who might otherwise be at the mercy of distorted and exploitative Hollywood representations and malicious mischaracterizations by political figures of welfare moms, street-corner men, and gangster kids. There remains an urgent need, however, to complement that work with studies of other social classes and neighborhoods beyond the city limits.

Chapter Outline: African American Suburbs in the Twenty-First Century

I begin by examining the work activists, residents, realtors, and others undertook in order for African Americans to move to Randallstown in the 1970s and shape their community in the subsequent decades. Exploring community issues helps highlight the meaning of race in the suburbs and the diverse views, paths, and threats found in Black suburbs today. Chapter 1 begins by considering earlier accounts of the expansion of Black communities. Sylvia Mackey and her husband, Hall of Fame football star John Mackey, were one of the first African American families to cross the color line into Baltimore County. While their fame and success made this an exceptional case, the Mackeys' motivation, the work that had to be done to make such a move possible, and the consequences for realtors, residents, and others were typical of moves up Liberty Road by later generations of Black suburbanites. Traditionally, when Blacks moved into all-white areas, white residents and social scientists alike described the process as blockbusting. "Blockbusting" referred to real estate brokers' efforts to "break up" a community so that they could profit as whites hurriedly sold houses and brokers resold at higher prices to Blacks (facing limited housing options) who moved in. But academic and neighborhood observers conflated two processes, so that the "problem" was widely defined not as the housing restrictions that banks and white residents had imposed to segregate Blacks but as the processes that led to the arrival of Blacks in previously segregated areas. The Mackeys' integrationist realtor was labeled a blockbuster and lost his business as a result. Accounts by African Americans who moved into such neighborhoods and by Black realtors who assisted them present a more nuanced picture, ultimately revealing that "blockbuster" was more of a slur than an actual role. Previous accounts have exonerated the larger white community by projecting widespread racial intolerance onto a single, imagined blockbuster. The examination presented here allows us to reevaluate the many interrelated processes included in blockbusting, some of which were indeed deleterious, others of which were not. In addition, African Americans describe the events that whites called blockbusting with a fuller sense of their own agency. Seeing residential racial transition through the frame of "blockbusting" seeks to identify predatory discrimination, but it must be replaced by a perspective that prioritizes the needs of African American home seekers and does not mistake desegregation for a problem. African Americans involved in moving into white neighborhoods were seeking to strike the best deal possible in a system that they recognized was structurally organized to their disadvantage.

With this perspective, the account in chapter 2 of African Americans' most recent moves to the suburbs demonstrates the considerable effort required on the part of Black residents, professionals, and others to create Black suburbs against opposition. Here the contribution of local civil rights activists to Black suburbanization becomes clear. The existence of a large, established Black suburb around Baltimore owes its success to the efforts of identifiable organizations, activists, and individual personalities. Key actors included fair housing organizations and civil rights activists, who implemented strategies to desegregate the county. But the desegregation of the Randallstown area also required the contributions of dedicated integrationists in surprising places. A Quaker activist nestled in the Social Security Administration's bureaucracy saw to it that when the organization relocated its national headquarters to the Baltimore suburbs, it actively promoted residential integration for their diverse workforce. The development titan James Rouse proved to be a liberal reformer in the private mortgage lending business and was one of the only sources for mortgages to Blacks or to whites in integrated areas. This study finds that local people's efforts (particularly middle-class activist professionals) can explain why middle-class African American families have been able to break through the suburban color line in some cities but not others. In seeking to understand differences in African American suburbanization rates from city to city, the efforts of local civil rights activists must be considered alongside national changes in law, policy, and financing.

Chapter 3 examines how activist residents have harnessed the power of the suburbs to allow racial integration even while fighting to maintain relative economic exclusivity. Randallstown residents used community associations, county zoning enforcement, and middle-class agency to either oppose or facilitate racial transition of their neighborhoods. A local homeowner association leader like Ella White Campbell became a political force because of her ability to mobilize residents, utilize zoning regulations, and force local officials to take notice. After racial transition, residents used the same tools to ensure that Black communities remained resolutely Black *middle-class* communities. Residents used the same associations, zoning, and political influence to enforce rules that facilitated racial integration but typically opposed economic integration, or the arrival of less wealthy residents. Campbell, for instance, described the strict suburban standards in her neighborhood: "We have a reputation. We do not play. . . . You don't drive around this community and see high grass." She went after an investor who tried to rent one of the split-ranch houses in her neighborhood but failed to maintain it. This kept the area neat but also kept lower-income families out and economically segregated the community. Suburban racial integration has often come at the cost of continued economic segregation, setting up an abiding tension in the success story of middle-class African American suburbs. This chapter measures the impact of suburban activists' efforts to create uniquely suburban, desegregated, stable communities by measuring several area-wide indicators. Results show that suburban racial transition did not follow the classic patterns of white flight or ethnic succession. Instead, the areas where the number of African American residents increased most were *also* the areas of fastest *white* growth. Home values show that while race still mattered, African American suburbs around Baltimore did not experience the sharp decline predicted by models of urban blockbusting. Residents of Randallstown made use of their suburban resources to exert influence over the process of racial transition and to maintain property values. The result has been a qualified success, a suburb that expanded housing options for middle-class African Americans and provided comparative community stability, while still clearly bearing the marks of systemic racial inequality.

In chapter 4, community political issues demonstrate how Black suburbs invert expectations about suburbs and African American communities alike. Along Liberty Road, the meaning of economic development, the community response to big-box retailers, the use of mass transit, and even the availability of liquor licenses all contradict the expected pattern in either urban African American communities or white suburbs. On each of these issues, African American middle-class suburbanites stake out different positions than either white suburbanites or African American urbanites. For instance, activists in cities have opposed Walmart because of the poverty-wage jobs the company creates in a race to the bottom. White suburbanites oppose Walmart because of what it signifies culturally. Unlike city residents or white suburbanites, African American suburbanites welcomed Walmart. A county planner noted that while in white areas "they'll fight a Walmart . . . in Liberty Road they want them. So it's kind of fun for a change. Do a Walmart groundbreaking and not get people killing you." Liberty Road residents likewise navigate their own path on classic community development issues, laying out a unique set of positions shaped by race, class, and suburban space. These local conflicts bring out both progressive and conservative political traditions in African American suburbs and demonstrate the potential of African American suburbs to alter the traditional framing of local political issues.

Chapter 5 reaches the outer boundaries of the suburban expansion. While Randallstown has become a secure Black suburb, few African Americans venture just a few miles farther up the road, a location that remains predominantly white. Between concerns of being profiled while driving and feeling uncomfortable in many predominantly white parts of the county, African Americans' suburban experience is severely constrained, in a manner that has resonance with the experience of Blacks living there a hundred years ago, when people could not always safely travel or live outside of small communities. The basic rights to travel, occupy and use public spaces, and make free use of the surrounding environment are today described by a growing global movement as the "right to the city." But like critiques of neoliberalism, the right to the city has, particularly in the United States, been described largely as a challenge to economic inequality. How do we understand the right to the city racially? Seeing segregation as a denial of the right to the city also helps us understand why—beyond real estate and mortgage discrimination—African Americans continue to live in overwhelmingly African American communities. At the same time, I seek to better understand white attitudes in terms of Negrophobia, a fear and anxiety of Blackness. This chapter finds long-standing attitudes that perpetuate segregated communities that still exist in the suburbs but have taken forms that are more rarely articulated—by residents or observers—and demand new attention.

With the bursting of the housing bubble and the start of the foreclosure crisis, the community's stability was thrown into doubt. Chapter 6 concludes that African American communities experience neither precipitous decline nor halcyon stability. Instead, constructed with great difficulty but particularly exposed to the predations of capitalism and its crises, these are spaces of what I term *punctuated equilibrium*.[85] Such communities are often characterized by relatively long periods of stability and acute moments of crisis. A neighborhood-level examination of the housing bubble, led by people in local foreclosure-prevention nonprofits, illustrates that the model of punctuated equilibrium explains why African Americans were at such high risk for foreclosure and what effects the crisis may have on places like Liberty Road. One former mortgage originator turned foreclosure counselor admitted in an interview that "lenders, especially up here in Maryland, when they would send out mailers they would target African American people." Another foreclosure counselor warned that the "four Ds" of death, disability, divorce, and debt put homeowners at risk, and African Americans are positioned to be at greater risk for each of those. Punctuated equilibrium is a new model that resolves the paradoxical coexistence of structural racial inequality and apparent neighborhood stability and establishes the historical continuity between dangers, like foreclosure, that contemporary African American homeowners face and those that confronted Hawkins and McMechen in their era.

In chapter 7 I consider the long-term political implications of African American suburbanization. African Americans continue to be strong Democratic voters. But people are rarely pure reflections of a single party's platform. Indeed, consistent with their middle-class suburban location, virtually all African Americans in Randallstown had some personally distinct subset of views that would be compatible with conservative positions of the pre-Trump Republican Party, specifically elements of its religious and economic conservativism.

The conclusion asks how African American suburbs might play a role in disrupting the highly racialized and rigidly defined party positions of national electoral politics. While party affiliations often seem unchangeable in the short term and decades of Republican campaigns have been founded on a politics of anti-Black resentment, as recently as 1960 significant numbers of Black Baltimoreans voted Republican. The overwhelming role of race in forming today's polarized political discourse all but prevents African Americans from affiliating with the Republican Party. But the changing demands of American voters, including growing numbers of African American suburbanites, suggest the possibility of a fundamental realignment of electoral loyalties.

In the twenty-first century, African Americans in the suburbs are reconfiguring responses to racial inequality in ways that demand a new understanding of the operation of race in contemporary America. Many aspects of racial inequality have direct lineages to George McMechen's era, but they have changed enough to prevent us from adequately understanding them using existing frameworks. Along the commercial boulevards and interstate highways of the suburbs, across the rolling lawns of single-family houses, African Americans seeking the good life still find that racial inequality, in its neoliberal manifestation, impinges on their lives. As they build communities, join organizations, get involved in local politics, raise families, and worry about their bills, their health, and their children, residents try to improve their communities in a myriad of ways. At times those new ways are inspiring, promising, and nuanced; at other moments the suburban landscape renders them contradictory, exclusive, or imperfect. It is remarkable that residents have been able to create a long-standing, stable community amid the divisive social organization of class- and race-segregated suburbs, coupled with the threat to social and economic stability posed by neoliberalism. Despite those successes, it is evident that the residents along Liberty Road have not achieved equality. *Liberty Road* provides the opportunity to better understand how people have made the progress they have and maps out the journey that remains.

1

Beyond Blockbusting

How Racial Transition Works

As a tight end for the Baltimore Colts, John Mackey made an unbeatable pair with quarterback Johnny Unitas. During the 1966 season, six of Mackey's nine touchdowns included runs of more than fifty yards. The highlight of the 1971 Super Bowl came when a pass by Unitas bounced off the fingertips of two opposing players. Mackey caught the ball and ran seventy-five yards for a touchdown. He was later inducted into the Pro Football Hall of Fame.

In 1964, as he started his career with the Colts, Mackey and his wife Sylvia were looking for a home in the Baltimore area.[1] Their daughter Lisa, the first of three children, was less than a year old. John had grown up in suburban Long Island, and Sylvia came from a long line of highly educated African Americans (her mother *and* grandmother were both college graduates). So, according to Sylvia, the couple was looking for a home in the suburbs from the start. Through a friend they met S. Lee Martin, a young African American realtor who worked for a firm owned by Mal Sherman, who was white. Martin began looking for a home for the Mackeys. But homeowners rarely wanted to sell to Blacks, and other realtors often refused to show homes in the county to prospective Black buyers. Around the time Sherman hired Martin, Sherman had decided to cross the color barrier that other realtors maintained.

Sherman described his introduction into housing desegregation as a revelation. He was well aware what the costs would be for himself professionally.

> I had gone to Baltimore Hebrew Congregation and heard a sermon from Rabbi Lieberman . . . and he said . . . "When the boxcars went to Auschwitz, the gentiles would turn their cheek and we cannot do this as far

as the Negro is concerned. We must step up to the plate and get them equality with whites."

The next morning I went in to see him . . . and I said to him, "What can I do about what you talked about?"

He says, "What do you mean, what can you do? You have more power than I have. . . . You can open up neighborhoods regardless of race, creed, or color." I said, "If I did this, I'd be run out of this town, the way this town is set up. I'd be committing business suicide."

And the rabbi says . . . "Well, you asked me what you could do."

I went home to my wife, and I told her what happened, and I said, "We really have to work on all this." She said, "We came here with nothing in 1949 [from New York]. You've done very well. If this is what you want to do, then go ahead and do it." . . .

So along came an owner out off of Milford Mill Road . . . [in the Randallstown area], and they were willing to make such a sale. It was Sylvia and John Mackey and I took them out there. . . . Before taking them out there, Holmgren and I showed a film to neighbors out there [on integration].

And then, I think we brought a priest and rabbi out there to get them ready for what was going to happen. . . . Oy vey. John Mackey was a member of the Colts football team. And they were doing great. So we showed him this house and they bought it.

According to Sherman, the Mackeys' moving in required some preparation.

John and Sylvia told me of their first meeting of the neighborhood association that they attended. And people asked them, "Why did you buy here—there are no colored children to play with your children." And Sylvia Mackey said, "Well why'd you buy here?" and they said, "Well, we liked the architecture, we liked the wooded lots, we checked the school system, we liked that, and so that's why we bought here." And then Sylvia said, "Well, we liked the same things that you liked. That's why we bought here." And then Sylvia said, "Well, how many of you ladies are college graduates?" I don't know, but maybe 20–25 percent of them raised their hands . . . and Sylvia said . . . "I'm a graduate of Syracuse University" and then John said, "Well how many of you men are college graduates?" and maybe 35–50 percent raised their hand. And he said, "I'm a graduate of Syracuse University also. We're both college graduates," which went to show that they were really a peck above the people that were living there, economically, socially, educationally, and so on. And John Mackey had been an all-America football player.

And so that sale showed us a lot of things. It showed us that, hell, without legislation, we're just not gonna get there.[2]

Their story demonstrates several truths about racial transition. First, the entrance of Blacks into white neighborhoods was hardly an inevitable shift. It required a determined (and financially able) prospective Black home buyer. Second, desegregation needed allied professionals committed to desegregation. Earlier studies have shown that white antiracists adopt their commitment to racial equality because of deep political or religious reasons. As Malcolm X said, "If you find a person without racism . . . usually they're a socialist or their political philosophy is socialism."[3] Sherman was motivated by his rabbi, who was involved in social justice. But Sherman, growing up in New York, also went to a communist-inspired elementary school. By Sherman's account, it was this early exposure to radical political views that fostered his commitment to racial equality. In addition to a willing realtor, the Mackeys' move made use of progressive clergy, a mortgage lender willing to make a loan for a house that crossed the color line, and a homeowner willing to sell to a Black buyer.

Mackey's fame and fortune did not leave his new neighbors so starstruck that they ignored his race. As is often the case, the Black pioneers were of higher socioeconomic status than their white neighbors, but the whites conceived of their arrival as a step down for the neighborhood's social status. While several of the neighbors were won over, others fumed. Even those who spoke to him at the neighborhood meeting were at a loss to understand why this fate—the arrival of an African American family, sports star or not—had befallen them. Nor could they deduce Mackey's motives, as similar to their own as they were.

For his part, Sherman's involvement cost him his business, as he knew it would. Before crossing the color line to sell a house to John Mackey, he had discussed with his wife the reality that to do so would be "business suicide," and in the short term it was.

Soon after he bought it, I started getting phone calls: "You broke the fuck-
ing block, now sell ours to schvartze [Blacks]." I said, "That wasn't my
purpose." "Oh yes, it must have been. You did that to get all the listings
and break everything up here and. . . ." "Not so, at all." He didn't want to
hear from me. "We want you to take our house for sale and sell it to a
schvartze." I said I wouldn't list it on that basis. So, I was finished with
that neighborhood. In other words, I couldn't get listings, I couldn't get
any more business . . . I didn't do it to. . . . But I was labeled a blockbuster.
And soon . . . and almost overnight, my competition would tell people:
"Don't list with Sherman—he's a blockbuster."

The embittered, taunting phone calls and facetious requests to "bust the
block" (by bringing in Blacks for the purpose of scaring whites into selling) that he received from resentful whites reflected his new reputation
among whites, labeled a blockbuster and accused of wanting to destroy
the tranquility of all-white neighborhoods for personal gain. Whites
would no longer do business with him. Builders of new homes in the
suburbs no longer worked with him. His business quickly shrunk from
an office of eighteen realtors to nearly none.[4] (Sherman also tried to
find a house in Baltimore County to sell to Orioles baseball start Frank
Robinson but was unsuccessful.)[5]

Sherman was labeled a blockbuster, a term of opprobrium in accounts
of twentieth-century residential racial transition. But what does the label
"blockbuster" mean? For both residents and researchers, the process
of residential racial transition has been explained, characterized, and
condemned by framing it as an initiative of the greedy blockbuster. The
blockbuster is a character of mythical significance in the epic story of
residential racial transition.

This chapter challenges the blockbuster narrative. The arrival of African Americans in a neighborhood took concerted efforts by people
in many different positions and considerable bravery on the part of the
new Black residents and others. By framing change as "blockbusting,"
the needs, desires, and actions of African American home seekers disappear. The model of the blockbuster is deeply flawed; it does not describe
what actually happened in transitioning neighborhoods. The concep-
tual flaw is so fundamental that reasonable inspection reveals that the
blockbuster did not exist. To understand what really happened when

parts of the suburbs turned Black, we must investigate, interrogate, and ultimately dismiss the myth of the blockbuster.

Defining Blockbusting

Blockbusting means different things to lawmakers, academics, and white and Black residents, making it ill-defined from the start. The term is widely addressed in scholarship and law. As one researcher succinctly defined it, "Blockbusting is a practice in which a real estate agent attempts to move a nonwhite, usually Black family, into an all-white neighborhood for the purpose of exploiting white fears of impending racial turnover and property devaluation to buy up other property on the block at depressed prices."[6] Courts have used similar definitions. The US Court of Appeals explained that "blockbusting refers to the practice of directly inducing or persuading an individual to sell his home by representations as to the entry into his neighborhood of blacks or other minority groups."[7] This description borrowed language directly from the federal Fair Housing Act, which, while not using the word "blockbusting," explicitly defined the practice as illegal.[8]

Academic researchers have also long used the "blockbuster" as the primary model by which to explain residential racial transition from white to Black. To the courts' definition, researchers add the impact of blockbusters on Black home buyers (which is curiously absent from the courts' definitions). Not only does a blockbuster sow seeds of racial fear (for instance, by ominously warning white residents that Blacks are coming to their neighborhood) to induce whites to move out, but blockbusters make extortionate profits buying the houses cheaply from whites and then selling them at inflated prices to Blacks.

White residents, like the courts, ignored the effect on Blacks. To white residents (who wanted to perpetuate their neighborhood's all-white segregation), a "blockbuster" was someone who failed to maintain segregation by selling or renting homes in white neighborhoods to Blacks. In her book, Amanda Seligman, for instance, presented the academic definition.[9] But she acknowledged that for residents of the white Chicago neighborhoods she studied, blockbusting was Blacks moving in. "Racial change, not sales tactics, stood at the heart of what most white West Siders counted as blockbusting."[10] The term thus became murky when researchers tried to insist blockbusting meant exploitative and manipulative sales practices, but their white research subjects used it as a despised synonym for racial integration. The experiences of Mal Sherman and others show that those tagged as "blockbusters" could be antiracist pioneers, not opportunistic profiteers. But residents didn't make distinctions between the motives of integrationism and profit. They didn't want Blacks moving in and blamed blockbusters. Neither white residents nor, ultimately, researchers who wrote about them actually limit discussion of blockbusting to the practices of blockbusters, instead using it as a general term for the whole process of neighborhood racial transition from white to Black.

Studies of blockbusting fall into two general categories. The first are institutional approaches that look at the exploitative practices of real estate brokers, local government, and mortgage lenders that uproot communities. The second are ethnographies of white ethnic communities that chronicle both white resistance to the arrival of African American pioneers and the loss of community (often portrayed as the social and physical destruction of the community) as experienced by whites.[11] Both perspectives are indispensable to the study of blockbusting, but we gain a more complete understanding by considering the objectives of African Americans involved in the process, which get left out of both of the most common perspectives.

The most dramatic accounts of blockbusting and violent white reaction to it have come from histories and ethnographies of white communities in the midst of racial integration.[12] Reflecting the call by theorist David Roediger to interrogate racism through the study of not Black communities but white ones, these ethnographies are invaluable for their presentation of whites' actions, racist ideology, and interethnic variation in response to the arrival of Black neighbors.[13] Rieder, for instance, presents a shocking account by a white who attacked a newly arrive family: "We ran right into the house and kicked the shit out of every one of them."[14] Other work in this vein dissects and presents white racial attitudes from the unmitigated animus directed at African Americans ("they wasted the bomb on Hiroshima")[15] to distinctions that can be found even among informants whose language is rife with references to "niggers" and "spics" between African Americans (categorically rejected as potential neighbors) and Mexicans (disliked but allowed to move into the neighborhood without violence).[16] Work like that of Thomas Sugrue identifies different responses by different white communities (Jewish communities were unlikely to use covenants to exclude Blacks because they knew covenants were used to exclude them too) and distinguishes between "defended" and "undefended" neighborhoods. Defended communities were those in which Black pioneers were met with systematic and prolonged campaigns of significant violence against property and people organized by ironically named neighborhood "improvement" associations. Reflecting the narrowness in the range of whites responses to Black neighbors, "undefended" neighborhoods were those in which Black pioneers also faced violence, often a half dozen incidents, most often against property, but by isolated individuals rather than an organized community group.[17] The distinction is valuable because Sugrue identifies characteristics that foster more or less violent reaction to Black neighbors. In these ways, accounts of white communities in the midst of racial transition are irreplaceable resources for understanding the dynamics of racism.

At the same time, in-depth investigations of white communities carry inherent shortcomings. In particular, accounts of blockbusting tend to be told from the perspective of whites. Thus the arrival of African Americans to a white neighborhood is characterized, by itself, as a problem. Seligman, for instance, noted that even legal remedies to blockbusters' scare tactics "did not address racial change per se . . . a major element of whites' postwar urban crisis ended up unchecked."[18] The crisis was not manipulative real estate tactics but the arrival of Blacks. Seligman went on to characterize "the movement of African Americans onto a block occupied exclusively by whites" as "a crisis that they had to confront."[19] While such accounts presumably represent white informants' views rather than the author's, one result of focusing on white communities (from which the valuable findings noted above are derived) is that simple racial change is presented as an "urban crisis." Also, whites blamed social change for physical deterioration: "[Whites] experienced a twofold urban crisis: one rooted in the landscape's physical decline, the other in an unwelcome social transformation." Similarly, Rieder described a broad swath called "Middle America" feeling "molested by formidable powers: Blacks and liberals and bureaucrats" and accepted whites' racism because the only alternative was to unrealistically expect residents to blame "slavery, labor markets, or similarly arcane forces."[20] There is no substitute for such intimate accounts of white reaction, but they are structurally ill suited for assessing policy.

The other type of blockbusting study has been a more macro-level, institutional analysis informed by both history and quantitative data on structural changes in the community and the city. Kevin Fox Gotham's work on Kansas City, for instance, is a valuable addition in this respect.[21] As Gotham points out, previous work on blockbusting had used the ecological model of invasion and succession, emphasizing consumer choice and market demands. Instead, Gotham focused on the role of institutions, such as the Federal Housing Administration, the mortgage and real estate industries, public school administrations, and real estate redliners to show that blockbusting and resegregation were not the natural outcomes of individual consumer preference but the product of institutions infused with racist assumptions that informed school boundaries, lending, and community boundaries. This is a necessary and vital insight into the nature of blockbusting and the role of large institutions like the federal government in establishing twentieth-century residential segregation in the first place.

The story of Randallstown's transformation into an African American suburb expands this institutional analysis in two directions. First, while Gotham is most interested in the institutions that contributed to conditions leading whites to leave, there are just as many institutions necessary to allow African Americans to move in. Just as early ecological models reduced white out-movement to natural processes of "succession" and ignored the role of institutions, so accounts of blockbusting have continued to reduce African American in-moving to "invasion," not sufficiently accounting for the institutions, social movements, and social changes that allowed African Americans to move out of existing ghettoes and into new neighborhoods. Similarly, revisionist historians point out that African Americans were not new arrivals but have always been in the suburbs.[22] This attention by historians has just begun to be matched by studies of African American suburbs by sociologists like Karyn Lacy.[23]

Admirably enough, courts and researchers described a kind of real estate broker as a "blockbuster" to focus attention on the actions of people they believed were using race-baited fear to victimize homeowners. But there are several significant problems with thinking of racial transition through the lens of blockbusting.

First, the image of blockbusting was simplistic and imagined the blockbuster to be a powerful, unstoppable malignancy. W. Edward Orser, who studied racial transition in Baltimore in detail, pointed out that the blockbuster played but one small role in the larger process. "Blockbusters lit the match, but, as the definition implies, they were only one ingredient in a complex set of circumstances. Indeed, blockbusting exploited the crevice of an otherwise pervasive and systematic system that governed race and residence. In mid-twentieth century urban American, a silent conspiracy sought to assure and preserve the segregated dual housing market."[24] (That silent conspiracy had been in place since McMechen and Hawkins had challenged more explicit segregation at the start of the twentieth century.) Despite their precise definitions, in actuality studies of blockbusting have examined a much broader range of important processes. These include attitudes, violence, and the gerrymandering of school boundaries to maintain segregated schools.[25] Crucially, some of these processes are not caused by blockbusters and would happen without them. For instance, the boundaries of a study of blockbusting must and do encompass the entire process of racial transition, even after, for instance, the neighborhood reaches the racial "tipping point" after which whites continue to move out and new whites will not move in even without exhortation from blockbusters.[26] Similarly, store owners quickly fled blockbusted areas, but leaving stores they had leased was not the result of blockbusting real estate agents.[27] Likewise, Rieder's account of the racial transition of Canarsie includes all of the worst elements of white reaction to classic blockbusting but describes the process entirely as a micro-level dynamic of white owners selling to Black buyers, without intervening blockbusters.[28] Rather than making the blockbuster the sole necessary and sufficient agent, blockbusting in practice is analyzed as just such a complex arrangement that maintains separate housing markets for whites and Blacks that results, at the borders, in sizeable racial transition whenever Black families begin buying homes on formerly white streets.[29]

Second, the definition presented by Gotham and others focuses on the actions of white blockbusters but does not include the overcharging of Black customers in its definitions. "Attempts to move a nonwhite, usually Black family" into a home that had belonged to a white family are not a social problem. It is the overcharging and dishonest business practices toward Black buyers that constitute the real crimes of the putative blockbuster.

Third, by highlighting the agents of racially intolerant real estate practices, African Americans and white homeowners are unintentionally drained of their own agency. People decided to make moves without the need for blockbusters. Although African Americans involved in blockbusted neighborhoods were aware of the work of blockbusters, the central experience of blockbusting for them was not the machinations of the blockbuster but the purchase of homes by themselves and other African Americans. Scholarly and popular definitions both put racial change at the heart of blockbusting and choose to define that change as a problem of such significance that the whole enterprise is morally compromised. In contrast, telling the story of the same neighborhoods in the same period but from the perspective of arriving Blacks does not depict what went on in the neighborhood, imperfect as it was, as a crisis, nor condemn blockbusters—even though Blacks resented their efforts to destabilize their new neighborhoods. As Seligman concedes,

> Black Chicagoans, for their part, expressed more mixed attitudes toward the real estate dealers and apartment owners who made housing available at the edge of the ghetto. Many were pleased with the opportunity to live in less crowded conditions, but others resented the psychological and financial costs associated with this housing. Blockbusting and its concomitant practices that exploited African Americans might have constituted a portion of their urban crisis as well, but the fact that Blacks needed adequate housing so desperately meant that getting access to their own property was as much a welcome solution as it was a problem.[30]

From this perspective, the actions of blockbusters do not warrant primary concern. Thus Steven Gregory's account of the racial transition of Corona Queens begins with how African Americans moved in, assumes white out-moving as a given, and mentions blockbusters only in passing.[31] Gregory goes on to assume that efforts to stop blockbusters were cosmetic and ineffective because the dynamic of white out-moving and Black in-moving happened independent of actions of such agents.

The comments of African American Ginny Young, whose husband Buddy had played for the Baltimore Colts before John Mackey, provide wonderful evidence of this. She remembered many details of her neighborhood, but not the process that was supposedly so central to it: "Beautiful. When we moved there—but of course it was—what did they call it? Some kind of *busting* when white realtors would come in and tell the owners that Blacks were moving in and actors would come in and say your neighbors have sold." Ginny readily shared stories of the era's patronizing racism and had heard the story of blockbusting and its dramatic street theater, but when I asked she couldn't think of anyone she knew who had seen it happen firsthand.[32] It was in the back of her mind, not on the tip of her tongue, elusive and illusory. From the perspective of African American residents, the role of blockbusters was not that important and certainly did not condemn the whole enterprise. Instead, "blockbusting" was the birth of a community.

Blockbusting is thus a tangle of overlapping definitions, a conflation of social problems and social progress, and an allegation that may not describe reality. Assessing it therefore requires that we disaggregate some of the explicit and implicit components of the practice as it has been understood. There are four major elements to blockbusting as it has been described by the courts, researchers, and the public.

The first practice ascribed to blockbusting is "fear peddling": blockbusters allegedly scared residents in a previously segregated, all-white neighborhood by introducing Black residents. It was because of their arrival that white residents left extremely rapidly (catalyzed, some argue, by blockbusters' racist, fear-mongering whispers, phone calls, mass mailings, and door knocking), selling their homes at fire-sale prices to the blockbusters.

Second and simultaneously, blockbusters did what whites expected respectable realtors not to do: they sold, rented, or showed houses in white neighborhoods to Blacks who might be interested in moving in. Interview projects from the 1950s, 1960s, and 1970s show that crossing the color line in this way was explicitly articulated as a violation of white community norms, of norms within the real estate industry. The National Association of Real Estate Boards until 1950 supported segregation with a written policy that prohibited members from introducing any ethnic group into a neighborhood where other fellow members did not already live.[33] Long after the practice was no longer official policy, it remained widespread.

Third, blockbusters engaged in *hyper-exploitation* by charging Blacks much higher prices for housing than whites. This could be accomplished simply by raising the price. But more often other practices were included. Since African Americans could not borrow money from banks and most other sources of conventional mortgages, brokers would either lend money at exorbitant interest rates or set up "contract sales," "buying on time," or "rent-to-own" schemes in which the broker owned the house and the Black would-be buyer paid rent that was credited toward an inflated purchase price. (A 1955 survey in Baltimore found that 95 percent of all purchases by Blacks from whites were with "contract sales.")[34] To add insult to injury, brokers would then add additional charges, overcharge for repairs, and systematically engage in similar misleading, dishonest, and criminal financial practices to further inflate the monthly cost or total cost, until Black buyers could no longer afford the home and were evicted, having lost everything. Accounts from at least as late as the 1950s suggest that these practices were widespread in several cities and that the courts, composed of men whose money was often invested in real estate schemes connected to the brokers, ruled against Black plaintiffs who claimed misconduct by such brokers.[35]

Fourth, whites expected that blockbusted neighborhoods would experience a precipitous decline. Buildings would deteriorate and public services from schools to trash pickup would falter. Crime and violence would skyrocket. Obvious questions were rarely asked about the responsibility of the new absentee landlords who neglected buildings, or blockbusters who left exploited homeowners with no money to make repairs, or of the state that maintained discriminatory tiers of city services. This component was important because if simple prejudice against Black neighbors wasn't enough to dislocate white residents, expectations about what a Black neighborhood would become was.

Recognizing the four distinct practices subsumed under the label of blockbusting allows a more useful analysis, particularly for applying our understanding of the elements of blockbusting to post-1970 real estate practices. Each of the four groups that described blockbusting—white homeowners, housing activists, elected officials, and researchers—addressed a different constellation of these four components.

White homeowners in areas that experienced racial transition denounced blockbusting largely because of its second component, that of allowing Blacks into segregated white areas. To deny that they and their neighbors were intolerant, they sometimes argued that white flight from their community would not have occurred had it not been for the first component—the fear peddling that blockbusters were said to engage in. As this chapter demonstrates, the extent of fear peddling appears to be wildly exaggerated.

For housing activists, there was never a problem with the second part of the practice, desegregating white neighborhoods and allowing African Americans to expand their limited, segregated housing options to include new, higher quality neighborhoods. It was the third part—the extortionate terms on which Blacks were "sold" homes—that required action. Meanwhile, housing activists often blamed blockbusters for the resegregation that followed the arrival of new Black homeowners. Activists claimed that, absent the fear mongering of blockbusters, more white residents would have remained after the arrival of the first Black buyers, creating more integrated neighborhoods rather than zones that quickly emptied of whites, filled with Blacks, and re-created high rates of segregation.

For their part, policy makers sought to stop the first part, fear peddling, with legislation. As Christopher Niedt explains, "Realtors had successfully blockbusted city neighborhoods in the Liberty Road corridor during the 1950s and 1960s, but as they advanced into the county, they were met with resistance. Resident outcry prompted the local legislative delegation to introduce anti-blockbusting measures in the state house in 1969."[36] Officials proposed legislation including prohibitions against "for sale" signs or "sold" signs that whites believed realtors used to signal that large numbers of whites were leaving and that others should sell their homes too. (It is telling that African Americans challenged the constitutionality of these sign restrictions as infringements on free speech because they saw the laws as efforts to keep Blacks ignorant of property sales that they might be interested in.) The second component of blockbusting, color-blind real estate dealing, is now enshrined in law, enforced through lawsuits, but in reality unevenly practiced. The third component, hyper-exploitation of home buyers and racially discriminatory lending, is contrary to public policy but, as evidenced in the subprime mortgage crisis, still widespread.

Most academic accounts of blockbusting have failed to adequately specify what is and is not problematic among the four components of residential racial transition. A new orientation for scholarship on community segregation must replace the indiscriminate hand-wringing of the blockbusting literature with a means to tell the story of African American neighborhood expansion from a more productive perspective, the view of African American home buyers, those whose options are most systematically and seriously curtailed. Such a perspective would better identify effective contemporary strategies for progress against racial inequality and the real obstacles to such progress.

In contrast to portrayals that construct blockbusting as a problem, describe it as a "crisis," and portray it as "threat," I assess racial transition—the web of activities collected under the banner of blockbusting—as a process whose benefits and costs are quite different from those otherwise supposed.[37] In undertaking to move into new neighborhoods, African Americans have achieved some of their goals and made measurable improvements, even while the manifest problems with housing segregation in America have ensured that the outcomes are far from perfect. This approach builds on revisionist histories of suburbs, particularly those by Andrew Wiese, Betsy Nicolaides, and Kevin Kruse.[38] Aided by these perspectives, we can reframe what others have chosen to call "blockbusting" as a valuable tool for increasing the range and quality of housing options for African Americans, in collaboration with open housing laws and civil rights movements. This perspective relocates the social "problem" of blockbusting more exclusively in white residents' reaction (both moving out and failing to move in) and mainstream mortgage lenders' discrimination, rather than in Black residents' arrival. Racial transition, including situations in which it has been labeled blockbusting, is a key mechanism by which middle-class African Americans have harvested what fruits they can of the civil rights movement.

Integrating revisionist understandings into the Baltimore case is facilitated by the work of a community of scholars who have focused on Baltimore City and Baltimore County. Louis Diggs, a local oral historian who has published several books on the historical African American communities of Baltimore County, provides a unique view of much smaller African American communities that preceded postwar suburbanization (and, for that matter, Emancipation itself).[39] Similarly, study of the broader range of institutions and larger social forces in Baltimore County benefits immensely from the work of several scholars who have begun examining how urban renewal, highway building, and disinvestment after the 1968 riots were intended to displace African Americans but also had the thoroughly unintended consequence of catalyzing African American suburbanization.[40] Finally, the comparison of the suburban and urban experiences of racial transition is aided by Orser's study of classic blockbusting in a Baltimore City neighborhood twenty years before the beginning of large-scale racial transition in Baltimore County. Beyond presenting a valuable point of historical comparison, Orser elucidates three pillars of the dual housing market and thus of the conditions that laid the foundation for blockbusting and rapid racial transition: (1) an institutional commitment to segregation by banks, realtors, and the government, (2) "the refusal of white residents to consider the possibility of residential integration," and (3) "pent up demand for housing opportunity by African Americans, long-restricted in terms of residential options but eager, even desperate, for improved housing and neighborhood amenities."[41] While institutional approaches examine the first foundation and ethnographies the second, study of the African American experience of blockbusting and racial transition fully renders that third pillar, while also contributing analysis of a broader range of institutions to the first pillar. The story in the racially transitioning suburbs suggests that the perspective of that third pillar—African American interest in homes outside the existing urban ghetto—is a more productive perspective from which to evaluate the outcomes from blockbusting than the second pillar of racist white reaction. Research motivated by the "blockbusting" frame has been misdirected, focusing on dramatic if vague stories (of fear peddling) and rarely considering some of the most important problems in housing segregation (like hyper-exploitation of Black home buyers). We come up short when talking this way about residential racial transition, but not just because we're missing part of the story. Blockbusting points us in the wrong direction because much of what we thought we knew about blockbusting is not true.

Tortured Confessions of a Blockbuster

Accounts of blockbusting typically focus on the white real estate broker who bought up houses. In fact, accounts typically focus on the *same* blockbuster, Norris Vitchek. Almost anyone who has read about blockbusting and the changing racial composition of American neighborhoods has read parts of Vitchek's account of the machinations of blockbusters. Vitchek's firsthand account of blockbusting gave the practice "national notoriety" and remains the definitive account of what blockbusters do.[42] But it is not clear that the description of Vitchek's blockbusting tactics is accurate, or even that Vitchek really existed.

Norris Vitchek, in a first-person expose in the *Saturday Evening Post* titled "Confessions of a Blockbuster," claimed, "I am a block-buster." He defined blockbusting this way: "I specialize in locating blocks which I consider ripe for racial change. Then I 'bust' them by buying properties from the white owners and selling them to Negroes—with the intent of breaking down the rest of the block for colored occupancy." Blockbusters were specialized real estate brokers who circled the city and moved in on neighborhoods, not profiting incidentally from racial change but triggering that change for profit. He wrote sneeringly that "we were not only making money, we were having fun doing what we were doing. . . . We would try to outdo each other with the most outlandish threats that people would believe and chuckle at the end of the day." The article described outrageous performances blockbusters would go through to scare whites about soon-to-arrive Black families. The author claimed he would pay Black women receiving "aid to dependent children" to walk their kids through the neighborhood or Black men to drive noisy cars down the street or make phone calls to homeowners asking for "Johnnie Mae," a stereotypically Black name. The performances were all in the service of scaring whites into selling their homes cheap. "Confessions" got the desired reaction, especially among white West Side Chicago homeowners. Over the years, it became the lapidary account of the manipulative practices blockbusters engaged in and how they flipped neighborhoods. The "Confessions" article has been cited in sociological texts, law review articles on real estate practices, and histories of racial change.[43] The article even spawned imitations, including another piece published twenty-five years later, also called "Confessions of a Blockbuster," that made the same incendiary claims about real estate brokers' behaviors while "busting" a block.[44]

Both articles had lives far beyond their actual readership. Vitchek's "Confessions" article almost seemed to have been circulated in battered photocopied form. Historian Andrew Wiese, for instance, found reference to Vitchek's article in a master's thesis by Roberta Raymond, who herself cited a copy of the article with no publication date indicated.[45] Richard Rothstein cited it alongside an *Atlantic Monthly* article that referenced payments for fighting women and noisy cars and calls to Johnnie Mae without mentioning Vitchek's article by name. Rothstein's otherwise meticulously researched book even claimed Vitchek said he "arranged burglaries," perhaps an embellishment he picked up from one of the other sources that had cited Vitchek secondhand.[46] Vitchek's story appeared in Amanda Seligman's book and others.[47] The second "Confessions" article lived on not even in battered secondhand form but by reputation alone. It was cited in Andrew Wiese's 2004 history of the suburbs, *Places of Their Own.* Wiese quoted a portion he found in Rosalyn Baxandall and Elizabeth Ewen's book.[48] Baxandall and Ewen found it, in turn, in Levine and Harmon's 1992 book. Levine and Harmon, the only writers who ever saw the original account, no longer have the article, nor does any library.[49] Though the piece, which turned out to be no more than an anonymous letter to the editor, claimed to recount events said to have taken place twenty years earlier, the story, published in an obscure industry publication that went out of business two years later, lived on for decades. The winding trail of secondary citations of these oft-told tales implies the story has the veracity of a legend. Researchers never sought out the anonymous author of the second article. But more is clear about the author of the first article—there was no Norris Vitchek.

As Amanda Seligman helpfully explained in her account, when the 1962 article was published about Chicago blockbusting, angry white West Side Chicago homeowners immediately tried to determine who the real blockbuster was behind the pseudonym. The neighborhood newspaper investigated. Suspicion soon focused on Mark Satter. "After a few weeks of hedging," Seligman wrote, "Satter admitted that he was indeed Alfred Balk's source [Balk was the editor of the story] but adamantly denied that he was a blockbuster."[50]

Satter was hardly a blockbuster. A leftist lawyer, Satter had spent years defending Black residents in court from the exploitative practices of people he would call blockbusters (who would pile on fees to make payments impossible, forcing evictions and loss of residents' equity). Satter did own properties that he rented to African Americans, but there is no evidence he did so on the exploitative terms his opponents did. Satter is best characterized as a crusading, if isolated, civil rights lawyer, pursuing a lonely and often unsuccessful campaign against blockbusting practices and Chicago's uncompromising residential segregation. Since Satter worked against segregation, to most white Chicagoans he was the same as a blockbuster—someone who dared work against their efforts to keep their neighborhoods segregated white.

In articles in the neighborhood paper the *Garfieldian*, Satter initially admitted he was the person in the article: "I wrote that *Post* article. Certainly I did!" ran the subheadline. I thus long assumed, from Seligman's book, that Vitchek *was* Satter.[51] Seligman concluded that the "Confessions" article was "a hoax."[52] In her assessment, Satter had written in the voice of a true blockbuster to publicize the abuses of disreputable real estate dealers and to show that the thoroughgoing racism of the whole system hurt white and Black residents.

But if Satter was the source for the article, then the original source for all the histories of blockbusting is a fabrication written by a foe of blockbusting, not an accurate account by an actual blockbuster.

Was Vitchek actually Satter? Mark Satter's daughter, Beryl Satter, said no. Beryl, a historian at Rutgers University, wrote *Family Properties*, a widely acclaimed, carefully detailed, and compelling story about her father Mark's life and one-man crusade against the Chicago business and political establishment, which profited from the exploitative practices directed at Blacks. According to her account, Alfred Balk, an editor at the *Saturday Evening Post*, had come to Chicago to write about blockbusting. He had met with her father. Mark had directed Balk to blockbusters he could interview but did not write the article. The blockbuster, she concluded, was someone else. Beryl explained that while Balk had been brought to court and ordered to name his source, he refused and won a victory for press freedom in his defense. She interviewed Balk before he died, and Balk refused to name his source, saying he had promised complete anonymity and would honor that commitment. Beryl said that her father had always assumed Vitchek was a composite of several people, but Balk insisted the blockbuster was a real individual (and that it was not her dad). In a letter to a reader, Balk once explained that the blockbuster had been willing to talk because "he paid the man for the story" and because the blockbuster "did seem genuinely angry at being scapegoated for what he saw as a business practice in which many, many people were implicated."[53]

Had Mark written the article? Beryl Satter believed he had not. As she explained in communications with me, in the papers of her father that she had examined for her book, she found working drafts of all his other essays, "clearly showing his authorship." She also found one typescript of the Vitchek article among his papers, but it apparently lacked the signs that Satter himself had written and revised it, and she believed Balk had provided it to her father. In fact, she wrote that her father was dissatisfied with the article because he believed it underestimated the profits blockbusters made by flipping properties from whites to Blacks.

What can we conclude? Chicago residents believed Satter was Norris Vitchek. Satter told the *Garfieldian* he was, or at least that he had written much of the story, but his papers suggest otherwise. And Alfred Balk, the *Saturday Evening Post* editor who came out to Chicago to write a story about blockbusting, insisted Vitchek was some other, real blockbuster. Without concrete evidence, what can we conclude?

With fifty years' hindsight, a highly likely answer emerges. Balk had come to write an article about blockbusting. When the article was published, it was written in the second person, addressing the reader directly: "If you are an average white citizen, with average prejudices, you may regard all this as the ruin of metropolitan neighborhoods. I think of it merely as more business for what already is a growth industry."[54] Evidence in the article shows the first-person narrator was almost certainly not a blockbuster, not even a person of typical white American racial prejudices, but someone quite radical in their thinking about Black residential segregation and the need for civil rights reform.

First, the narrator described blockbusting uniquely: "I make my money—quite a lot of it, incidentally—in three ways: (1) by beating down the prices I pay the white owners by stimulating their fear of what is to come; (2) by selling to the eager Negroes at inflated prices; and (3) by financing the purchases at what amounts to a very high rate of interest." This is not how a blockbuster in Chicago would have defined his job. First, all three components are described in the most contemptible terms. People in all sorts of jobs that the general public finds contemptible justify what they do; the more contemptible the job, the more they rationalize it positively. The blockbuster could have done so as easily as saying that he engaged in the classic model of "buy low, sell high" or that he sold homes irrespective of color or creed (as integrationist realtors in Mal Sherman's time often did). Indeed, these are precisely the justifications articulated by the speculators Satter sued on behalf of Black home buyers who had been overcharged for homes.[55] Likewise, any real blockbuster at the time, talking to whites, could have readily justified the higher prices charged to Blacks not as "inflated" but as necessary to compensate for some imagined negative stereotype about Black customers—their being financially unreliable, unsophisticated, unable to keep up their home, or a host of other things. Again, one speculator who overcharged Black home buyers used exactly those stereotypes to justify his inflated costs in an interview with Beryl Satter.[56]

The description given in the Vitchek article is unlikely to be by an actual speculator for other reasons as well. Recall that whites (then and later) defined blockbusters in terms of their violation of the white racial consensus not to let Blacks into white areas and by the "ruin" that they caused them, not in terms of the harm they did Blacks. Yet two-thirds of Vitchek's definition considers the harm done to Blacks. The speaker's definition of blockbusting is hardly that of a white person who shares white Chicagoans' prejudices.

To the contrary, the narrator seemed well acquainted with liberal perspectives. Later in the article, Vitchek cited a report by the Fund for the Republic, a liberal think tank, that said 80 percent of transitioning neighborhoods kept or gained value rather than decreasing in value as Negroes move in.

In line with these apparently liberal sympathies, the narrator concluded by challenging the reader to act with questions that would be posed by a liberal, like Balk, or a civil rights lawyer, like Satter, but not a blockbuster: "Would you try to influence your bank or savings-and-loan association to begin lending to Negroes? Would you help remove the pressure on 'busted' areas by welcoming a Negro family into your block?" In all, the article concluded with no fewer than eight proposals for equal rights reform. The article presented indictments, couched as challenges by the blockbuster, of the Real Estate Board for requiring members to discriminate against Black buyers, banks for refusing to lend to Blacks, police for failing to protect Black residents in new neighborhoods, and the city council for failing to pass fair housing laws. The author criticized neighborhood improvement associations that were actually "all-white" conspiracies to keep Blacks out, the Board of Education for discriminatory treatment of Blacks schools, white investors for bankrolling blockbusters, and newspapers that wrote only about Blacks in terms of "crime and welfare problems" rather than Black churches, business, or educational successes. The author was not a blockbuster; the author was a civil rights advocate.

The article in the community paper about whether Satter wrote the piece contradicted itself and may well have misrepresented Satter, whom the paper already strongly disliked as an opponent of the white exclusion their readers largely supported.[57] In the article in the *Garfieldian* in which Satter at first admitted to being the person in the article, he clarified his role:

> "While I wrote the article, I was not the individual quoted from experience—not the practicing blockbuster. However," he said, "the story I submitted and on which I collaborated recounted my experiences with Negroes in this housing situation."
>
> Satter said he had supplied all the information.
>
> But when pressed by the reporter, he again denied he was the anonymous "blockbuster" who allegedly told all in the *Post* article.
>
> "I told you how to find the blockbusters," he said. "Just check the *Daily Defender* [a Chicago African American paper where real estate dealers would have advertised to Blacks]. . . . The writer Alfred Balk, who penned the piece, I'm sure, made the blockbuster in the story a compilation of all real estate men who prey on the Negro housing problem."[58]

While the statements the article attributes to Satter are contradictory, the theme throughout them is that Satter did not see himself as the actual narrator of the story but that he aided Balk and may have made significant contributions to the description of what blockbusters did, even writing out something for the editor.

Balk may have spoken to real estate dealers who did business with Blacks—as Satter said, they could be found by reading advertisements in the local paper. But he was hardly transcribing a monologue by one of them throughout the article. The writing may have been by Balk, but it reflected, with considerable consistency, the way Mark Satter described the practices of blockbusters. Balk had talked to Satter about blockbusters, and Satter's contributions to Balk's understanding of the issue were significant enough that Balk sent Satter a draft of his work, presumably before it was published for feedback or comment. "Confessions of a Blockbuster," the article to which most sources turn for a firsthand exposé of blockbusting, is clearly more an indictment of those practices by one of its sharpest critics, not an account from the inside. If the writer was the editor, Balk, he was a rhetorical genius, concealing a call for desegregation within a first-person account of real estate practices that most readers would find manipulative and heartless. The author proposed the reform of a vast array of racist institutions, casting an ambitious civil rights agenda as the logical means for self-interested white homeowners to save their investments.

We know less about what really went on in transitioning neighborhoods than we thought. In other cases we know more about what real estate brokers did, but the charge of blockbusting is no more certain. In Baltimore in the mid-twentieth century, Morris Goldseker was the person most widely denounced as a blockbuster. As Ed Orser tells the story in *Blockbusting in Baltimore*, residents protested and were arrested in front of his office, charged he made excessive profits, and sued to stop him. Goldseker bought homes in white, often Jewish areas. He sold homes to Blacks. He was, in economic parlance, an *arbitrageur*, one who profits from buying in one market and selling in another. Arbitrage may take the form of people buying a commodity like gold in one country where the price is lower and selling it in another where it is higher, or buying cars inexpensively in one geographical region and driving them to a region where used cars are more rare, more in demand, and thus sold for higher prices. People who buy gas, bottled water, or generators and drive them into areas struck by natural disasters to sell at higher prices are arbitrageurs. In Goldseker's case, he bought homes in Baltimore's white, Jewish market and sold them in the

African American market, where such housing was more expensive. There is evidence that he made a profit, among other means, by moving from one market to the other, in classic arbitrage fashion.

The suit was brought against Goldseker by a multiracial group called the Activists. The heart of their case was that Goldseker had sold homes at "excessive" markups.[59] Although the Activists pointed to markups as high as 80 percent, Goldseker's company responded that the prices reflected risks, expenses, and a reasonable profit. The case collapsed when the Activists were unable to hire an expert who could study and quantify whether the markups had been excessive. To the larger public accusation of being a blockbuster, Goldseker admitted to selling homes through "buy-like-rent" arrangements but pointed out that his buyers had few opportunities to secure conventional mortgages. Goldseker's nephew defended the company's practices, insisting, "We were the first liberals. We were the first pioneers. We were supplying a need."[60] The justifications of Goldseker and his nephew—of profits reflecting risk and motives that were liberal and entrepreneurial—were much more typical of brokers who crossed the color line than the description given in Norris Vitchek's article. What Goldseker and Vitchek share, however, is that once again, on closer inspection, someone who was supposedly a notorious blockbuster faded into thin air.

That "Confessions of a Blockbuster" was not written by a blockbuster matters because the *Saturday Evening Post* article regularly frames the discussion of blockbusters. There is a more reliable source about realtors who crossed the color line in the era of Norris Vitchek, and it paints a very different story. For her 1969 book *Racial Policies and Practices of Real Estate Brokers*, Rose Helper interviewed ninety real estate dealers in Chicago—the same city in which Satter and Vitchek operated—who worked in Black or racially transitioning neighborhoods.[61] This more realistic account of real estate dealers varies seriously from the account in Vitchek's article.

Who were real estate dealers who sold homes in racially transitioning neighborhoods in the era of the Vitchek "Confessions" article? In Helper's extensive interviews, they were there by happenstance. They had been real estate agents in white neighborhoods and would have remained so, except that the neighborhoods in which they worked started to become nonwhite.

Brokers didn't describe the kinds of theatrical tactics Satter alleged. Roberta Raymond, who studied real estate in Chicago in the years just after Vitchek claimed to be practicing there, said panic peddling was a "rumor" of which "no documentation has yet been provided."[62] Real estate brokers in transitioning neighborhoods saw themselves not as extraordinarily malevolent people but as real estate men who found themselves and their colleagues with a choice to make: while they had previously dealt only with whites, white buyers were disappearing as Black buyers were showing up. They could sell to Blacks or do no more business in the area. They held a range of views, from accepting to derogatory. Some sold to the new customers, some did not. The dealers, then, were not professional blockbusters who pursued racial change into new neighborhoods but local realtors who chose to work with African American clients when there were few prospective white renters or buyers coming to the neighborhood anymore. This does not mean that African American home seekers were not mistreated or that the brokers were not prejudiced—many were explicitly so. But they came to this position accidentally, not, as the blockbuster model implies, as agents who sought out racial change and exploited fear and the dual housing market. They didn't find blockbusting, blockbusting found them.

Their accounts challenge several of the fundamental assumptions of the conventional understanding of blockbusting practices. The inflammatory "Confessions," for instance, supports the claim that blockbusters actively practiced fear peddling. The Vitchek article makes the oft-repeated claim that a blockbuster would pay Blacks to show up in the neighborhood: that one blockbuster paid "Negroes with noisy cars to begin driving up and down the street a few times a day. He also paid a Negro mother who drew aid-to-dependent children payments to walk the block regularly with her youngsters." That the article was at least enriched by someone who wanted to highlight the excesses of blockbusters raises questions about the veracity of the claims. Helper's interviews not only found no evidence of such behavior but make clear that doing so would have been unnecessary. In white neighborhoods near growing Black neighborhoods, whites often attributed malicious intent to the most benign and quotidian activities by Blacks. A statement by one real estate broker in Helper's sample is particularly revealing. In describing the means by which Blacks sowed fear, he explains, "There is a certain period of *fear*. It seems like *a calculated procedure* that's followed by the colored people before they *break into* a neighborhood—such things as shopping in the target neighborhood. Yes, Negroes come in *deliberately* to shop in the stores. They also drive up and down the streets for no apparent reason. They'll also utilize *some* of the public playgrounds *on a limited scale once in a while*."[63] Yes, Blacks shop in stores, drive down streets, and play in playgrounds. The speaker cannot imagine why they would do any of these things. That Blacks might have had their own reasons, without white inducement, to walk or drive down the street of a transitioning neighborhood—that was typically adjacent to the larger Black ghetto—never occurred to residents. That those reasons might be as banal as wanting to go to the store or the playground was unimaginable to whites like that realtor. When Blacks drove down a street, they presumably were going somewhere; the speaker makes clear that the reason for Blacks driving was "not apparent" to him. (Meanwhile, it sounds unlikely that Blacks would drive through such hostile white neighborhoods without good reason.) This notion, that any banal activity by a Black person in a formerly white area is a calculated provocation, is enshrined in Vitchek's account of blockbusting. Interviews with whites reveal what I came to describe as "egocentric causality," in which cause and effect are confused. An observer imagines that someone else's actions are *caused* by the *effect* they have on the observer: if whites are afraid when Blacks walk down the street, then Blacks must be walking down the street *in order to make them* afraid, not for any reason internal to the life of those Black pedestrians themselves. The disconnect between the banality of the actions and the imagined maliciousness of the intent is inescapable today but was invisible to white residents at the time.

This casts doubt over the first practice in blockbusting: fear peddling. In accounts I have collected of whites living in racially transitioning neighborhoods, activities that would otherwise be called fear peddling were often much more banal than they were interpreted to be. Postcards sent by realtors to a neighborhood encouraging owners to contact the realtor and promising that now is a good time to sell could be interpreted as efforts to instill urgency in already-nervous homeowners. But such postcards are widely distributed, in transitioning and nontransitioning neighborhoods, to generate business. Likewise, a white woman recalled a story that had become legendary in her family: they had lived in a white neighborhood as Blacks were beginning to move nearby. The family was not racist, she explained, but had to move when they were victims of an attempted arson, in which Blacks had tried to burn their house down as a message that they should move. Regretfully, the family moved, and for decades afterward they told the story of Black threats to their home. The arson event? A family member had found three birthday candles stuck to their back door (perhaps with wax), the candles recently extinguished. If they had not blown out, or not been discovered as soon as they were, "they could have burned the house down," the woman explained. When I noted that arsonists rarely set fires with three birthday candles and that gasoline is accessible to anyone wanting to start a large fire, she was perplexed.[64] The incident may have been bizarre but was more likely the product of children playing (whether they would have been white or Black, or what the nature of game was, it is impossible to know) than an attack on the family's home.

Other whites have claimed that explicit fear peddling does occur: one white homeowner living in a white neighborhood that bordered non-white neighborhoods in New York, for instance, told me that he had received calls in the 1990s warning that "they're coming." The homeowner told me the story to arrive at the antiracist punch line that he told the caller he hoped they did because he didn't much like the close-minded white neighbors he currently had. The account suggests that some fear peddling may have happened (though that neighborhood remained predominantly white, casting further doubt that realtors could flip a neighborhood on their own even if they wanted to). Could a realtor make such phone calls? Perhaps. In general, however, the claims of fear peddling discussed here suggest that it was probably rare because it was largely unnecessary. Whites took banal or ambiguous events (Blacks driving in cars, candles stuck by the door) as signs of blatant hostility. They embraced egocentric causality to conclude that Blacks' actions were in fact calculated acts of fear peddling. And white residents near African American neighborhoods or in transitioning areas knew that African Americans lived nearby, knew if African Americans were moving closer, and knew the changes in home values and white demand for their neighborhoods as those demographic changes occurred. White residents could generate their own fear, and it was unlikely that local real estate brokers, who unintentionally found themselves working in racially transitioning areas, took the initiative to seed fear rather than focusing on the difficult question of how to operate in the racially shifting context they now found themselves in. It is conceivable that ominous phone calls or barrages of mailings from real estate brokers could have accelerated white departures, but given that it is nearly impossible in the United States to find neighborhoods that have remained racially integrated for any length of time, there's no evidence such a transition wouldn't have happened in relatively short order anyway.

Helper's book provides a much more believable self-portrait of real estate dealers who dealt with Black clients than does "Confessions." There were variations in their own decision to work with African American home seekers. Some cited their professional duty to serve their clients—including Black clients—well. Others looked to their conscience, another to the laws of equal protection and the constitutional injunction that all men are created equal. Most argue that Black customers' money should be just as legitimate as white customers' money and that Negroes—not just whites—should have the right to live where they can afford to live. "The colored man shouldn't have a right to live in a decent community?" asked a dealer in a newly Black area. "That's a lot of baloney. I say he's got a right to buy as long as we all use the same American dollar."[65] Others concurred with segregationists that the broker should ensure that newcomers were of high caliber but used character rather than race to determine that: "It's my obligation when I sell to anyone to find out who he is, what character, not race or color," explained a dealer from a predominantly Black neighborhood.[66]

Several described the threats and consequences of selling to Blacks. Colleagues chided them and assumed their business must be faltering. City building inspectors fined the apartment buildings they managed where Black tenants were moving in. "They threaten you. They bring pressure to bear. You get calls. All of a sudden a lot of building inspectors visit your building and find something wrong. They bring pressure on you. They get the savings and loan institutions to ride you. Insurance companies make it difficult for you to get a loan."[67] Others were called racist names, threatened, ostracized socially, ridiculed by other brokers. One received requests from the Real Estate Board to stop his activities, another was the target of a community effort to get lenders and insurers to hinder his operations. While the brokers carried on through all of this, it is hard to believe that an actual broker like Vitchek would not have mentioned these sanctions in a tell-all like "Confessions of a Blockbuster."

Furthermore, none of these brokers described their work in the avaricious terms Norris Vitchek did; his was a description by an opponent of blockbusting, not a real estate broker working in a transitioning neighborhood.

It is critically important to note that these brokers stood in sharp contrast to the much larger number of white real estate brokers (a sample of whom Helper interviewed) who would not sell to Blacks. While the larger group's views varied from pragmatic to ideological and religiously justified segregationism, the racism was stark and impossible to ignore. They didn't serve African American customers for a range of reasons, from a desire not to anger potential white clients in the neighborhood to an apparently exaggerated fear of retaliation and explicit segregationist beliefs that Blacks and whites should not mix. Most said they would not have wanted Blacks to live in their own neighborhood and therefore supported those whites who wanted the same for themselves.[68] While the blockbuster group would sell to Blacks under at least some conditions, others preferred business suicide to taking on Black clients as a neighborhood transitioned: one broker said his firm let go of their three salesman. "They can't sell, because we don't allow them to sell to colored and whites are hard to sell to."[69] Capitalist self-interest was no match for racist solidarity.

Rose Helper's book offers a reminder about race in this period that is helpful in getting to the bottom of the mysterious blockbuster. If blockbusters were villains, then there were no heroes. There were two types of "real estate men" at the time: those whom researchers and white residents called blockbusters and those who were explicitly racist, steadfast segregationists who, even in a neighborhood where Blacks wanted to buy, refused to allow them to do so because they wanted no part in undoing segregation. In any description by white residents of the times or by historians of the period, if blockbusters are criticized, it is this strict segregationist group who are left, implicitly or explicitly, as the default norm of real estate behavior. Helper's interviews make clear that while plenty of those who did business with Blacks remained openly prejudiced, all of those who refused to do business were prejudiced. There were blockbusters and segregationists. There was nothing in between.

When example after example of blockbusters do not bear out, the impression grows that the blockbuster is a legendary figure, used by white residents to explain a phenomenon for which he is not needed. The exploitation, manipulation, and exclusion in these neighborhoods issued not from the fabled, largely imagined blockbuster but from the members of the larger white society themselves. Whites imagined that some malicious actor must be required for racial transition to take place and that the malicious actor must be some *other*. But the racists were themselves. Panic, selling for a loss, violence, and resegregation happened in neighborhood after neighborhood, in mere weeks, city after city, not because of a well-oiled network of blockbusters operating in exactly the same way but because of uniform white consensus about racial segregation and prejudice. The blockbuster was a myth. The outcome was real. Whites' collective refusal to socialize, live, educate, or work with Blacks was the cause.

In reviewing historical tales of blockbusters and period allegations of blockbusting, again and again the villain melts into thin air. Vitchek is the prototypical blockbuster but didn't exist in any recognizable form. Mark Satter was widely denounced as a blockbuster simply for not being a segregationist and furthermore for defending Blacks who were victimized by contracts and the courts. In Baltimore County Mal Sherman, like Satter, was called a blockbuster for acting on his commitment to equality and civil rights. For decades researchers thought mistakenly that the blockbuster was an actual occupation they should study. It turns out that blockbuster is no more than a slur.

Still more is at issue in the account of the white blockbuster. While focusing on the blockbuster may have given white homeowners and other residents a way to direct their anger away from their own racist practices toward an imagined other, for academics the blockbuster served a different purpose—it personified the racist practices in the real estate and mortgage industries. But there were problems with such a framing. Focusing on a real white real estate dealer on the selling side of the equation orients such accounts toward the conventional narrative of the rapaciousness of blockbusting realtors, the perceived loss by white homeowners, and, afterward, the exploitation of Black homeowners. The real estate broker is the villain, the white residents are angry, and white liberal readers can conclude that not even Blacks benefit. When it comes to residential integration, this model imagines, we're all losers.

But changing the narrator changes the story. As Orser notes in the case of Baltimore, blockbuster stories "presented African Americans as *necessarily* unwitting tools, victims in the process." Those stories "tended to obscure the active choices most initial African American settlers were making about their housing status."[70] To understand the role African Americans played in their own housing decisions, we must replace the narrative of the blockbuster.

Replacing Blockbusting: Real Realtors and Transition

Black realtors who represented the buyers told the story differently. An African American realtor and pillar of Maryland's real estate community, James Crocket described the process:

> Realtors . . . had an unwritten agreement that they would never sell to Blacks, so what they would do is they would find a Black person [a broker] that would work with them and they would say, "I have a vacant house or I have a house that's going to be sold in a neighborhood. Would you like to pick up the listing?" So I would say, sure I would pick up the listing, and they would say, "Do me a favor, when you sell the house, let me know because I might have a house that the people can buy." You understand? . . . It created relationships with certain people. And they would tell their agents, look, call Jim Crockett, tell him you have a listing he can pick up if he wants it. And that's what happened. . . . They were assuming I would have a Black buyer, and they could get the resale of the person selling the house. . . . So it created relationships with certain people.[71]

By Crockett's account, in contrast to the apocryphal story of a white blockbuster, Black realtors were using white realtors' greed as a weapon against their racism. Their actions opened up white neighborhoods—formerly rigidly closed to Black home seekers—to Black buyers. Crockett saw his actions not as malicious blockbusting but as a straightforward responsibility to his clients that is left out of accounts of blockbusting

Figure 1.1. Pioneering realtor James Crockett, in his office in Baltimore. He wears an Obama button and a green tie for Saint Patrick's Day.

that are described in terms of *inducement*. "My position then and now is to improve the living habits of people. If they want to go in this particular area, I will find them a house in this particular area." This process also opened up part of the market to Black realtors like Crockett, who until the early 1960s were barred from the Maryland Real Estate Board and their valuable multiple listing service. Even later, many were prevented from working in the suburbs by sellers' agents who contrived to keep Black realtors and Black buyers from setting foot inside homes that were for sale. Contrary to the narrative told from the departure point of the greedy and destructive white blockbuster, in Crockett's account white and Black realtors made money and the home buyers got the kind of housing they wanted.[72]

Other African American real estate brokers provide similar accounts. Sociologist Kevin Fox Gotham, for instance, cited Carl Feldman, who described how "I worked with a lot of white realtors . . . and the [white real estate] companies would call me, 'I got a house that I want you to sell for me.'"[73] Similarly, Amanda Seligman noted in passing that "some African Americans made a good living helping other Blacks find homes in restricted housing markets."[74] Yet a study told from the perspective of white homeowners who viewed integration as an "urban crisis" cannot bring out the historic significance of Black realtors' opportunities.

In fact, African America real estate brokers objected to characterizing the work they did as blockbusting at all (in contrast, apparently, to white blockbusters like Vitchek), arguing that what they did was not exceptional or objectionable. "You see," said Crockett, "when a white person moves into a neighborhood, it's not blockbusting. When a Black moves in?" He paused in his sentence and gave a pointed look, inviting the question of why selling homes to Blacks was defined as a problem. When Blacks moved in, the presumption was that there must have been malfeasance (by a blockbuster) to explain their arrival and the result was characterized as a problem because whites expected home values would decline and living conditions would deteriorate and objected to white children playing with Black children. Crockett's observation pointed out a key problem with the definition of blockbusting used by courts and researchers: the "problem" was located in the arrival of Blacks (induced, it was presumed, not by Blacks' own needs but by the conniving of a manipulative white broker), not in the actual problems and challenges new Black homeowners—and their real estate brokers—faced. To Crockett and others involved in satisfying the housing needs of African Americans, the concept of blockbusting was a problem itself; it misdiagnosed the ill as the means by which African Americans moved into a neighborhood, not the means by which they were kept out.

Antero Pietila, who followed up decades as a journalist reporting on Baltimore with *Not in My Neighborhood*, a deeply knowledgeable book about racial segregation in Baltimore in the first half of the twentieth century, concurred: "They were blockbusters, who created panic among whites. *That was the white view*," Pietila said. "The black view was that blockbusters were agents of liberating desegregation that gave blacks better housing."[75]

From the perspective of African Americans, who were most disadvantaged by the segregated system of the dual housing market, their best chance to improve the quality and range of housing available was through the process that came to be called blockbusting. And as seen in later chapters, in the suburban context the ultimate result was not the "widespread physical deterioration" others warned of. Housing in a racially segregated society remained highly troubled and far from perfect. But the result of moving to the suburbs was neighborhoods that, while they did not eliminate the inequality and challenges of being Black in America, continued to be preferred by residents to the urban neighborhoods that would have been their only alternative in the absence of racial transition and resegregation.[76]

Hyper-Exploitation

The practice of charging African Americans more for their homes or even of establishing exploitative terms that made it difficult for them to pay back the loans turns out to be the real social ill nested inside the tangle of practices called blockbusting. There is good evidence that African Americans were charged more—often much more—for loans to buy houses, from Baltimore to New York, Chicago, and beyond.[77] For instance, in 1963 the New York City Commission on Human Rights study of eleven property sales found that Blacks bought houses from dealers for 66 percent more than the white seller was paid:[78] dealers bought houses from whites for an average price of twelve thousand dollars but sold them to Blacks for twenty thousand. (The "estimated fair market value" of the homes was close to what the whites were paid, so it is not clear in those eleven cases that whites were underpaid, but Blacks were clearly overcharged.) In addition, the study found frequent practices of double mortgages and balloon payments at the end of the sales term. In Baltimore in the same period, Morris Goldseker engaged in similar practices, including double mortgages, which allowed him to extract additional capital from houses immediately while his Black buyers continued to pay.[79] And in Chicago, of course, Beryl Satter found that Blacks who went to court after being pushed to the brink with end-less, manipulative added charges were denied relief by the courts, which were happy to evict anyone the white broker/dealer wanted.[80]

Yet even this, the most damaging part of the story, does not fit well into the blockbusting model and is better seen in another light. Afri-can Americans have always been charged more for property. Indeed, these practices fit into a long, ignominious history of financial hyper-exploitation of African Americans buying property. This has several implications. First, it is not particular to blockbusting. After all, people were denied less expensive, conventional credit both in racially transi-tioning neighborhoods and in established Black neighborhoods, so the practices were in no way specific to blockbusting. Second, the practices are tied to the financier, not the real estate agent, even if in some his-torical moments that person was likely to be one and the same. Finally, teasing out exploitative lending as a distinct practice much more wide-spread than blockbusting answers a question. During the collapse of the housing bubble in 2007–2008, as the nature of unsustainable subprime, variable-rate, interest-only, and balloon-payment mortgages came to public attention amid a wave of home foreclosures, reasonable questions hovered at the edge of the conversation: Why would people take out these overpriced loans? Who would purchase a house when the terms were so biased against the buyer that successfully paying off the mort-gage seemed like a long shot? In 2008 such loans were heavily concen-trated among minority borrowers. The answer is that people of color bought property on these terms because bad terms are the only terms people of color have been able to find when looking for a home. There is an unbroken continuity from the subprime crisis back to the "buying on time" schemes of the 1950s and 1960s, and back further to denial of credit and costly terms in the decades and even centuries before that. The role of the real estate dealer in establishing manipulative and ex-tortionate mortgage terms was a momentary convergence in the classic, urban blockbusting era of the 1950s and 1960s. As African Americans gained access to loans from banks and other financial institutions, the real estate dealers vilified in the blockbusting model no longer provided financing. Lending practices that appear to be a historical blip when seen as part of blockbusting are revealed as a century-old practice when described as discriminatory lending.

Integration?

The goal of neighborhood racial transition was different from the African American perspective than from that of white observers. Blockbusting has typically been condemned because it did not produce long-term integration. African Americans' perspective on blockbusting challenges the metric by which blockbusting is measured. Gotham articulated the white progressive view when he wrote, "The *crucial question* regarding the suburbanization of African-Americans is whether this racial movement represents neighborhood integration or resegregation and the growth of suburban African-American ghettoes."[81] This is a vitally important question, and the normative goal of encouraging Black in-moving without triggering white out-moving is a valuable one. But African Americans have not articulated it as the primary question.

Integration was never articulated as a primary goal of African Americans, a fact that on reflection should not be surprising. The "crucial question" posed by African Americans is whether suburbanization could provide better quality housing, improve services, and expand residential choices for African Americans who have too long and violently been constrained in overcrowded, overpriced urban ghettoes.

After three decades in the suburbs, Leronia Josey considered why she and her husband had moved and made such sacrifices. "This is why we came out," she said. "It wasn't anything other than a better life. . . . I wanted good schools for my son. I wanted peace and quiet in the neighborhood, you know what I mean, and reasonably nice surroundings and stuff. It had nothing to do with wanting to come to an area that was 80-some percent white."

Reflecting this goal, multiple African American realtors explained that their primary goal was to be able to offer their Black prospective buyers the homes they wanted, and at midcentury those were overwhelmingly suburban homes. James Crockett concluded that his African American clients "were looking for decent housing. That's all. Number one looking for decent housing, and an educational system, a place where they could raise their families. And a house that they could afford, most of all." The goal of Black suburban home buyers was to get a better price or a better home than they could find in the city, particularly compared to the already-Black neighborhoods available to them in the dual housing market.[82] Suburbanization achieved that goal (though it was still laced with inequities).[83] In addition, moving to the suburbs itself was often an explicit objective of African American home seekers, as one former realtor who first tried to sell Black clients fixer-upper Victorians in the city—like the one he had bought—found out. Integration was at best described by African American pioneers as a secondary goal, may have been a tactical goal, and often has been an incidental one. Since McMechen's move across the color line in Baltimore in 1910, integration has never been the primary measure of the success of blockbusting for African Americans.[84]

But while integration was never the primary goal of home seekers (or even of African American open housing activists), it has an even less prominent place today than it did in the past. Twenty years ago, in their landmark book *American Apartheid*, Douglas Massey and Nancy Denton began with the observation that "during the 1970s and 1980s, a word disappeared from the American vocabulary. . . . The word was segregation."[85] By the twenty-first century, that word's antidote, "integration," had also disappeared.

I asked several people, "What does integration mean today?" The answer given by Patricia Ferguson, president of the Baltimore County chapter of the NAACP, was a common one. Ferguson paused, composed herself, and answered, "Nothing."

She explained that the reality was "still segregation. . . . It doesn't mean anything. What does it mean? Okay. I can go to the same stores you go to and shop now. I still can't go to the schools. I still am not paid the same." Ferguson was fed up with the lack of progress that had been made under the promise of integration.

James Crockett gave the same answer, with an almost identical justification: "Nothing. Because you haven't integrated, you've resegregated. You haven't changed the thinking processes of people."

People didn't talk about integration, even when community leaders talked about the negative effects of segregation on community members, church parishioners, and others. Where had integration gone?

Integration was a way that some civil rights organizations framed a set of issues but became meaningless when it was no longer a meaningful component of the civil rights movement. It had fallen from prominence in the language of national civil rights organizations. But it also did not serve residents at the local level: they had "integrated" by moving into the formerly white suburbs, but whites' gradual disinvestment from the area had reversed the process of integration. Second, residents thought a great deal about less well-off African Americans who might move from the city. They weren't moving to white areas but were moving closer to Randallstown. Whether residents wanted to help poorer African Americans or were wary of their possible arrival, it was not clear how a campaign under the banner of integration would be relevant. Improving schools, fighting crime, improving police behavior might all mitigate some of the concerns they had about newcomers moving out. But integration seemed irrelevant to those issues. With no national movement discussing integration, there would be little purpose served in talking about it, worrying about it, or seeing it as the cause of immediate problems. Meanwhile, many residents referred to whites moving out of Baltimore County to whiter, more distant "exurban" counties, so that while residents often suggested things had improved over time, it was also clear they hadn't changed all that much.

Contrary to Malcolm X's claim that the bourgeoisie was "integration mad," integrationism was much more of a strategic goal than an abstract end in itself. As evidence, the concept fell out of use once movements were no longer framed, strategically, in terms of integration. The focus in the suburbs was on what had once been considered the fruits of integration—quality schools, quality housing—irrespective of the racial mixes in which they might be obtained. A perspective focused on African American home seekers changes the objectives of their search—from integration to quality housing and neighborhoods. The point of comparison then changes as well, from an idealized but nonexistent racially mixed, middle-class neighborhood to housing in existing Black neighborhoods, and in so doing alters the assessment of the process of racial transition.

Changing Practices

Existing framings of blockbusting—for all their value in presenting it as a battle between residents' defense of a neighborhood's use value against capitalist speculators' exploitation of its exchange value—nonetheless fall prey to the tendency, to extrapolate from Du Bois, of defining

African Americans and all things Black as inherently "problems."[86] While African Americans themselves face problems and reactionary white neighbors may cause problems, we should be careful not to make the mistake of defining the neighborhood itself *as* a problem and resist whites' expectations that blockbusting itself—the arrival of Black neighbors and whatever follows—be discussed as a problem.

What does it mean to say that blockbusters do not exist? Social roles do not exist in nature; we define them socially by establishing concepts and boundaries for those concepts. The conventional definition of "blockbusting" did not capture the actual social problems that spring from the racism of our housing market. To the contrary, since blockbusters sold to African Americans at a time when the National Board of Realtors forbade its members from doing so, the concept of blockbusting included an antidiscriminatory practice rarely practiced by anyone else.

Thus to say that blockbusting did not exist is not to say that there were not real estate brokers who sold homes to Blacks—only that doing so by itself was not a problem. Nor is it to say that discriminatory lending practices were not systematic—but these practices are not captured by the definitions of blockbusting. Instead, these practices are better understood this way: Communities of white homeowners, since Hawkins and McMechen's time, had collectively opposed selling homes in white neighborhoods to African Americans. Banks and conventional lenders had refused to lend to them, both to support that de facto ban and, some realtors explain, because banks did not want African American customers. For their part, African Americans were understandably interested in moving into better quality housing than the dilapidated and overcrowded stock owned by absentee landlords in existing Black neighborhoods. They sought to move elsewhere. In white areas with soft resale markets, some real estate brokers were willing to broker deals from whites to Blacks, but because African Americans could not get conventional credit, such brokers could profit from "installment" financing at much higher prices. The installment financing instruments could be resold profitably on a secondary mortgage market, expanding the sphere of investors who profited from these practices and further prejudicing judges and other elites, who were likely to own such investments, against African Americans' claims that the arrangements were hyper-exploitative and illegal.

That description accounts for both the agency and desires of African American home seekers and the structural discrimination directed at them. The blockbuster never appears. There are more and less accurate ways to model the world. When Pierre-Simon Laplace, the French astronomer, presented his model of the mechanical workings of the universe to Emperor Napoleon, Napoleon is said to have asked why he had made no mention of God in explaining the motions of the planets. Laplace replied, "Je n'ai pas eu besoin de cette hypothèse"—I had no need of that hypothesis. In the more terrestrial case of real estate and residential racial transition, we can say the same thing of the blockbuster: we don't need that hypothesis. Because the blockbuster has no effect on the system, because we can explain the workings of the system more thoroughly with a model in which he is absent, the blockbuster does not exist.

From the perspective of African Americans involved in the growth of Black communities, what happened was something very different from blockbusting. They were confronting challenges. African American elected officials, religious leaders, and community activists in Randallstown, like their counterparts in many communities, all detailed problems that they were working on and that their community was facing. But none saw blockbusting as responsible for those problems, nor did they take the existence of problems to mean that all the components of blockbusting were all problems, much less the historic "crisis" that others have described it to be.

The distinction is significant because, though Du Bois meant something different when he asked, "How does it feel to be a problem?" there is a tendency to define mundane aspects of Black life as problems, rather than to see African Americans as facing problems in even mundane aspects of their lives. Thus "predominantly Black high school" becomes synonymous with "problem," just as Daniel Patrick Moynihan, in his influential report on Black America, transformed "matriarchal households" from a family type that may face problems into one that was a problem.[87] The creation of African American neighborhoods that may face problems did not create those problems. Nor is the creation of those neighborhoods a problem itself—to the contrary it is a solution since the restrictive dual housing market has created a shortage of such neighborhoods and thus many of the problems themselves.

The perspective of African Americans who moved into transitioning neighborhoods suggests that the problems associated with blockbusting are actually the provenance of other phenomena such as disinvestment, mortgage discrimination, white prejudice, and a segregated housing market.

For instance, the resegregation of transitioning neighborhoods such that they become predominantly Black rather than remaining mixed is caused not by blockbusting and only secondarily by the flight of whites from new Black neighborhoods. That transition is caused primarily by whites in the larger metropolitan-wide housing market refusing to buy homes in neighborhoods with noticeable Black populations. The refusal of that group is nearly invisible in accounts of blockbusting, but their actions are the most significant factor in the resegregation of blockbusted neighborhoods and mean that most mixed neighborhoods will not remain mixed but become uniformly African American.

Similarly, people were overcharged whether the neighborhood was "busted" (racially transitioning) or not. Nor are other concerns typically considered by studies of blockbusting rightfully the responsibility of blockbusting itself: reductions in municipal services reflect reduced provision of municipal services to African America neighborhoods generally, corporate disinvestment reflects corporate disinvestment in Black communities generally. Neither is particular to blockbusted areas. Fighting blockbusting to a standstill would do nothing to reduce segregation, the dual housing market, white Negrophobia, or uneven development; in fact opposing blockbusting could reinforce all four. Contrary to the blockbusting narrative, racial transition brings significant if not unlimited advantages to African Americans and rare opportunities for more integrated communities to all races, and traditionally produced no effects for African American residents that were any worse than they faced in other neighborhoods already available to them.

Moving Forward

As a concept, blockbusting is a mess. It describes integration as a social problem, engages in egocentric causality to imagine bogeymen where there are none, and obsesses about the loss of community allegedly imposed on whites by the desegregation of their neighborhoods, while saying comparatively less about the measurable financial harm and government double standards dealt to African American home buyers. The concept attributes incredible powers to marginal real estate brokers who operated outside mainstream practices in lower-prestige neighborhoods, while stripping African Americans of any credit at all, imagining that they are summoned to white residents' doorstep by the conjuring blockbuster. It is time to retire this relic of racial hysteria.

This assessment of blockbusting is not a denial of residential segregation and the active efforts of whites to segregate African American households. Whites and white society did engage in those efforts. Audiences have asked questions about my work that make clear they are concerned that when I dismiss blockbusting I'm also dismissing the reality of racism in the housing market. I do my best to make clear I am not. The stakes are high in writing about, and fighting, racism, and work that might impair the struggle is justifiably critiqued for its inaccuracies.

This reexamination is not a criticism of the work of my colleagues and other researchers who used the blockbusting frame. I used it for many years. Political and historical context influences the proper framing of an issue, and attention to blockbusting identified structural racism and how discrimination was integrally woven into profitable banking, real estate sales, and development industries. Moving beyond blockbusting enlarges that structural understanding, demonstrating how the racially discriminatory outcomes of the housing market are not the result of racist exploitation that's concentrated (and therefore seemingly isolated) in one bad actor but the result of a broad distribution of white supremacist assumptions across numerous, intersecting institutions and everyday actors.

If the blockbuster is not the evil, mustache-twirling villain behind the scenes, we can stop organizing against him, as activists did in the twentieth century, with legislation banning "for sale" and "sold" signs, public protests, and denunciations of alleged blockbusters. Often those efforts targeted real estate developers for failing to toe the color line that white residents thought they could tacitly rely upon. Instead, we can target the practices that actually drive and maintain segregation, overcharge African Americans for housing, and unjustly distort access to housing and resources.

New and old residents in racially transitioning neighborhoods like Randallstown still expected trouble in their changing neighborhoods, and inequality was the reality for African American home buyers, residents, and communities. People had to confront racist resistance to them entering Randallstown, realtors who kept Black brokers and buyers out, discrimination that prevented buyers from getting mortgages, financially strapped homeowners or absentee landlords who would not maintain their property, and a mass white exodus that could flood the market and devalue all properties in the area. Blockbusting might be dead, but the real problems of a racist dual housing market remain.

Telling that story with a sense of African American agency allows us to see how residents addressed each one of these challenges, from the arrival of John and Sylvia Mackey to the foreclosure crisis.

2

Building a Black Community

Activists Bring Racial Transition to the Suburbs

In 1970 Herbert Lindsey moved to Maryland. After completing his graduate studies in one of the nation's premier sociology departments, at the University of Wisconsin–Madison, he had taught at the Tuskegee and Hampton institutes, two historically Black colleges. He had also been involved in civil rights work and community organizing. As an undergraduate in Chicago, he worked with Nicholas von Hoffman in Saul Alinsky's organization, the Industrial Areas Foundation, as well as the American Friends Service Committee, a Quaker organization. Lindsey explained that as a result, "In addition to my [training in] sociology, when I came here I . . . had some political experience in Alabama and Virginia, so I was very sensitive about certain things." Fresh from civil rights efforts, Lindsey knew where to expect discrimination. "So when I arrived, here, I tried to get housing in this area."

I spoke with Lindsey in the offices of the NAACP's Baltimore County chapter in the Benjamin Banneker Community Center. The center is a block from Winters Lane, a Black neighborhood of small streets lined with neat, older, single-family houses. (Lindsey also pointed out that John Wilkes Booth, Abraham Lincoln's assassin, had attended school just a few blocks away.) It was midsummer, and outside a summer camp was having a Hawaiian-themed party. African American kids ran around squirting each other with water guns. Counselors joked lightly with them. The mood was relaxed and festive.

Lindsey had first arrived in the Baltimore area to take a position in the sociology department of the University of Maryland's Baltimore County campus. Immediately he had difficulty. He wanted to find a place in Baltimore County, but no one would rent to him. He went to a large complex of garden apartments. "I was looking for an apartment on Rolling Road, Town and Country apartments. . . . Town and Country said, 'Nope, we don't have any.'" "Why don't you try over there in Howard County?" the apartment management suggested, and steered him to Town and Country's apartment complex in that county. In the end, Lindsey could find no one who would rent him an apartment in Baltimore County. Thus his first apartment was in the Town and Country complex in Ellicott City, a town founded by Quakers with a small if significant African American community. (The scientist Benjamin Banneker, after whom the community center in which we met was named, was born in Ellicott City, and Howard County's first "colored school" was built there in 1879.[1] Records show the school board badly neglected the school, supplying running water only in 1950.) Lindsey's inability to rent in the Randallstown and Rolling Road area left him frustrated that the county was enforcing a color line.

"So that was my taste with Baltimore County at an early stage," explained Lindsey. Other people had similar experiences. It was clear that until at least 1970 African Americans were not welcome, and whites would not allow them to rent or own homes in most of the county.

To Lindsey in 1970, Baltimore County appeared to be resolutely closed off to African Americans. In the next ten years, however, the African American population nearly tripled. By 2010 the county was home to 209,000 African Americans, some 80,000 of whom lived along Liberty Road in the Randallstown area. This chapter takes a new look at the causes behind the growth of Black communities. Mechanistic accounts of "population growth," "white flight," "people coming out of slums," and the Great Migration fail to explain why African American suburbs arose, why they grew when they did, why they developed outside some cities and not others, and why they flourished in some parts of the suburbs and not others.[2] I use the Baltimore suburbs as a case study to better answer these questions. African Americans suburbanized not because of one driving force but thanks to a complex web of choices and structure.

Hidden Diversity in the Suburbs

Herbert Lindsey's story of being shut out of Baltimore County is not so simple. At the same time he was being turned away, African Americans *did* live in Baltimore County, even on the same road where Lindsey had looked for an apartment. Lillian Rogers Dorsey was born in 1906 in a house on Rolling Road, near Liberty Road. All of her parents, grandparents, and great-grandparents had also been African Americans born in the Liberty Road area. The house she grew up in had no electricity or running water; Dorsey's mother did the wash in the same wooden tub that Dorsey's ten brothers and sisters bathed in, with water carried from a neighbor's pump. The family had one stove, in which she burned wood to cook with during the day and coal at night to keep warm.[3] Lillian knew that her grandparents had not been slaves but did not know about her great-grandparents. (The name Dorsey has roots in a large slave-holding family in Maryland.) The adults in her family "would never talk about slavery, it was as though it would hurt them to mention slavery."[4] The Liberty Road area had been home to free African Americans since at least the early 1800s. Slaves lived in the area in that period as well, and probably as early as the founding of Randallstown in the early 1700s.[5]

Despite the physical challenges Dorsey described in an interview with local African American historian Louis Diggs, she emphasized her pleasure being part of an intimate, rural Black community. The family was active in Union Bethel AME Church, one of the oldest Black churches in the county, founded in 1826.[6] (Church records suggest Union Bethel had received financial assistance from W. Ashbie Hawkins in 1890.)[7] Her father was the church secretary, her grandfather an assistant to the pastor. The surrounding Black community was relatively small. Church members would often walk several miles to Black churches in neighboring towns for the opportunity to socialize and worship with other African Americans (see Figure 2.1).

Lillian attended a school for colored children that was held in the St. Thomas Odd Fellows lodge behind the church. Another school for colored children was just down the road. (Her school went only to sixth grade, and there was not a high school in the county that allowed Black students to attend until later.) During dances at the St. Thomas Lodge, young people who were too shy to go inside often danced outside to the music. The memories of Lillian Dorsey and others who lived in the Liberty Road area often emphasized their fondness for the area and the community life they had constructed.

This paradox—that African Americans like Herbert Lindsey were excluded from Baltimore County when other African Americans like Lillian Dorsey already lived there—highlights the multiple routes by which

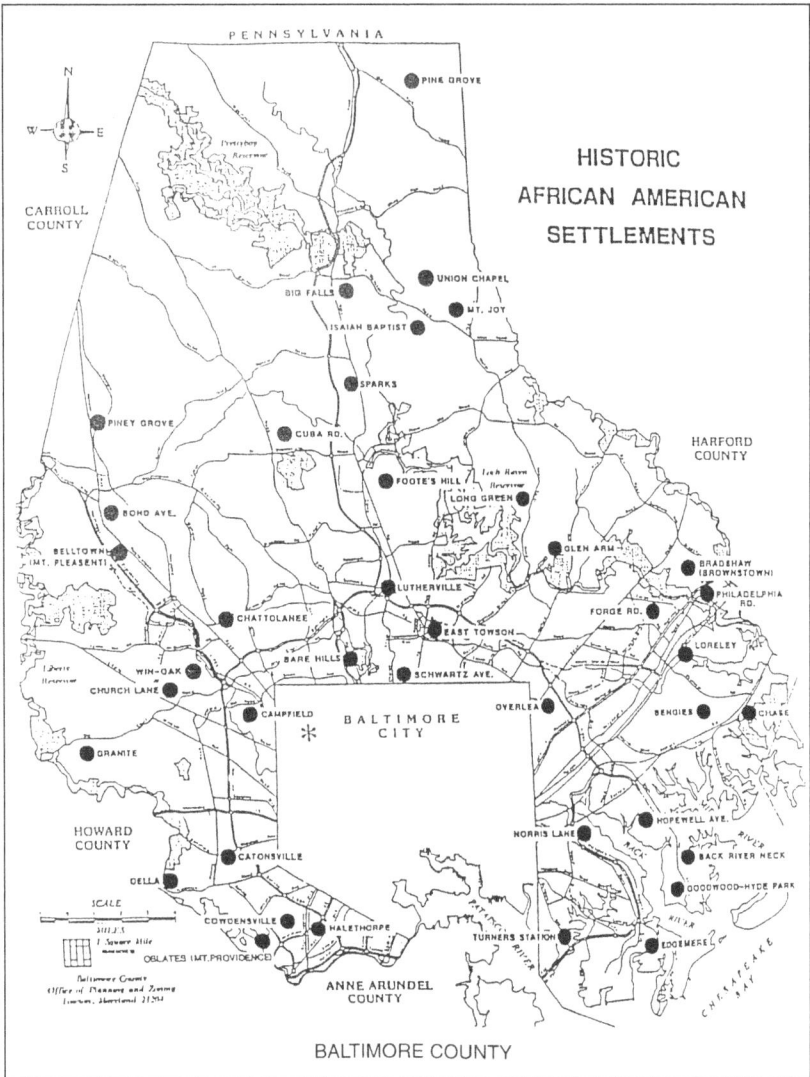

Figure 2.1. Forty historic African American communities identified by
Louis Diggs dot Baltimore County, surrounding the city. Most of these small,
formerly rural communities still exist today and predate the end of slavery.
Source: E. H. T. Traceries, Baltimore County Office of Planning, and the
Landmarks Preservation Commission, "Baltimore County Architectural
Survey: African American Thematic Study, Final Report" (August 4, 2003).

Black Americans have come to the suburbs. Historian Andrew Wiese details at least three major patterns of African American suburbanization. Lillian Dorsey's family represents the oldest example: small, rural enclaves of Black families that were eventually surrounded by expanding suburbs. Just as Latino activists in the Southwest—whose presence predates US sovereignty there—say, "We didn't cross the border, the border crossed us," rural African Americans could point out that they never moved to the suburbs, the suburbs moved to them.

The second pattern of suburbanization was that of working-class industrial suburbs. Heavy industries relocated to spacious factories outside the city, and workers—Black and white—followed them. Examples in Baltimore County are at the far corner of the county from Randallstown, to the southeast. Sparrows Point and Turner Station grew up with the arrival of Black workers at the Bethlehem Steel Plant. Sustained by relatively well-paying jobs at the steel plant, Turner Station is said to have been one of the wealthiest "self-contained" African American communities in the United States.[8]

These industrial suburbs also exhibit suburban advantages identified by Wiese. For instance, in suburbs at the beginning of the twentieth century African Americans could buy land more cheaply, allowing higher rates of homeownership (often with self-built homes) and reducing the cost of living through growing vegetables and raising chickens and other food sources in small backyard farms. Several of the earliest residents of Turner Station Diggs interviewed grew up in homes built by their fathers. The families grew crops, raised chickens, and slaughtered hogs in the backyard. Their mothers often worked in the homes of nearby white families.[9] Suburbanites could establish some degree of independence and financial security, but to do so required working multiple jobs and establishing a semi-self-sustaining household in a new, suburban area.

Herbert Lindsey was part of the third and largest process of Black suburbanization. Called "spillover suburbs," postwar suburbs like Randallstown were most often continuations of growing Black communities in US cities.[10] Black neighborhoods expanded, and as they neared city boundaries they often "spilled over" and continued into formerly white suburbs.

The term "spillover" is unfortunate but already widely used. My aesthetic dislike of the term is its implied sloppiness, like a cup of coffee that has slopped around and splashed into the saucer or left a dark ring on a white tablecloth. But it is also misleading in the way in which it suggests a natural or inherent process. Agency is lost, and the term suggests that Black communities that were growing by natural increases easily continued that process as they crossed the city line.

Nothing could be further from the truth. County boundaries had been used as racial boundaries for some time. And while the line drawn by early twentieth-century whites in Baltimore along Eutaw Street (intended to keep out people like George McMechen) was both unofficial and prone to perpetual backward revision, county lines were different. First, they represented two separate municipal governments. County governments could therefore continue to implement segregationist policies that, by the mid-twentieth century, would have been politically difficult in cities with growing Black electorates. County lines also allowed white suburbanites to keep their local property taxes to themselves, apart from city residents who were Black, poor, immigrant, or politically disadvantaged in other ways. Finally, the Supreme Court ruled in 1974 (in *Milliken v. Bradley*) that while racial integration of schools might be mandated by courts within racially diverse cities, courts could not require all-white suburbs to integrate with other districts—such as city school systems. White suburbanites concluded from this ruling that county boundaries could legally be used to maintain segregation in ways that previous dividing lines no longer could.

It was against this reinforced boundary of race, municipality, schools, and property taxes at the county line that Baltimore-area civil rights activists worked to gain the advantages of suburban homeownership in the 1960s.

Integrating the Suburbs

As late as the 1970s African Americans viewed Baltimore County as part of the unreconstructed South. State Delegate Emmett Burns, a veteran civil rights activist, said Baltimore City was run "like a plantation" and Baltimore County was no better. The county executive refused to build public housing (pushing poor residents to seek housing in the city) and, according to the *Baltimore Sun*, "did everything except stand in the school house door to preserve his county as a white-only suburban enclave" while the county used "exclusionary zoning" and low-budget renewal projects to decimate twenty historic African American communities. The county's policies reflected the attitudes of newly arrived whites who had doubled the county's population between 1950 and 1970.[11] When one prominent African American showed interest in a house in a white community, he was told by whites that if he wanted a mortgage he would have to wait "a long time."

African Americans were completely shut out of new suburbs, but the historical Black communities were nearly as constrained by segregation. In 1972, County Executive Dale Anderson issued an executive order requiring that any real estate broker who sold to a Black buyer had to report his actions to the police. A Civil Rights Commission representative scoffed at the idea that this was to protect home buyers from racial violence; the purpose was to "clearly intimidate rather than help the potential black buyer in the county."[12]

Yet a decade later Baltimore County's Black population had grown by 178 percent—over 34,500 people—from 19,416 to 53,955, while the white population held steady near 590,000. Thus a second paradox: in the face of rigid residential segregation, the African American community had more than doubled in a decade.

One way to confront segregation was organized activism for fair housing. The community group Baltimore Neighborhoods was founded in 1959 to unite community members and support neighborhood integration. By the mid-1960s Baltimore Neighborhoods set their sights on the suburbs. Their strategy was to open up the entire county by finding homes for Black residents all around the county. According to member Malcolm Sherman, the thinking was that "if we could get Blacks in developments all around the Beltway, there'd be no place to run anymore." He considered what had actually happened: "How's that for naïve?"

Baltimore Neighborhoods and other groups, invigorated by the passage of the federal Fair Housing Act in 1968, used testers to gain evidence of discrimination by housing developments and apartment complexes in the county. Lenwood Johnson, another member and an early African American resident of the suburbs, joined when he and his wife found they were repeatedly denied apartments. He explained that testers from Baltimore Neighborhoods relied on the momentum of desegregation activism rather than gambling that courtroom challenges would prevail.

In one such testing project, Johnson's wife called the rental agency of an apartment complex. On the phone the agent didn't know her race and assumed she was white. Johnson explained that "everything seemed to be okay." Then his wife "let the person know that she's African American, and was that going to be a problem. And the guy told her 'Well no, as long as your money is green, I'm with you.'"

But the landlord was suddenly less accommodating. "Now we wanted to go to see the house [but] the guy's schedule is crowded, he can't make it the next day." So Lenwood Johnson called back using the assumed name Calvin Marshall and "my white voice." "Now the same guy, who could not see us the next day, he could see me the next day. . . . So we called the guy back to let him know that Calvin Marshall and Lenwood Johnson were one and the same."

Johnson made use of the fact that housing discrimination was now illegal but didn't pursue the case in court: "We didn't have time to prosecute the guy," he explained, clarifying that "since open housing was still kind of a new concept, there wasn't any real precedent for doing this kind of thing." Activists were mobilized to challenge housing segregation by the legislation that their own efforts had produced. But their successes in changing landlords' and developers' practices relied on informal pressure rather than the route of untested courtroom challenges.

Even before he was thrown into testing residential segregation in the county, Lenwood Johnson was already a veteran activist. He had worked in war-on-poverty groups in Baltimore. Because of his commitment to such work, Johnson explained, he had resisted moving to the suburbs: the action, for a war-on-poverty activist in the 1960s and 1970s, was in the city. The city was where activists worked, where war-on-poverty organizations operated, where large numbers of Black people lived. The suburbs seemed distant from those commitments.

He and his wife were led to challenge the color line in the county because they were unable to buy a home in the area of Baltimore in which they were interested, along the Alameda. Redlining, in which banks refused to make loans in Black and racially mixed neighborhoods, had made it impossible for them to get a mortgage. In a sharp reversal of earlier redlining patterns, by 1973 the place Johnson and his wife *could* get a mortgage was in the suburbs.

When Johnson began work on a major surveying project for the county government, he came upon living conditions in the historical Black communities that he had not expected. Within the forty areas now identified as historic African American communities, like the one Ms. Lillian Rogers Dorsey lived in, Johnson found primitive conditions. He recalled scouring the county, traveling down "little dead end roads" and feeling as though "you had gone into another century because you saw people living in conditions right out of slavery." Houses had no running water, and residents had to go to other homes even to access well water. There were no sanitation facilities.

The very fact that conditions in Baltimore County had not changed prompted people like Johnson to bring their activism to the county. He reported the conditions he had observed to county officials, but found there was no response. So he began organizing the new suburban African American residents. "In 1978 there were a number of people who had been involved in civil rights movements back in the sixties and seventies," Johnson explained, "who had now moved into Baltimore County and they were living large now. They had the split-level [house] and they had their top shelf liquor on the shelf in the club basement, and five figure automobile in the driveway, so we all had it made until I had to go back and tell people that we've got people living in conditions right out of slavery. And we can't—at least I can't—live in peace unless we try to do something about it." It was these conditions that led him to work to establish a Baltimore County–wide chapter of the NAACP.[13] Leronia Josey, who would become a county judge and political candidate, experienced the same shock when she first saw those historical communities—still lacking compared to the new suburban areas surrounding them—several decades later. She recalled that where she had grown up in Virginia, Black neighborhoods were easy to identify because "the concrete stopped, and you had the gravel road, you know what I'm saying? And then when I ran [for office] in 2006, and I went over to Owings Mills for people to take signs for me and stuff, I thought, Lord have mercy, I would have never thought that African Americans were living in homes like this." It reminded her of where she had grown up. Josey argued that such conditions—and their own memories of them—motivated African Americans both politically and personally—politically to improve those conditions, and personally to earn enough money to ensure that their own children had middle-class comforts.

The NAACP chapter used federal equal opportunity requirements to open jobs in the county fire department and police department to African Americans. Opening up housing was part of a larger push for equal access and equal opportunity, as Baltimore City activists joined those already in the county, relocating their attention (and often their own families) to the county. The influence of open housing activism and legislation was significant. As Lenwood Johnson recalls, "President Johnson signed open housing legislation. . . . And what happened is that quite a number of middle class Blacks were anxious to move someplace else, so when open housing legislation [passed], next thing I know it was almost like a nineteenth-century land rush up Liberty Road. The only thing was missing was a chuck wagon following . . . the Conestoga wagons heading out Liberty Road." For African Americans, suburban homesteading had begun.

Activist Bureaucracies

In addition to integration activists in groups like BLEWS (Blacks and Jews) and Baltimore Neighborhoods, there were individuals in professional positions who used their positions to help African Americans gain access to housing in the suburbs on a more equitable basis with whites. One unexpected source of help came from the Social Security Administration. Social Security's contribution to open housing was not evident from its job managing federal retirement and disability checks. On the ground, Social Security not only provided jobs for thousands of African Americans but also worked aggressively, in an unappreciated role, to desegregate neighborhoods in the Randallstown area.

Because Baltimore is only an hour from Washington, DC, since at least the Second World War it had housed back office operations for the federal government. Much of the Social Security Administration, then only a few decades old, was scattered across buildings in downtown Baltimore. The federal government sought to consolidate those offices. A local developer supplied a large tract of farmland for the new headquarters, hoping such large-scale development would increase the value of his other nearby holdings.[14] In 1960, Social Security's new headquarters opened in Catonsville, near the historic community of Winters Lane and twenty minutes west of Randallstown.[15]

Civil service jobs with the federal government had long been a niche for middle-class and working-class African Americans. After the Civil War, in the late nineteenth century and into the early twentieth, northern politicians with pro-Union sentiments had awarded a tiny collection of government jobs to African Americans.[16] More recently, the fact that civil service jobs could be obtained by taking a test rather than through the personal connections of the largely white professional world made these positions more accessible to African Americans than office jobs in the private sector. Ever since Social Security had been centered in downtown Baltimore, the offices had had significant numbers of African American employees.

Colonel James Pennington was one such employee. After leaving the military, Pennington went to the Social Security offices, told them that he had been in charge of security in the military, and was hired to head security at the new headquarters. He worked there for fifty years, until 2009. At retirement his salary was close to the median household income. He was able to build a large split-level ranch house nearby in the county's historic Winters Lane community. Pennington was proud that he had been able to raise his children and support a family with his work. Sitting in the living room of his home, looking out through the sunroom he had enlarged, he said, "I began to notice that African Americans were being included in the work force. They were being hired in great quantities in all the areas. . . . As far as I would be concerned, they were successful African Americans." With a stable job and household, Pennington was also able to get involved in civil rights and education issues in the county. He joined the county chapter of the NAACP and eventually became president. But while Pennington lived in Winters Lane, the tiny community was far too small to accommodate the number of African Americans employees coming out to the suburbs with Social Security.

The Social Security Administration's significant involvement in fair housing issues didn't follow automatically from the fact that it had many Black employees. Liberal administrators decided to make the federal government's stated commitment to open housing an active part of their office's mandate. Structural, individual, and social movement forces intertwined to make the Social Security Administration's headquarters a significant force for local desegregation.

Robert Ball served as director of Social Security for a decade starting in 1962. Ball and his deputy, Lou Zawatsky, were already involved in fair housing groups including Baltimore Neighborhoods and the Citizens Planning and Housing Association. John Michener was a Social Security administrator at the same time. Eighty-seven years old when I interviewed him in 2012, he recalled with evident pleasure the means he had used to discreetly push the Social Security bureaucracy from passive support for open housing to more effective advocacy. Michener, a Quaker, prided himself on always having lived in integrated neighborhoods. (When I spoke with him he had recently pushed to create more economic and racial integration at the Quaker retirement community where he lived, but had been defeated.) A decade after losing a job at the University of California, Berkeley, for refusing to sign a McCarty-era loyalty oath, he transferred to the Baltimore County Social Security headquarters. While Ball and Zawatsky were good liberals who supported open housing in theory, Michener, who like Ball and Zawatsky was white, quickly saw how to put the weight of this large federal bureaucracy behind fair housing in practice.

First, pressure mounted on Social Security to match their words with action. "Word has gotten around the community that we as an organization support open housing; now people are starting to ask what we're doing about it. Are we doing more than giving lip service to a noble objective?" wrote Zawatsky in a memo. "The enclosed letter from . . . the Windsor Hills Improvement Association is an example of the kind of reaction we are getting. [Windsor Hills] wants to see some action on our part."[17] Michener was put in charge of writing a response. What his supervisors didn't know was that Michener lived in Windsor Hills and had gotten the association to write the letter in the first place. He was then put in the position of responding, on behalf of Social Security, to his own letter.

Writing in response to the demands he had written, Michener proposed several Social Security policies. Growing out of those proposals, Social Security set up a Housing Office with counselors to provide housing referrals to their employees.[18] They added an office to investigate reports of discriminatory treatment and refer cases to federal agencies for prosecution. At the time white realtors would not show homes to Black buyers and would not share information on what houses were for sale—the multiple listing service that printed out lists of homes in realtors' offices—with Black realtors. To rectify the problem, Social Security went so far as to contact a local realtor who was facing legal sanctions for discriminatory practices and convince them to install one of their own multiple listing printers in the Social Security offices.[19] Now African American employees could sidestep white realtors' obstructionism and find out what was for sale through Social Security's Housing Office.

Beyond these measures, the administration actively supported the cause of desegregation. Under Ball, employees could attend meetings of open housing civil rights groups as part of their regular work day, and Michener remembers driving to such meetings with Ball and Zawatsky.[20] The Social Security headquarters provided office equipment and furniture to National Neighbors, a network of integrated neighborhoods around the country.

To those who would have thought that such direct involvement in activism was inappropriate for a federal agency, policymakers at Social Security responded that they were merely validating the recently passed Civil Rights Act of 1968, which said that it was "the policy of the United States to provide . . . fair housing throughout the United States." Administrators felt strongly that they needed to employ "all legal means necessary to open to black workers the same choice of housing, in the same areas, available to their white coworkers."[21] With a large and racially diverse staff nationwide, Social Security needed to pursue policies that supported those employees and would allow them to continue to attract employees regardless of race. The policies were disseminated nationwide, and at least one administrator urged that "SSA should locate future installations only in those communities where black employees will have the *same* opportunity as white employees to secure housing."[22] It was true that Social Security's housing activism was motivated by its director's personal commitments, but they justified it as required for a large, diverse organization.

Michener made the critical point that Social Security's advocacy for open housing could not happen in a vacuum. In a letter to me he wrote, "Without the complex interactions of the organizations and individuals

mentioned above SSA's Housing Office could never have been establish."[23] The Social Security Agency voiced support for open housing
because of its leadership.[24] They were pressured into action by neighborhood associations and activists like Michener who were already working
on fair housing issues. Social Security could pursue open housing under
the mandate they deduced from recently passed federal legislation. And,
critically, Michener argued that Social Security could pursue its goals
only by supporting nonprofit organizations like National Neighbors,
which were in turn significantly strengthened by the resources, people,
and prospective homeowners Social Security provided. Seeking to understand how the color line was breached in Baltimore County leads not
to one single event or organization but to a network of people, groups,
laws, and employers that exerted pressure on various parts of the barrier
to African Americans seeking homes.

The impact Social Security made on the desegregation of Baltimore
County was significant. Michener estimated that when the housing program started in the late 1960s over a thousand of the office's six thousand
employees were African American. Many were in clerical positions, including about half of the staff who did key-punch and card-punch data
entry. While fewer were in high-level positions, Social Security provided
a critical mass of African Americans with secure, relatively well-paying
civil service jobs. Over the next decade Social Security's suburban headquarters introduced hundreds of African American employees to the
suburbs. The administration actively sought to overcome housing discrimination and find homes for employees wherever they wanted to
live. Because white neighborhoods are highly sensitive to the presence
of even a small number of African American residents, it would have
taken only a handful of families in any one neighborhood to effectively
open up the neighborhood to other families. Social Security employees
made up a significant number of the African American pioneers who
crossed into the suburbs around Randallstown. It was in the decade after
Social Security first implemented their policy that the African American
population in the county first grew, and grew dramatically.

Outside of Washington, DC, Prince Georges County's position as
the only majority-Black, majority-affluent suburban county in the nation owes much to the availability of secure civil service jobs for African
American workers. In other cities, other major employers, including

major private employers like industrial steel mills, had to address the housing needs of their employees and confronted, in more and less accommodating ways, the segregation of the US housing market. Thus major employers—and in the case of Social Security, their activist administrators—could use their power to open up formerly segregated suburbs.

The Suburban Ideal as Escape from Urban Renewal

Other factors encouraged the movement of African Americans from the city to the county. Most striking was how many families had been uprooted in Baltimore through urban renewal and other upheavals. Baltimore had been using eminent domain and urban renewal since the era of Hawkins and McMechen, when the city arranged for a poor, dilapidated African American neighborhood to be torn down and replaced with a rail yard.[25] Those projects particularly targeted low-income African American areas. The rate of displacement and its racially targeted character reached extremes during the height of urban renewal. According to the Baltimore Urban Renewal and Housing Agency, between 1951 and 1964, 89 percent of all displaced households in Baltimore were African American.[26] Some 25,000 people were displaced in that period, and an even larger number were scheduled for relocation in the following decade. Displaced poor Blacks had to move to other neighborhoods—often less poor Black neighborhoods. The arrival of lower income residents then prompted established residents to seek new neighborhoods, either better Black blocks or transitioning, formerly white blocks nearby. Whites in turn left at the appearance of new Black neighbors. By 1980 an incredible 10 percent of Baltimoreans had been displaced through urban renewal.[27] Most of those 94,000 people were Black. An even larger percentage, Black and white, moved because of indirect displacement caused by either urban renewal or white flight. As early as 1911 W. Ashbie Hawkins identified most of this movement of whites and Blacks as being toward the northwest of the city, up Liberty Heights Avenue, following Jewish neighborhoods. Eventually, the search by displaced residents for new homes carried them toward the suburbs. Thanks to civil rights activists' work in opening up the county, they could move there.

While displacement via urban renewal may have pushed African Americans from their homes and jobs and the suburbs may have drawn them, cultural preferences played a role in American suburbanization regardless of race. After all, postwar white suburbanization is often described largely with reference to the "suburban ideal," the supposed American preference for low-density housing and the single-family home. The new autocentric, low-density suburban communities were rife with inconveniences: the distance from shopping, the isolation from extended family, the lack of cultural resources, the paucity of ethnic food and resources, the absence of public transportation, the expense of auto dependence, and the diminished opportunities for sociability, among others. Postwar Americans, observers believed, were willing to forgive those inconveniences in exchange for a green lawn, a quiet, affordable house, and a place to park their car. Researchers like Herbert Gans have pointed out the inaccuracy of explaining the growth of the suburbs exclusively from the side of consumer demand. He argues that in an extremely tight postwar housing market developers could sell whatever they could build cheaply, and initially conducted no market research whatsoever to determine customer preferences.[28] But the suburban ideal was not wholly imagined either. While the ideal cannot be separated from the exclusive racial and class connotations of the suburbs that conveyed status on such suburbs, the preference for the suburban physical and social environment became widespread throughout society.

Angelo Hernandez was surprised by the resoluteness of people who embraced the suburban ideal. Hernandez, whose father was Cuban and mother was Black, grew up in the Baltimore area. In 1981, after college, he began working as a realtor in the Security Boulevard area, named after the nearby Social Security headquarters. He sold primarily to people of color and primarily in the Randallstown area. By this time African Americans had been moving into Randallstown for a decade. Hernandez already knew the area well; his first trips to Randallstown had been to the homes of white classmates from his Catholic school to rehearse their Beatles tribute band (see Figure 2.2). But the suburbs weren't for him: he and his wife bought an old Victorian in the city across from a large park and spent years renovating it, room by room. He sought clients interested in buying the spacious, aging homes in his city neighborhood, but to no avail. "Long story short, I probably sold

Figure 2.2. In 1981, Angelo Hernandez began his career in real estate selling homes in Randallstown to African American families. As an adolescent in the late sixties and early seventies, Hernandez (at left) visited classmates' homes in Randallstown, which was still overwhelmingly white, to rehearse with his rock band.

two Victorian or Edwardian row homes. Maybe three. And then two dozen out in the Randallstown corridor." His clients sought the suburban ideal, not historic homes ripe for gentrification. "I would show them my house, I was so proud of my work. . . . They had no interest in that, they wanted to live in suburbia. They wanted to go to the mall, to be close to their place of work, which, in many instances, was Social Security. Security Square Mall had just been built . . . in '72. And it was a very popular place at the time." Hernandez had grown up in a family that looked askance at suburban homes, which may have explained his preference for city living. But he recognized that in the 1980s he was in a distinct minority. What home buyers wanted "was that pseudo-contemporary, split foyer, split level type of homes. My mother would refer to them as 'prefabs.' I don't know if that's appropriate. But they were basically brick-fronted, vinyl-sided, aluminum-sided, and they were very 'tract housing' built by developers who would put up subdivisions of anywhere from fifty of 'em to three hundred of them at a time. And people would purchase them and have a quarter-acre, a third of an acre walk-around plot of land."

The suburban ideal existed in harmony with material differences between the city and the suburbs. Hernandez argued that primary concerns on the minds of parents contemplating buying a house in the city or the suburbs were the familiar litany of late twentieth-century urban woes: "Violence, drugs, quality of education, post-riots. Remember we were only '68. 'I want a better life for my kid than I had for me,' you know.'" While his customers remembered playing jacks on the classic white marble stoops of Baltimore City rowhouses, they imagined that halcyon childhood was now available only in the suburbs. Clients told him, "I played jacks and played on the stoop, I want marble steps, I want my kid to have a lawn. Be able to ride his bike without someone taking it. So he could set the bike on the steps and come in for a soda, or water, and not come back out and it's gone. Or somebody's pulling him off of it." Hernandez's African American clients were moving out of the city only a few years after serious riots following the assassination of Martin Luther King; the city was suffering from severe underinvestment as businesses were not rebuilt, others left, and the commercial and residential tax base shrunk. Suburban schools were recognized as better funded than city schools. The suburban ideal was a means to articulate culturally differences that existed materially.

Those cultural differences turned material advantage into cultural status, reinforcing the cultural magic of the suburbs. Moving to the suburbs "was definitely a status thing." Hernandez imagined a conversation among new suburbanites who returned on Sunday to the city to go to church. "It was the whole aura . . . we've got the new cars, and you would come into town on Sunday to worship at the church from the old neighborhood. So you've got this large migration of traffic coming back down into Liberty Road on the weekends to go to church. And that was a sign of status, quite frankly." Suburbanites could then deploy their suburban amenities in friendly offers that showed off their newly acquired status. "You'd say, 'We'll have you at the house!' You know, 'we'll have a cookout.

A barbecue in the backyard. We'll have you out over the holidays, come on out. It's beautiful.'" Markers of suburban life—the car, the commute, the barbecue, the backyard—also functioned as symbolic substitutes for larger material advantages that government policy, mortgage practices, and middle-class flight and political power had secured for the suburbs. As new homeowners returned to the old neighborhood with invitations to barbecues and stories of tranquility surrounded by a green lawn, the material and cultural advantages of the suburbs became intertwined, and drew more households out to the county.

Thus as civil rights activists and Black professionals pushed down suburban barriers to Black home buyers, urban renewal pushed middle-class residents out of their old neighborhoods. The cultural hegemony of the suburban idea and its material advantages attracted Black families, like white ones, out to suburban lawns and strip malls.

Access to Mortgage Capital

As activists breached the racial barrier into Baltimore County, and Baltimore African Americans embraced the suburban ideal, prospective home buyers needed one more critical ingredient in order to be able to move out to the suburbs: money. Once again, access to mortgage capital came through a confluence of activist efforts, resulting legal pressure, and individual people's commitments to nondiscriminatory housing. Among this web of factors, particular people's personal commitments to open housing suggest specific features in Baltimore County that allowed an African American suburb to grow around some cities, while none developed around others.

Buying a house requires not only a willing buyer and seller, but a home loan to finance the purchase. When Angelo Hernandez discussed the different status and racial composition of neighborhoods, he cited the Prince song "Uptown." When he discussed his life in the suburbs, he talked about the Beatles. And when he discussed mortgage capital, he quoted Wu-Tang Clan: "Cash rules everything around me." The key to selling homes was getting financing. Hernandez was successful because this critical part of the process was "kind of my forte. . . . I could help them get their financial house in order and could get them a loan. A first mortgage and no kind of creative, or subprime kind of financing or anything like that . . . primarily FHA-insured mortgages, Fanny Mae–insured mortgages."

At least as late as the 1950s, African Americans buying Baltimore City homes in transitioning neighborhoods often bought from middle-men.[29] But groups including the NAACP, CORE (the Congress of Racial Equality), and a local fair housing group called the Activists initiated a three-year campaign against exploitative home sales. The campaign cul-minated in a lawsuit against the Morris Goldseker Company, which the Activists found had profited as an arbitrageur in over a third of the sales in one transitioning neighborhood. Though the suit eventually stalled, sustained, organized opposition to blockbuster profiteering coupled with increased access to mortgages by the 1970s changed the prospects of African American home buyers, who could use mortgages to buy di-rectly from homeowners rather than middlemen.

This improvement fostered a second one. As long as African Ameri-cans were financing their purchases through blockbusters with uncon-ventional, expensive, and insecure financing schemes, exploitation was endemic. Once realtors initiated racial change with a call to Black re-altors like James Crockett, the middleman was largely removed from financing. Crockett was able to arrange loans through conventional lenders, and at more conventional rates. Real estate dealers' profits began coming from conventional sales commissions, not arbitrage buy-ing and reselling. This was likely beneficial to white sellers and Black buyers: in the old model, outgoing whites were paid too little for their homes; African Americans paid too much. By arranging financing for direct sales between the two parties, it was less likely that both sides were being taken advantage of. In the past, middlemen had actively wanted Black buyers to default, so that they could reclaim the property and sell it again.[30] The elimination of such intermediaries reduced some of the most extreme manipulation African American home buyers were subjected to. The process also likely reduced the middleman's interest in stoking prejudice among white potential sellers.

But what banks or lenders wrote mortgages to African Americans? Ever since Baltimore's apartheid legislation was ruled unconstitutional by the Supreme Court in 1914, whites in Baltimore and the rest of the country had employed a set of informal racist practices to maintain segregation. Among these was banks' consensus not to lend to African Americans—rarely at all, certainly not at interest rates as low as those afforded whites, and never to African Americans seeking to live in white neighborhoods.

Like Angelo Hernandez, James Crockett attributed some of his success as a real estate broker for African American clients to his skills in obtaining mortgages for prospective buyers. Early on he became adept at a game of nod-and-wink. Crockett, who worked more in the city than in the county, recounted,

> You had lending institutions that had their own restrictions. They would not finance a house where there was not a Black living in that block—to a Black buyer. So they knew your reputation. And they would say to you, "Are there any Blacks living in this block?" And you would say yes. You could say, "Herman Smith." Okay? And they wouldn't take the address or anything, they would say okay, Herman Smith live there. So eventually this name Herman Smith kept cropping up, so when you went down to place an application, they'd say, "Jim, who lives in that block? Herman Smith?" [Laughs] You know? So they wanted to make money, too. And that's how they made it.

But while Crockett's account suggests that there were ways to play on banks' desire to make money to induce them to violate the "gentlemen's agreement" to segregate home buyers, this process worked only for realtors, like Crockett, who had relationships with banks. And given the degree to which neighborhoods remained segregated, it likely worked only in some transitional neighborhoods and could not be relied upon to finance African Americans' moves to the white suburbs.

The first indication that financing for African Americans moving to the suburbs had come from a particular source arose in conversation with Lenwood Johnson, one of the founders of the county's NAACP branch. During an interview in his office in the county planning department, Johnson was recounting how he had moved out to the suburbs. Their desire to live in the city and stay connected to activist groups was frustrated by redlining. When looking for loans to buy a home in the city, said Johnson, "We were turned down more times than the bedspreads at

the Waldorf." Columbia, Maryland, was a new development that explicitly sought to be an integrated community. James Rouse, who had grown
from a mortgage lender to a large-scale real estate developer, announced
that Columbia would be integrated. But as Johnson points out, making
that a reality required Rouse to put his money where his mouth was.
Rouse was beginning to gain a reputation for ambitious planning projects and a liberal commitment to fair housing. Columbia was not simply
a housing development but a whole new town. And Rouse worked carefully to ensure that his new town would be integrated. Johnson argued
that Rouse's "multiethnic utopia in Columbia—that would not have happened if African Americans who wanted to live in the area had to rely
on traditional lending institutions for mortgages. So Rouse's company
made mortgages available to African Americans who were looking to
move into Columbia."

Unfortunately, Columbia was too far from Baltimore for Johnson
and his wife to commute to work every day. So they began looking in
Baltimore County. The Johnsons knew that Rylan Homes had built the
section of Columbia into which Ms. Johnson's sister had moved. In 1972
the Johnsons visited a new housing development being built by Rylan
Homes in Randallstown. They had seen the development advertised in
the *Baltimore Afro-American*. "We figured that if the Rylan Company
was going to take out a full-page ad in the *Afro*, they must be looking for
our business," he said. They chose a lot and a design for the house to be
built on it. Rylan built the house and arranged the financing, so it was
only once everything was in order that they learned who the lender was:
the mortgage company of James W. Rouse. After a few years, Rouse's
company sold the mortgage to another lender. Johnson said he was not
the only Black home buyer whose purchase was financed by Rouse.
"Several people I've come to know—same thing had occurred: Rouse
made mortgages available to them. I'm just surmising . . . it was probably
more people than I could possibly guess at this point." I heard a similar
account from William A. Ross Sr., who bought a new house near the
Social Security headquarters: Rouse had supplied the mortgage, not only
for him but for most of the fifteen other households on his block.

As I continued my research, it appeared that African Americans
were not the only people who benefited from Rouse's willingness to

lend to buyers crossing the color line. When John Michener decided to buy a house in the integrated Baltimore City neighborhood of Windsor Hills, he called twenty lenders—but none would give him a loan. One bank said they would be happy to lend money to him, assuming he was, of course, south of the street that at that time divided white and Black West Baltimore. When Michener said the home he wanted to buy was on the other side, the lender said frankly, "Oh, we've stopped making loans there."

Michener then brought his mortgage difficulties to the attention of the housing group Baltimore Neighborhoods, and they promptly arranged a mortgage through Rouse, who was not only a board member but a founder of the group.[31]

Why did Rouse make loans when others would not? There were likely several reasons. First, banks were least likely to make loans to African Americans, claiming, according to Black realtors at the time, that they didn't want white customers to even see Blacks inside the banks. Mortgage brokers like Rouse, on the other hand, did not have such public offices, or customers with other kinds of accounts. Mortgage lenders typically made agreements with investors to write a certain number of mortgages, financed by the investor, by a certain date. From that moment, the clock was ticking, so mortgage lenders could become much less discriminatory about whom they leant to as the pressure to reach the loan target grew.

Certainly, though, Rouse personally made a difference. Although he grew up in the segregated and conservative Eastern Shore of Maryland, Rouse had been interested in social issues and integrated neighborhoods from early in his career. He worked on a Baltimore plan to fight blight as early as 1951, and though this business-led initiative could be seen as either a beneficent plan by elites to improve slum conditions or an effort by developers to increase property values and foster development, the project stimulated Rouse's interesting in more equitable housing for Blacks.[32] (This interest in African American equality may explain a 1959 Rouse company outing to Harper's Ferry to see the initial restoration of the historic site of John Brown's antislavery raid.)[33]

In addition, Rouse had more experience than most lenders writing mortgages to African Americans. In 1935, while still in law school, Rouse managed to get a job with the fledgling Federal Housing Administration (FHA), a New Deal project to use government money to subsidize mortgage writing activity.[34] When he left the FHA for the private sector (soon cofounding the Moss-Rouse mortgage company), Rouse was singularly well positioned to make use of the new federal program. In his work writing Veterans Administration (VA) loans (to people like William Ross and the fellow veterans who were his neighbors), Rouse wrote many loans to African American home buyers. Thus he had experience working with Black clients that most home lenders willfully lacked.

S. Lee Martin, the realtor who worked for Mal Sherman and had represented the football player John Mackey when he looked for a home, recalled that "back in the sixties most of the Black people got mortgages through FHA." He recalled that "the Rouse Company had a big FHA banking portfolio," and knew that Rouse had gotten his start in FHA lending. In the sixties, much of the housing industry was strictly segregated—most of the largest realtors had no Black agents. Rouse was working extensively with African American customers when many others did not.

As early as 1954, Rouse was recognized as an authority on minority lending. That year, the head of the Mortgage Bankers Association appointed him president of the Committee on Financing Minority Housing. The committee was charged to identify what difficulties minorities faced in borrowing money, what could be done to change the situation, and how additional investments could be induced for minority mortgage lending.[35] Rouse worked on the project with some enthusiasm. A survey Rouse's group sent to 1,372 lending institutions nationwide gave some indication of just how rare it was for banks and brokers to lend to African Americans. Rouse's own analysis of the survey concluded that "no more than 10% to 15% of the originators [were] making loans to Negroes as a regular part of their business."[36]

Lenders gave various explanations for why they did little business with Black customers. In the collection of letters from the responding lenders, there were only a few disparaging comments made about Black borrowers, but many made few or no loans to Blacks. Among the surviving letters, the most insulting was the Monroe, Louisiana, firm that concluded in their letter that "these people do not think, act or have the necessary intelligence to recognize and take care of their obligation in our opinion." A Cleveland company wrote that "so far as we can recall, we have only made one loan to a colored person . . . so we do not know what attitude our principals might take."[37] Others did not make loans to Negroes, and therefore protested that they did not know how to start: a firm in Utah had an opportunity to write mortgages to "the better class of colored railway employees" living in Ogden. But "we did not have experience with . . . the paying habits of Negro borrowers generally or any particular market for loans to colored people." Others saw segregation as a given and blamed Blacks' limited housing options: a Kansas City company wrote that while their office "has been making loans to Negroes for many years with equally as satisfactory results as to white borrowers . . . the basic problem in Negro housing . . . is not lack of financing bur rather, lack of available housing. Unfortunately, in Kansas City very little land seems to be available for new Negro housing without encroaching upon white neighborhoods." A firm defensively suggested that "actually, of course, most of us will make loans to Colored people if we can find them in a good district and can have a good borrower." A very few letters that accompanied the survey then argued that Negro borrowers were not reliable customers, though most said that they were. Some particularly revealing letters pointed to an apparent structural obstacle at the national level: firms that lent money and then resold the mortgages on the secondary market (much as mortgages were infamously resold during the real estate bubble that burst in 2008) said they did not know to whom they could sell mortgages made to African Americans. Several firms that did lend to Blacks kept the loans on the books themselves because they could not be sold to the same investors who bought whites' debts. If buyers on the secondary market did not want to buy mortgages made to Black buyers, lenders had no market in which they might sell loans they might make.

The responses to Rouse's survey, including his own response, were destroyed to ensure confidentiality, so unfortunately we do not have Rouse's response to quantify how many loans he was making to Black buyers. But those who worked with Rouse said he did substantial business with Black home buyers through VA and FHA loans.[38] The survey suggests that lender behavior made a difference in housing options. A Louisiana lender said that they "wanted to [make loans to Blacks] because they all looked like they would be excellent borrowers, but we had absolutely no facilities to make colored loans." (What was meant by facilities was unspecified.) After the firm began working with a New York state bank that already had "colored loans" on its books, they began lending to Blacks. Likewise, a lender in San Bernardino, California, wrote that he had no doubt that "this area could easily use not less than 10,000 or more homes for colored and Mexican buyers. The economic advantages to this community of getting these people into clean, attractive surroundings staggers the imagination." The firm knew several builders "who would immediately construct these homes if we were able to give them GI loan allotments from lenders willing to accept these investments for their portfolios."[39] Lack of mortgage capital was choking off access to housing for people of color.

Once again, the Mortgage Bankers Association initiative was motivated by a combination of activist pressure that mobilized personal commitments and legal challenges that suggested change would be required. While an MBA official suggested that "the fact that MBA is going into this without any special prodding created an excellent initial impression" with Black leaders, in fact the minority housing committee was formed in response to pointed criticism of the mortgage industry in a report by the National Urban League.[40] The Quaker organization, the American Friends Service Committee, with which John Michener had been involved even before joining Social Security, also sent an early letter to Rouse's committee wanting to know more about what the mortgage bankers intended to do about the problems faced by nonwhite prospective borrowers.[41] The committee secretary regularly supplied the dozen members of the committee with legislative updates, on topics like the Supreme Court's landmark 1954 *Brown v. Board of Education* ruling, just as the committee was beginning it work. (The committee noted that as rulings eliminated legal segregation of schools, neighborhoods, and public projects, southern support for public housing dried up. A southern senator had supported public housing when it could be used to warehouse Blacks and bulldoze their former neighborhoods, but reversed his position and opposed it as soon as *Brown* was announced.)[42] Attention to the inadequacies of lending to African Americans did not originate with the bankers, but was their response to a context of activist pressure and legislative and judicial change.

Around the time the first African American suburbanites moved to the county and the Social Security Administration began their efforts to desegregate housing there, Rouse's mortgage company was one of the largest lenders in Baltimore County. Most of the few companies larger than his specialized in private, high-end mortgages. But Rouse, building on his expertise with FHA loans, made only FHA and VA loans and made $1.4 million in such loans in Baltimore County in 1974 alone—more than any other lender.[43] Nationwide, African Americans had been virtually shut out of FHA and VA mortgages by discrimination, lower wages, and the preference in those programs to finance the purchase of new homes—many of which were in developments that refused to sell to Blacks.[44] Only with the passage of the Fair Housing Act in 1968 did loans became somewhat more available to African Americans. William Ross, himself an African American military veteran, said Rouse and his company "were the VA specialists" as early as when he bought his home with a Rouse VA mortgage in 1956. Ross, who later oversaw the Urban League's nationwide housing program, recalled that when he began work on an urban redevelopment program in Baltimore City, he felt Rouse's firm was one of two where African Americans "could go to get a fair deal."[45] "He was the socially conscious mortgage broker in the Baltimore area," said Ross, who later went to work on (and live in) Rouse's Columbia, Maryland, development.

By the time African Americans began moving into Baltimore County, Rouse had been recognized as a leader for almost twenty years on the issue of minority lending. He had regularly made loans to African Americans well before most lenders in the Baltimore area did so and was a board member or founder of several fair housing organizations in Maryland. Rouse's concentration in VA and FHA loans, which attracted more African American buyers, and his explicit interest in increasing minority access to loans (which was financially beneficial to him as well) made him a regular source for mortgages for suburbanizing African Americans.

Suggesting that Rouse played a significant role in desegregating Baltimore County is not to idealize him. As Nicholas Bloom has pointed out in the most trenchant study of Rouse, Rouse was a capitalist with a liberal ideal. His critique of inequality did not extend to a critique of capitalism. Bloom argues that early Rouse projects displaced African American residents and concludes more generally that such for-profit ventures are inadequate to resolve housing crises in the United States.[46] Rouse was a socially conscious businessman, and his projects reflected the limitations of trying to improve social welfare while prioritizing profit. But that conflict did not prevent him from contributing financing to the desegregation of Baltimore County's once all-white suburbs. Rouse was an early, substantial lender to African Americans and the largest source of federally insured mortgages in the county. A metropolitan area that lacked such a player would lack an institutional source of mortgage capital to allow African American home purchases.

Ethnic Explanations for Desegregation

As Mal Sherman ruefully noted, activists had been unable to open up the whole county to Black residents. Instead, almost all African Americans who came to the suburbs moved up along Liberty Road, crossing from the northwestern corner of the city to the southwestern part of the county, which included Randallstown. Understanding why African American suburbs grew and flourished here but almost nowhere else in the county identifies the conditions necessary to break suburban racial barriers, and why so many US suburbs remain distinctly segregated.

Several factors explain why growth occurred in this section of the county and not others. The proximity of both the Social Security headquarters and the large and growing Northwest Baltimore Black community played a role. Other factors related to particularities of the housing and labor market in Southwestern Baltimore County. The fact that for more than a century, Blacks had moved into white neighborhoods that had previously been Jewish seemed significant to everyone I talked to, and a variety of folk theories—some flattering to Jews, some not—developed about why African Americans moved into Jewish neighborhoods but not others. Untangling this collection of explanations helps explain the complex and partial process of desegregation.

Conventional wisdom explains the growth of the Black community in this part of the county because it had previously been Jewish. Local observers offered two different explanations based on that observation.

The first and most common was that Jews were "more liberal" and tolerant, and so Blacks *could* move into Jewish neighborhoods whereas white Christians kept Blacks out of other parts of the county. Certainly Jews had a history of civil rights activism (as the name of the group BLEWS itself attests). Blacks and whites, Jews and non-Jews endorsed this explanation.

Contrary to the account that Jews were more tolerant than other whites, a county official warned that such an account idealized a much more venal situation:

> I think that's an urban myth . . . because the blockbusting was started by Jewish people, namely the Jewish landowners. And there has always been a group of people that have always been the educated and the more liberal of any ethnic group. But as a whole I think one would be a little naïve to think that all these love and kisses and all that. . . . Part of my interest in this is my husband lived in this area growing up; and . . . his parents tried to buy, as whites, one of the houses from Goldseker [the Baltimore developer, who was Jewish] and he would not sell it to them because they were white and he was breaking the blocks . . . So I would suggest that there is a lot more behind what sounds very nice.

Goldseker had indeed been the most prominent target of antiblockbusting campaigns in the 1950s.[47] Both of the characterizations of the role of Jews in racial transition—as either tolerant liberals or profiteering blockbusters—trade on well-established cultural stereotypes. But either of those cultural explanation would still beg the question of why a group embraced values that led them to act as they did. Instead of going down that path of infinite regress, structural economic factors seem to provide a more solid understanding of how Baltimore residents responded in a racially and ethnically structured housing market.

Accounts from other cities suggest that Jewish residents responded to many of the same practical considerations and popular prejudices that other white homeowners did. To the extent that there were differences among different white ethnics, they were at the margins. Jonathan Rieder's account of Jewish and Italian New Yorkers' opposition to neighborhood integration did not suggest Jewish homeowners were tolerant of integration. Jewish and Italian American residents hoped their neighborhood would remain all white, and many took collective action to keep it that way.[48] Conventional wisdom at the time did hold that *lower-middle-class* Jewish homeowners just barely had the resources to move out, while *working-class* Italians stayed and fought integration. The impression in that neighborhood was that Italians fought while Jews ran. Any difference resulted from means, however. Even if such a difference existed, it is hardly the liberal embrace of Black neighbors suggested by the initial explanation of Randallstown's integration, which held that Jews welcomed neighborhood racial integration.

A different explanation for the growth of the African American community in the wake of the Jewish community is the conventional story of ethnic succession, in which upwardly mobile Jewish residents moved out of a neighborhood and into nicer, newer developments father up Liberty Road's diagonal path out of the city, and upwardly mobile African Americans replaced them.

A significant but overlooked aspect of such ethnic succession is the tripartite nature of Baltimore's housing market. It is well recognized that the United States has a *dual housing market*, in which there are two virtually separate housing markets, one for African Americans and one for whites.[49] The two markets operate separately—whites rarely buy in Black neighborhoods, Blacks generally cannot buy in white ones—and have differences in price (which allowed for the arbitrage of earlier real estate dealers who were labeled blockbusters) and different financing (from conventional mortgages to "buying on time" and subprime loans).

But observers have noted that Baltimore, at least, has not two housing markets but three.[50] In addition to white and Black neighborhoods, there is a Jewish market. As one resident who moved to Baltimore from Brooklyn found, Jewish people in Baltimore lived in very segregated communities. Once a neighborhood became largely Jewish, it was no longer part of the white housing market. Thus while upwardly mobile Gentile whites might move to a larger home and sell their home in the large white housing market (whites constituted over 75 percent of Baltimore County households), to the extent that Baltimore's Jewish community moved outward from the city and further out into the suburbs, there was slack demand for the homes they were vacating. While other whites could draw from a larger pool and find less affluent whites to buy their homes, it was difficult to find buyers for homes in older Jewish neighborhoods. Whether motivated by a commitment to social equality or not, at certain points in the process of ethnic succession residents in this, the smallest of the three segments of the Baltimore housing market, had few prospective buyers if they did not consider selling to African Americans. As Antero Pietila points out, Baltimore's tripartite housing market meant that neighborhoods would go from non-Jewish to Jewish, and as Jews moved outward and upward, there was no market for the homes in existing Jewish neighborhoods *except* African Americans—who already lived nearby in housing an earlier generation of Jewish residents had moved out of as well.[51] Without denying the role that Jewish activists played in fighting segregation, African Americans found homes where they could and Jewish residents sold homes to whom they could.

This had been the pattern since the days of Hawkins and McMechen in the late nineteenth century. As Pietila described the process in a speech to the Baltimore City Historical Society,

> Gradually the whole area became perceived as Jewish and other white homebuyers and renters shied away.
>
> They were not only averse to living among Jews but also worried about the proximity of the black district that kept expanding. This aversion led to a peculiar Baltimore real estate tradition. In most American cities a dual real estate market existed—one for whites and a separate one for blacks. In Baltimore a separate real estate market also emerged for Jews who were limited to certain sections in the northwest and prohibited from neighborhoods east of the Jones Falls, a stream that divides the city.
>
> This three-tiered real estate market produced situations in which blacks and Jews became uneasy neighbors. Whenever neighborhoods that were perceived as Jewish experienced real estate downturns, the lack of other white buyers and renters repeatedly tempted some owner—who may not have been Jewish—to tap the black market. McCulloh Street [the story of George McMechen breeching a white neighborhood's boundary] was repeated time and time again.[52]

Beyond Baltimore, there is no evidence that Jewish neighborhoods necessarily play a decisive role in creating Black suburbs. While in

Baltimore Black suburbs grew up in Jewish suburbs, that is not the case elsewhere. (See Figures 2.3–2.6.) In nearby Washington, it appears that Jewish migration out of the city was toward the northwest, while African American suburbs grew to the east.[53] In Philadelphia, Jewish suburbs to the west and northeast of the Center City area are near Black communities but remain non-Black; African American communities stop abruptly at the city line rather than continuing toward Jewish suburbs. Boston displays no Jewish suburbs the size of those of the other three cities and has very little in the way of Black suburbs either. The absence of Jewish and Black suburbs arguably makes Boston the only case that supports a correlation between Jewish and African American suburbs, but the evidence is weak. To the extent that Jewish neighborhoods were causally linked to the growth of Black neighborhoods in Baltimore, it was one possible element out of the many locally specific conditions that enable or inhibit the growth of African American suburbs.

Even inside Baltimore County there is evidence that the Jewish–African American connection tells less of the story than popular accounts suggest. For instance, the Catonsville-Woodlawn area, near Randallstown, has a large African American population, but there is no evidence that this area was ever home to a significant Jewish community. The newer suburbs around Randallstown have been developed in adjacent areas such as Granite, which were rural and Gentile when Randallstown was Jewish. Residents attribute significance to the fact that Randallstown was largely Jewish before it became Black, but the pattern is hardly consistent.

As another example, the community east of Randallstown (called Pikesville) was also heavily Jewish and had experienced both new Jewish residents moving to Pikesville from the city and residents later moving away from Pikesville, farther out to the county. But Pikesville has undergone much less racial turnover so far. (By the late 1990s Baltimore was home to a growing community of Jewish immigrants from the former Soviet Union, which provided a new pool of prospective home buyers in the Jewish section of the segregated tripartite market that still endures.)[54] As a counterfactual to the significance of Jewish tolerance, consider the eastern part of the county, which Randallstown residents (white and Black) see as a white working-class area hostile to Black residents. It was also long home to Turner Station, which earlier in the century had been the largest African American community in the county. Both African Americans and those working-class whites had moved there to take jobs at the steel mills.[55] People don't have to like each other to live nearby each other. Neither claims of Jewish tolerance nor allegations of Jewish blockbusting nor ethnic succession processes sufficiently explain why African American suburbs grew up around Randallstown and not other places.

That Randallstown had been Jewish played some role in the fact that it became an African American suburb while other parts of the county remained steadfastly white. But the arrival of African Americans along this suburban corridor is too complex to be explained by the ethnicity of the previous residents alone, whether on account of tolerance, opportunism, or upward mobility.

Instead multiple factors interacted to make Black suburbs possible in Baltimore and to lead to their growth along the Liberty Road corridor. Urban renewal and the suburban relocation of the Social Security headquarters functioned as material push factors for a group of Baltimore City African American residents with the means to buy a home. The suburban ideal, which was both a cultural preference and a cultural expression of the material perks of moving to the suburbs, turned people's search from city to suburb. Civil rights activism cracked the wall of everyday white practices that had excluded African Americans and made mortgage capital available for conventional sales rather than exploitative "contract sale" practices that had immiserated Black neighborhoods in the past. Ongoing suburban white resistance still made such a move difficult in much of the county, and few Black families wanted to be the only Black household on the block. But the tripartite housing market made demand soft in formerly Jewish neighborhoods that were easily accessible from both a large existing Black community in the city and a major employer of Black professionals. Black families pushing and being pushed out from Black neighborhoods in the city found the Liberty Road corridor both was accommodating and met their needs, and builders constructed new developments to sell to white and Black buyers.

The growth of Black suburbs around Baltimore is representative of many cities, but not all. Some metropolitan areas developed spillover suburbs like Baltimore did, but others lack them. Other Black suburbs developed for different historical reasons. Willingboro, New Jersey, an original postwar Levittown suburb located between Philadelphia and Fort Dix and McGuire Air Force Base, for instance, was desegregated as a result of a state fair housing case and became a predominantly Black suburb. New York City has atypical suburbs in part because it is surrounded by many places that are cities in their own right, thus Black communities outside New York may be cities that had their own processes of Black migration, deindustrialization, and white flight earlier in the century.

Black suburbanization is a nationwide story, but there are important regional variations to recognize. Cities that were destinations in the Great Migration typically had central urban cores that developed large, concentrated Black neighborhoods within them from which residents either did or did not extend to the suburbs. Sun Belt cities of the Southwest often have convoluted, seemingly gerrymandered boundaries, so that there appears to be little rhyme or reason to whether an urban neighborhood is or is not within the legal city limits. Thus Houston, Los Angeles, and San Antonio may have Black communities that cross over the city limits not because they are classic spillover expansions but because the boundaries themselves twist and turn over the landscape, rendering one block city, another suburb, with little difference between the two. The most significant Black communities in urban areas are in the South, or in the cities on train lines radiating northward that were destinations in the twentieth-century Great Migration. In contrast, cities from Arizona to California, including large ones like Phoenix, San Diego, and San Jose, have fewer Black residents and smaller Black communities in the city and suburbs.

Baltimore's Black suburbs demonstrates that "spillover" is not inevitable or natural but develops from particular conditions. The process illuminates material and political factors that were likely significant in many other cities since the draw to the suburbs, the push from the city, access to the housing market, and the availability of mortgages cannot help but be central to the growth of such suburbs. Beyond whatever local variation there might be, people still racially segregate neighborhoods

Figure 2.3. African American communities in Boston generally stop at the city border (shown as a solid line).
Source: SocialExplorer.com.

since any metro area that does have meaningful numbers of Black suburbanites has a concentrated Black suburb.

The growth of African American suburbs has been significant. In 1960 only three cities had suburbs that were more than 10 percent Black: Miami, New Orleans, and Houston. By 1980 there were seven: Washington, Miami, Newark, Atlanta, New Orleans, St. Louis, and Baltimore. There are significant African American suburbs in as many as twelve of the twenty largest metro areas. African American suburbs now exist outside cities like Charlotte, Chicago, Dallas, Detroit, New York, and

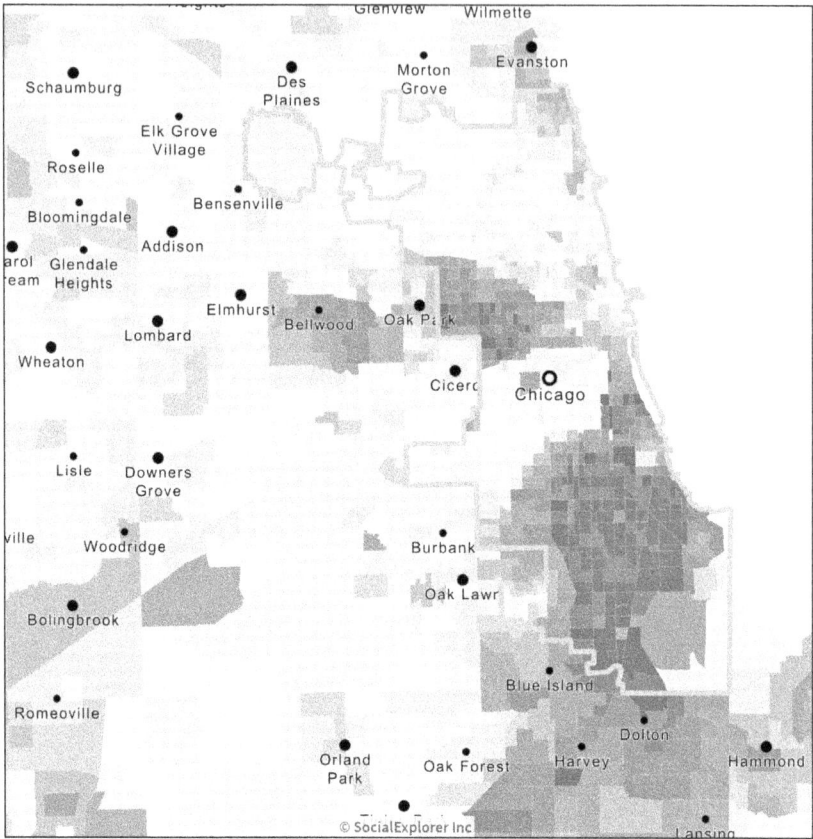

Figure 2.4. Chicago has extensive African American suburbs south of the city boundary (shown as a gray line).
Source: SocialExplorer.com.

Orlando (see Figures 2.3–2.6). Today, 40 forty percent of African Americans live in suburbs.[56] Black suburbanization is more the norm than a rare exception.

Each city with sizeable African American suburbs does not need to have the exact same constellation of factors that Baltimore did. Experiences in nearby Prince Georges County, outside Washington, in which white residents resisted the arrival of Black residents and stable government jobs provided the economic basis for a Black middle class, suggest there are patterns across cities. Certainly, jobs, mortgages, and efforts to integrate would seem necessary for Black suburbs to grow. Processes like urban renewal and highway building pushed people to new neighborhoods. Today, factors like immigration and gentrification influence the location and racial composition of neighborhoods where Black people live.

As in other cities, a new chapter in Baltimore's Black community began as African Americans "spilled over" into the suburbs. Civil rights gains, real homeownership free of hyper-exploitation, and increased

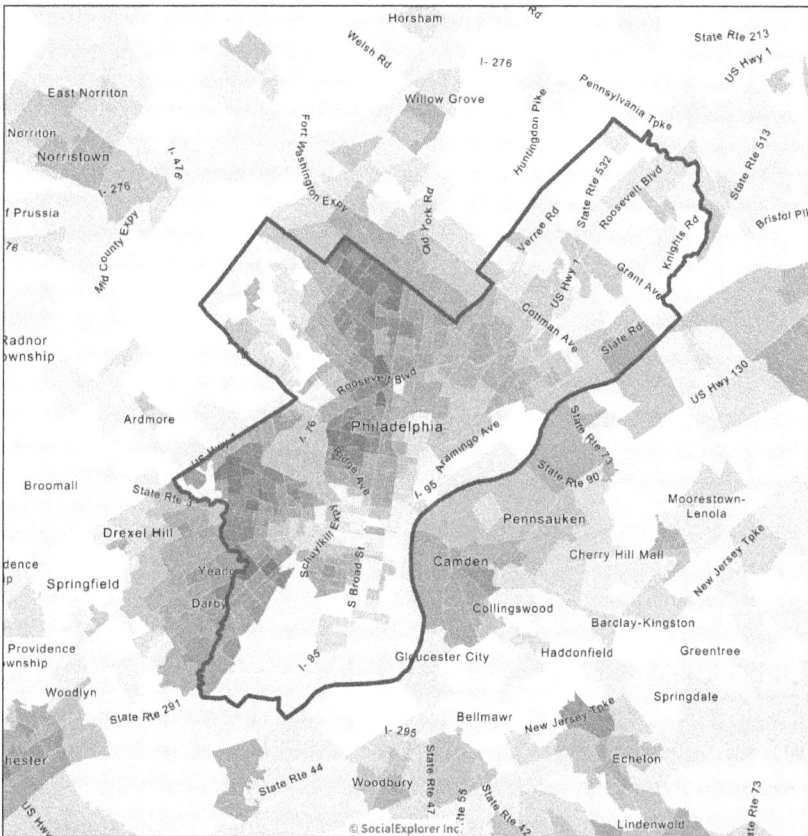

Figure 2.5. African American neighborhoods in northern Philadelphia have just begun to cross the residential street that marks the city boundary (shown here as a black line). Black areas east of the city are actually Camden, NJ, a separate city across the Delaware River.
Source: SocialExplorer.com.

Figure 2.6. Washington, DC, has extensive African American suburbs to the west in Prince George's County, MD.
Source: SocialExplorer.com.

economic stability created new possibilities along Liberty Road. The unique spatial organization of the suburbs and relative class homogeneity for a group with the resources of the middle class meant that this new community would develop differently than previous, urban Black communities. In Randallstown, the stage was set for a new Black experience, a middle-class suburban enclave outside the center city, confronting old prejudices and inequalities but with a suburban set of tools with which to respond.

3

Desegregation

Resident Activists Craft a New Story in the Suburbs

As civil rights activists made progress against the suburban color line, residents' approach also shifted during this period. By the definition of historian Thomas Sugrue, Randallstown was an *undefended* neighborhood: community associations did not organize to keep African Americans out. But they did organize to maintain their property values during and after racial transition.

Conventional wisdom predicted that racial transition inevitably brought the deterioration of housing stock, rapid white flight, and the decline in social class of inhabitants. Countering those expectations, resident activists in Randallstown found ways to maintain neighborhoods, slow white flight, and preserve the socioeconomic class of their communities. As a result, some of the negative consequences often attributed to racial transitions were alleviated. Resident activists' qualified success indicates other communities have the means to encourage racial change without suffering much-feared declines in property values. Along the way, the strategies employed by resident activists demonstrated how suburban social institutions and norms could be harnessed to create economically stable racially transitioning communities.

The ability to use suburban strategies was not without its hazards, however. Given that postwar suburbs were constructed to exclude—by race and by class—suburban strategies of property value preservation can carry uneasy aspects of class intolerance. African American suburbanites in particular recognized, and often wrestled with, the ambiguous position of trying to preserve a neighborhood's property values by keeping poorer people out.

Community responses were described by two inspiring people who should be heroes for their personal dignity and integrity, Ella White Campbell and Emily Wolfson. The two decades-long Randallstown

Figure 3.1. Ella White Campbell's neighborhood.

residents, the first Black, the second white, were each the kind of determined, one-person community institution who seemed cut from the same cloth. But as can be true in such cases, that similarity was more evident to outside observers. The effect of decades of passionate advocacy by each of them was that they had occasionally ended up on different sides of local issues. They had not spoken to each other in years and maintained a tacit cease-fire by observing a civil distance.[1] Working independently, they lived in similar communities on opposite sides of Liberty Road.

Does Racial Change Lead to Economic Change?

The two neighborhoods in which Campbell and Wolfson lived provide useful data about how racial transition has and has not affected communities financially. Subsections of the suburbs are often named by the developers who build houses there. Campbell lived in Stevenswood, Wolfson in Courtleigh. The two communities underwent dramatic racial change but did not experience dramatic income declines. The two communities have followed similar if not identical paths over the past thirty years (see Figure 3.2). Both went from having virtually no Blacks in 1970 to being 75 to 80 percent African American in 2000. From 1980 to 2010, county median income grew by $1,314, while median incomes in Stevenswood and Courtleigh increased by $7,525 and $3,653, respectively. Behind the overall rise, however, are some decades when incomes have risen and others when they have fallen.

Racial change alone did not determine median incomes. In fact, in both communities the decades of the fastest growth in the percentage

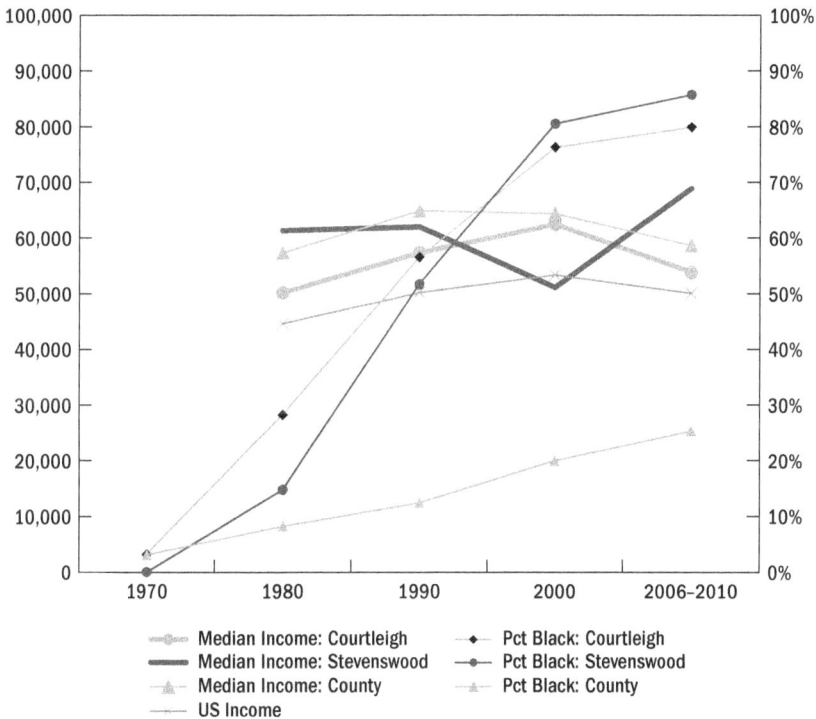

Median Income: Courtleigh — Pct Black: Courtleigh
Median Income: Stevenswood — Pct Black: Stevenswood
Median Income: County — Pct Black: County
US Income

Figure 3.2. As the percentage of residents who were African American in two neighborhoods—Courtleigh and Stevenswood—rose, incomes continued to stay close to the county median. (Note that in 1970 the census calculated average income, not median, and average income tends to be higher than median income. Thus, in the graph the 1970 income measures are comparable only to each other, not to other years.)

of African American residents (1980–1990) are associated with income *growth*, not decline. The percentage of African American residents in Wolfson's neighborhood of Courtleigh doubled from 28 to 56 percent between 1980 and 1990 and incomes rose by $2,000. Campbell's neighborhood of Stevenswood grew from 15 to 52 percent African American and incomes remained unchanged. Stevenswood did experience a significant drop from 1990 to 2000 but made it up the next decade to rise back above the county average. The racial composition of these communities changed from all white to nearly all Black, but race did not push down the income medians in the communities.

Race matters, but its effect can at times be subtle. The two neighborhoods' incomes stayed close to county averages, but of course the county's racial composition was changing, and as the percentage of Blacks rose incomes at times declined. Whiter counties may (or may not) have been more prosperous. There were also difficult decades in these neighborhoods, but their meaning is nuanced. By 2000, for instance, Stevenswood's income dropped considerably. In "nominal" dollars, residents' median earnings increased from $27,000 to $49,000. But when considering buying power, inflation meant that residents could buy less and were not doing as well as in other parts of the county. In a small, single census tract, this could be accounted for by local factors such as a cohort of homeowners who were retiring and thus experiencing a drop in income even if they were well prepared for retirement. Whatever the case, the median income of residents there rose sharply in the next decade.

Elsewhere around Randallstown, incomes did decline at times. Multiple factors play a role, not the least of which being the declining desirability of homes built in the 1950s and 1960s in some of the older suburbs, the aging of residents into retirement (and thus out of their highest earning years), and the increased placement of retirement communities and other "group homes" that would reduce income figures.

Randallstown offers evidence of the reality of a Black-white gap but shows strong evidence of a robust, viable community. In this setting we can examine how local residents exercised their middle-class, suburban agency to ensure that the declines people expected during racial change did not materialize. There is other lapidary work that details the structural disadvantage of African Americans and the reality and implications of income inequality.[2] Here I seek to understand how residents act within the constraints of those structural realities to mitigate their impact on the neighborhood and preserve a strong community against such challenges.

Local Strategies for Class Stability during Racial Change

Residents described several strategies through which they have maintained the class composition of their neighborhoods while not resisting the racial transformation of the communities. Emily Wolfson, eighty-six, was a leading activist in her community for years. Wolfson grew up Jewish in Brooklyn, and when she moved to Baltimore as an adult had no patience for the degree to which she found the Jewish community to be "ghettoized." Though her own social circle was Jewish, she felt uncomfortable in a setting whose extreme segregation was a contrast to her more diverse childhood in New York. In 1958 she moved out of a Baltimore City Jewish neighborhood to the Courtleigh development in Randallstown, a new, more diverse white community that eventually became largely Jewish as well.

Wolfson was already familiar with white responses to new Black neighbors. Decades earlier she had known a friend who played cards every few weeks with a group of other local women. She rented her home, the others were homeowners. African Americans started to buy homes in the area, and at the next card game the friend found out that everyone else in the card group had sold their homes in a single week. "She said, 'I was the one left in the club.'" The story was typical of how quickly racial transition happened in the 1950s, in Baltimore and other cities.

In contrast, when the first African American moved into Wolfson's neighborhood, residents took action to prevent white flight while allowing racial change. First, residents organized to prevent whites from fleeing in fear. Wolfson described how they did so after Baltimore Colts player John Mackey moved nearby:

WOLFSON: There were enough people I think that made a real effort to calm it down. Why did the women go door-to-door and say, "Oh, Mr. Mackey is moving in. Isn't that wonderful? Let's really be nice to him."

Q: Did they actually do that?

WOLFSON: Yes, yes. Two Jewish ladies. Both of them well educated, both of them understood what was going on. They didn't want trouble in their neighborhoods, they wanted everybody to live peacefully. And they stayed in their neighborhoods.

Wolfson credits the community's organization—the work of people like those "two Jewish ladies" for stopping white fear selling. For her part, Wolfson was a longtime community activist, particularly working to ensure high-quality local schools, which also contributed to neighborhood stability. With whites not moving out as a group and telling others not to, home values and the incomes needed to buy them remained constant.

Around the same time, another resident fought to ban the display of "for sale" signs that could foster fear selling. As Wolfson explained, "What they would do is put a big for sale sign on one house, then they would go to the others: 'If you don't sell now you'll lose all your money and be living with Blacks.'" Resisting racist warnings, residents of Courtleigh were able to significantly dampen fear selling, the first mechanism to depress home values in racially transforming neighborhoods.

The actions Wolfson recounted do not mean that all whites welcomed Blacks. Many may have objected. Furthermore, the actions of some residents are muddy in a way that typically makes it difficult for an observer today to assess the motivation, or impact, of actions at the time. The "sign ban" Wolfson described would have legally prohibited the use of either for sale or sold signs. Such signs were indeed widely reputed to be tools in blockbusters' playbooks. A block sprouting a dozen for sale signs signaled to remaining residents that it was time to get out and sell for whatever the local broker was offering. From this perspective a sign ban simply stripped blockbusters of one of the means they had of stoking racial fears. But signs also communicated to African Americans that homes were for sale. Since Black real estate dealers long had difficulty getting access to other dealers' listings, taking down signs removed an important way of finding out about properties for sale. The objective was likewise ambiguous: slowing down sales may have been helpful to whites opposed to fear selling. But trying to slow blockbusting meant keeping neighborhoods white longer—which meant keeping Blacks out. To the extent that sign bans worked, they reduced the number of houses available to a Black market where there was typically considerable demand.

It was with this justification, in fact, that the African American realtor James Crockett went to court to oppose a sign ban introduced in Baltimore City. In 1972 the county banned for sale signs in the Liberty Road area. The city followed suit two years later. Crockett protested by posting a for sale sign in front of a house on McCulloh Street—the same street to which George McMechen moved at the turn of the century— and brought his challenge all the way to the Supreme Court.[3] Crockett argued the ban infringed on free speech rights. Most often, white realtors didn't call to tell him of homes for sale, and Black buyers needed for sale signs to find out about houses for sale in white neighborhoods. The ban was an infringement on First Amendment–protected speech. From Crockett's perspective, a sign ban fought blockbusting by maintaining the segregated housing market that excluded Blacks from white neighborhoods. Bans on for sale signs were ruled unconstitutional.

By Emily Wolfson's account, however, residents in Randallstown soon recognized that racial transition was a reality. After some walked door-to-door to reduce their white neighbors' anxiety about the process, communities in the increasingly Black suburbs then organized to make sure that maintenance of their community did not decline at any stage of racial change.

Ella White Campbell moved to the Stevenswood neighborhood of Randallstown in 1986, twenty-eight years after Emily Wolfson had moved into the Courtleigh neighborhood on the other side of Liberty Road. The racial composition of Campbell's neighborhood shifted slowly from white to Black over the twenty-one years she lived there because, according to Campbell, white residents stayed until it was time to retire or move out of the region, just as Wolfson said they had done in her neighborhood.

Ms. Campbell was a recognized force in the community, able to organize her neighborhood and turn out hundreds of residents at a county government meeting. An African American woman, she had been active in education and community groups, was honored by her sorority, and had once run for state delegate. We spoke in the kitchen of the split-level ranch house she and her husband had shared for twenty-one years. Outside was the motor home they used for family trips, bringing children, and now grandchildren, to see historic and natural sites around the country. She sat straight in her chair. Speaking in precise, carefully chosen words, she explained how her community association had played a central role in stabilizing the neighborhood.

Several community members described their approaches to the task of maintaining the status, appearance, and reputation of their communities after racial transition, but none so vividly or effectively as Ella White Campbell. Campbell was a respected and influential institution in her community. She had been president of the Stevenswood Improvement Association since she moved to the community, when she began organizing against a neighboring hospital's medical waste incinerator. Campbell could turn out three hundred people for a meeting in twenty-four hours, and politicians accorded the Stevenswood homeowners group, made up of little more than one hundred households, the respect of a much larger institution. The association's cohesion and Campbell's power as a community organizer proved to be key ingredients in residents' ability to maintain the status and appearance of Stevenswood.

According to Campbell, Stevenswood had succeeded in remaining a strikingly clean and orderly community because the association ensured that it remained so, and the group made county officials understand that they must support the association's efforts.

Campbell explained how the vigilance of the Stevenswood Association prevented neighborhood decline. "We have a reputation: We do not play. We mean business," she said. The strategy of Campbell and the Stevenswood Association was to aggressively enforce community standards, association rules, and county regulations. "We tell the neighbors our standard is, if there's a complaint, and it reaches the . . . association, [we have] a three-strike process." Campbell described how the association acted politely but quickly and rapidly escalated their actions to force homeowners to maintain their property. If a resident didn't mow and rake the lawn, brought trash cans out to the curb too long before trash pickup, or failed to maintain their home in a more serious way, the association noticed the violation of local rules and took action. "On the first strike you're going to get a call from either me or one of the officers." Then came the second strike. "If things don't change, then you get a visit from two or three of the officers. And we repeat the complaint, okay? But before that visit takes place you get a letter in the mail from the organization detailing the fact that we have contacted you on whatever date it was, this problem has not been rectified, so we'll be paying you a visit to find out if you need our help in rectifying it." According to Campbell, the association did not hesitate to compel compliance. "If that doesn't work, the third strike you're out because we will report you to the county. In other words, we will find the legal source of the violation and we'll see to it you're penalized, so it's one, two, three. Three strikes you're out. And we stick to that rigidly."

Stevenswood appears to stand out from other communities in the county government's particular responsiveness to its problems, and this is likely in large part a result of Campbell. When a neighbor is not maintaining their house to community standards, she is confident that with the county, the association can "find" a code violation encompassing the offense. Campbell vividly illustrated Stevenswood's particular abilities to convince the county to act in their interests:

> So you don't drive around this community and see high grass. In fact there's only one house in which you might see that, and that's because we had the house condemned. Down the street. And we are trying to force the owner to sell it, because of poor maintenance and the fact that the owner kept putting undesirable tenants in the house. So we went to war with him, with the owner. And got the county to condemn the house, and took the owner to court, so that the owner *can't* rent it out. And we're on the county to force the owner to sell the house. But that's the kind of thing we do.

In the suburban context, Campbell's story of a home being condemned is stunning. Unlike severely disinvested neighborhoods in Baltimore where abandonment and condemnation left blocks of boarded-up buildings, in suburban communities like this one more homes are condemned to enlarge floodplains than for inadequate maintenance. Nor was the building abandoned; it was condemned while the owner was still actively seeking to rent it because he had run afoul of the local homeowner association.

The condemnation illustrated how maintenance and behavior were regulated by the community association. As Campbell made clear, residents wanted the house condemned not only because of inadequate maintenance but because of the "undesirable" tenants. Similarly, the residents "advocate being nosy neighbors," enforced an association-established curfew for children, and got involved with other households when there were significant problems in the home. In these ways, homeowners used the association to regulate, restrict, and sanction the behavior of their fellow neighbors. They did so for fear that to be any more permissive would set into motion a cycle of neighborhood economic and social decline. In this way the suburban institution of the homeowner association, which already had a well-established history of imposing strict regulations on residents, was used in African American suburbs to assure residents that middle-class norms would be maintained in their community.

In the suburbs, residents could use community associations—some of which are set up by developers with mandatory membership and dues by homeowners—and the willingness of the suburban county government to strictly enforce narrowly written municipal codes. The space of the suburbs and the fact that residents were largely of the home-owning classes meant that they could harness suburban community institutions and the county's enforcement mechanisms to shape the community as they saw fit. While Campbell was exceptional as an organizer, I never noticed widespread neglect in other neighborhoods. Even empty homes for sale at the height of the housing crisis may have been identifiable by the empty rooms visible through curtain-less windows, but the lawns were mowed.

Campbell's aggressive approach to neighborhood maintenance in part reflected her own personal style. It also reflected a sense that the community was under threat—that because there was the ever-present possibility that lower-income residents would move in, or that absentee investors would buy up and rent out houses without maintaining them properly, extra vigilance was required. A neighborhood that had experienced a racial or ethnic transition of this type was inherently at risk of declining in class status, and residents worked with a sense of urgency to maintain the social standing and symbolic presentation of their community.

The strategies used by residents to maintain their neighborhoods are at once effective and disturbing. The approaches of both Wolfson and Campbell helped maintain the communities as middle-class enclaves and even allowed residents to welcome (or at least not oppose) the ar-rival of African American homeowners with the reassurance that ra-cial change doesn't need to threaten their class status or home equity. Yet neighborhoods achieved this racial inclusivity through aggressive class exclusivity. Renters were strongly discouraged, neighbors of lesser means who didn't keep their homes up to others' standards were finan-cially penalized, and conformity with hegemonic middle-class norms was demanded.

The spatial prerogatives of the suburbs shaped residents' views as well. Wolfson, for instance, supported expanded mass transit in the area and had no tolerance for parochial intolerance (which she occasionally experienced when she had been at the vanguard of Jewish in-movers to Randallstown a generation earlier). Yet she opposed plans to build "townhouses" in Randallstown. Townhouses are rows of attached houses, and the density of such developments reminded her too much of the city. She already believed, like many professional urbanists, that inner-ring suburbs in the county were often, functionally, part of Baltimore City. But Wolfson was emphatic that she did not want townhouses—which, as she knew, were the kind of house I had grown up in and in which my parents still lived—anywhere near her neighborhood and believed they were inappropriate for a suburban setting. Neighborhoods' racial toler-ance was achieved through class intolerance, and the American dream of homeowner independence was secured in African American suburbs through singularly restrictive rules governing homes, appearance, and behavior. To sustain the class status of their neighborhood, residents not only used norms of property maintenance and single-family suburban living but expanded their repertoire to make use of several distinctive features of suburban space.

The Role of Suburban Space

Residents repurposed classic elements of suburban communities—community associations, county zoning regulations, class homogeneity, and homeowner concern with property value—to shape their neighbor-hoods as communities transitioned from white to Black. The distinctive social organization of the suburbs that residents used was joined by distinctive suburban spatial features. These spatial elements were the context in which a very different process of racial transition developed than that which characterized cities in the era before large-scale African American suburbanization.

In 1969 researchers Karl and Alma Taeuber noted that racial transition could happen not just as "succession" or "invasion" (in which the number of Blacks increased while the number of whites in a tract shrank) but also as "growing," where the numbers of both groups grew, but African Americans at a faster rate.[4] This case confounds the predictions of that model. Taeuber and Taeuber expected conditions of "growing" in cities where the Black and white populations were both growing overall. But in Baltimore County between 1970 and 2000, the number of African Americans jumped from 19,000 to 152,000, while the number of whites *dropped* from 600,000 to 561,000. The most common type of transition in Baltimore *City* was succession. Between 1940 and 1950, 53 percent of census tracts the Taeubers studied gained Blacks and lost whites.[5] But this pattern was not immediately reproduced in the suburbs. For cities, racial transition occurred as succession or invasion, but in the county it led, at least initially, to growth.

New construction allowed this growth and changed the pattern of African American in-moving. In the breakthrough decade of the 1970s the African American population grew by the same numbers (and a higher percentage) in the formerly all-white tracts furthest toward the rural fringe along Liberty Road as inside the Beltway in the inner-ring suburbs. Outer-ring suburbs were newer, larger, and more desirable: realtors suggested that people moved as far up Liberty Road as their income and wealth would allow. The inner ring had little room for new homes. In the outer ring, by contrast, developers continued buying farms and building homes a hundred at a time, bringing thousands of new residents to formerly all-white, semirural areas.

The presence of land for relatively large-scale new construction that characterizes these suburbs even today means the arrival of Blacks in previously white suburbs differs from urban transitions in three ways. Rather than Blacks replacing whites, Black and white populations grew at the same time. Second, new homes specifically can facilitate Blacks moving into previously all-white areas. And contrary to common expectations, after neighborhoods became all Black, home values did not collapse. By synthesizing these three processes, we can identify three different stages of racial transition, each delineated by African Americans' access to new housing.

Elsewhere, racial transition (or ethnic succession) meant Blacks replaced whites. The number of people living in the neighborhood often fell.[6] In the suburbs, the populations grew during desegregation. Randallstown grew *rapidly* as a Black suburb even though, paradoxically, residents said that whites did not move out rapidly. The large-scale suburbanization of African Americans in Baltimore County reveals a unique element that suburbs contribute to processes of racial residential change, further highlighting the importance of knowing the landscape in which such transformations are taking place.

Looking more closely at the rapid growth of the African American community in a county that had blatantly excluded Blacks, a surprising paradox emerges. Comparing maps of the 1970 and 1980 censuses, there are two areas along Liberty Road in which the African American community grew most (see Figure 3.3a–b). The first is not surprising and is typical of accounts of African American suburbanization: tracts adjacent to the city line, adjoining the largest existing Black community in Baltimore, grew from 2,000 to 12,000 Black residents (see the area of Figure 3.3a–b marked with a rectangle). But farther up Liberty Road, farther from the city, in Randallstown, the story was different. Baltimore County's uncompromising segregation was maintained in tracts that already had very small numbers of African Americans; in these there was no increase in African American residents. But a group of geographically large tracts that actually had *no* African Americans at all showed amazing gains. In these formerly entirely white tracts (marked with a circle), nearly 3,000 African Americans moved in, making the areas a quarter Black. In a county known for its segregation, Blacks had made the fastest inroads in the whitest areas.

The explanation for this paradox points to the way in which the space of the suburbs alters the manifestation of racial conflict and tells at once two contradictory stories, one of a successful challenge to segregationism, the other the first chapter in the end of integrationism. First, in absolute numbers whites were not "fleeing": the same stretch along Liberty Road where 4,700 African Americans moved in the 1970s *gained* 2,500 new whites as well. Second, as indicated by an increase in the number of whites *and* Blacks, Blacks weren't moving into homes whites as a group

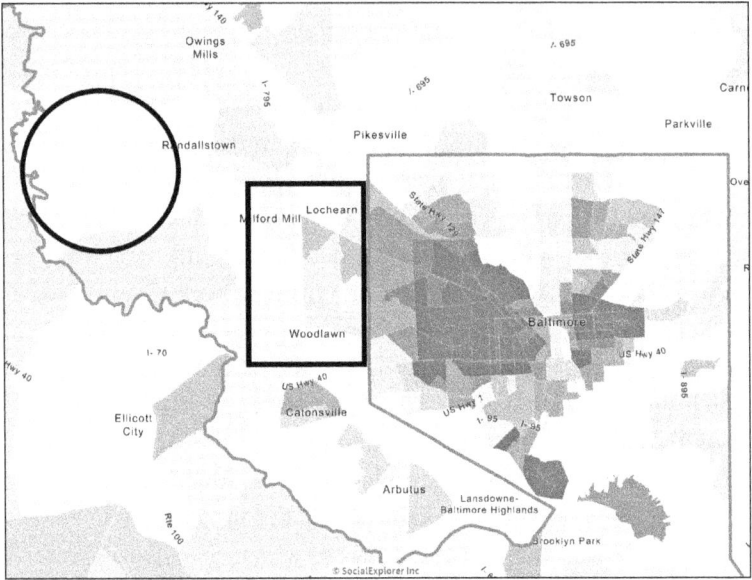

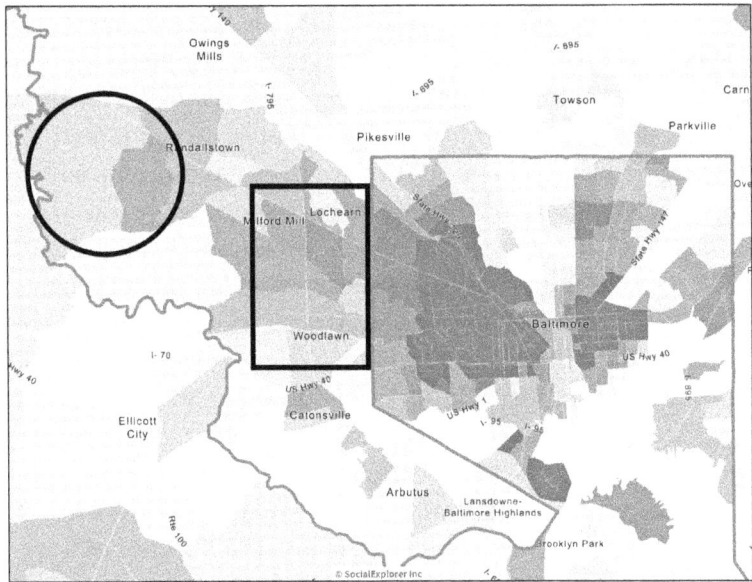

Figure 3.3a–b. Maps of 1970 (top) and 1980 (bottom) censuses. Areas of greatest growth in the African American suburbs between 1970 and 1980 were the tracts closest to the city's existing west side Black community (in the rectangle) and, paradoxically, the tracts farthest out Liberty Road that in 1970 had no African Americans (circled area). Other areas in Baltimore County that already had small, long-standing Black populations in 1970 (like Winters Lane, the trapezoid shape south of the rectangle) showed virtually no change in this period. Source: SocialExplorer.com.

no longer would live in. Here is a key difference between suburban ex-amples of racial change and the urban examples detailed in books like Jonathan Rieder's *Canarsie*. In the urban case, housing is nearly a zero-sum game: all the land is spoken for, and little new housing is likely to be built in a moment of racial turnover, so for Black families to move into a neighborhood, white families must decide to move out. In built-up areas (like cities), pioneering Blacks must move into existing white neighborhoods.

The non-zero-sum pattern occurred throughout Randallstown. Blacks' most dramatic periods of growth could be accompanied by growing white populations too. In 1970, the five whitest census tracts along Liberty Road were home to nearly 16,000 whites, but only *31 peo-ple* who were African American.[7] One decade later, the Black population had grown by an astronomical 152,611 percent to 4,731 African Ameri-cans. But while those 4,700 African Americans moved in, so did 2,463 additional whites, so that while the Black population grew to over 4,700, the white population grew from 15,724 to 18,187. Of those five tracts, all five gained Black residents, and three out of five gained white residents. Contrary to the expectations of white flight, in 1980 the two tracts that lost whites had the *smallest* number of Blacks, the smallest growth of Blacks, and the smallest percentage of Blacks. The tracts with the most and biggest growth and highest percentages of African Americans gained nearly as many whites as Blacks. Particularly because of the high premium put on new housing in the culture of the suburbs, whites and Blacks wanted to move into the same types of housing, and middle-class whites and African Americans had the means to do so. Racial transition happened alongside population growth.

In suburbs like Randallstown, housing was not (and is not today) a zero-sum game because in this car-centric landscape there remain large undeveloped plots of land available for new housing. African Americans could stymie segregationists in part by doing an end-run around them, choosing new developments where change (from rural to suburban) was already inevitable rather than in established communities where white institutions were hostile and closed to African Americans. Rather than moving into a neighborhood that whites had claimed, pioneering Blacks could move into an area that was no one's yet (see Figure 3.4). While the racial turnover of existing neighborhoods absolutely did occur in

Figure 3.4. Homes constructed in predominantly African American census tracts around Randallstown.

Randallstown, the rate of racial change would have been much slower had African Americans needed to find an existing home for sale. The suburbs provided a different option. Whites like Emily Wolfson could stay in their homes rather than flee, yet African Americans could still move into the area. In this way the space in which events play out affects actors' options and the nature of the outcome. In this case the suburbs gave African Americans additional means of gaining access to the suburban American dream.

New housing is indeed an attraction for home buyers who may not be welcome in established neighborhoods. Some affluent African American families specified that they had been looking for "new construction" when they bought their home. One reason these home buyers preferred new homes was that they believed maintenance would be lower and more predictable than it would be for an old house whose heating, roof, plumbing, or other major systems might be on the verge of needing emergency repairs. But residents also said that new developments offered new possibilities. New residential neighborhoods seemed less likely to be racially hostile because they were not yet established turf.

The strategy was used not only by African Americans. Emily Wolfson described being able to move out of Baltimore's strictly segregated Jewish neighborhoods fifty years ago because Randallstown was new: "The difference in part was that we moved into new housing. This house hadn't been built when we bought it, we bought it from a model. And so it was people coming who really didn't know who their neighbors were going to be. And that's how it happened on this block. Some were Jewish and some were not." In contrast, she noted, when African Americans began to move into her neighborhood several decades later (as opposed to new developments farther up the road), they faced more opposition because the neighborhood was no longer new: "When the Black families moved in [to that neighborhood], they weren't moving in to new housing, they were moving into housing that had already been established. And I think that's a little different, because the neighbors had staked out their place in life, because they owned the house. Then, Black family moves in, 'Oh we're going to have a changing neighborhood.'" Some gathered together, dug their heels in." While the cases are not wholly comparable, Black families that moved into new neighborhoods were making use of the same strategy Jewish residents had decades earlier. The shine of new homes also held the promise to African American buyers that the houses wouldn't fall victim to the cycle of downward class status implied by the ethnic succession model of change. To African American suburbanites even more so than other potential home buyers, older homes signified the risky proposition of a potentially deteriorating neighborhood.[8]

Racial tolerance and ethnic succession prove to be insufficient explanations for the rapid growth of these Black suburbs, and new construction provides previously underappreciated alternatives for Blacks seeking greater residential choice. Ethnic or racial transformation of suburbs is not a zero-sum game because the sum of housing can dramatically increase.

From my interviews with residents, planners, and realtors with direct experiences in Randallstown in different periods, I conclude that the availability of new homes to African Americans delineates three periods of suburban residential racial transition. In the earliest phase, African Americans began looking at largely white areas. Some realtors began introducing Black buyers into existing white neighborhoods. During the middle period, neighborhoods close to the city were already 40 to 60 percent Black, and Black realtors and Black buyers had easy access to the local market, and Blacks were the most likely buyers. According to realtors active in these periods, Blacks initially gained access to existing homes, not new homes. Further out in the suburbs, new housing was being sold to whites and Blacks. Finally, in the late phase, Black realtors based in the suburbs sold homes already owned by Blacks to other African Americans, and new housing developments were nearly 100 percent Black as soon as they were sold. Black realtors represented buyers, sellers, and new home developers. Thus in the first phase most real estate agents resisted change. Eventually, in the first and second periods they selectively steered African American customers. In the third phase Black buyers had broad access in this neighborhood, but white buyers had largely disappeared. The fact that African American residents remain highly concentrated in only a few parts of the county suggests a color barrier still existed. These three phases are useful distinctions in the suburban case. Perhaps they are found in cities as well, but the lack of new construction and often rapid transition in cities would make such phases difficult to distinguish.

While new construction proved an effective tool for outwitting segregationists, it was paradoxically not a tool to maintain integration. After the decade of transition, whites did move out of Randallstown, even if not with dramatic speed, and without new whites moving in, the area emerged as a Black suburb. This did not invalidate the new construction strategy but merely showed that it achieved one set of civil rights objectives (providing quality housing to African Americans and opening up white suburbs to African Americans) but didn't achieve another (permanently integrating neighborhoods). Just as the space of the suburbs, with the room for new construction, influenced desegregation, so the rate at which neighborhoods changed from one race to another in the suburbs revised the conventional story of racial transition.

The Speed of Racial Transition

In historical studies of midcentury urban residential racial transition, communities changed from all white to all Black in less time than it took to update the census. W. Edward Orser found in his history of one Baltimore City neighborhood that twenty thousand whites left and twenty thousand Blacks moved in between 1955 and 1965.[9] In the next decade, historian Andrew Wiese found a similar number traded places in East Cleveland.[10] Amanda Seligman found racial transition in Chicago took less than a decade for every neighborhood she studied, as it did in other cities.[11] Kevin Fox Gotham found approximately seventy thousand whites and Blacks moved out of and into homes in twenty years in the southeast section of Kansas City, but individual neighborhoods within that larger area changed faster.[12]

In contrast, the two census tracts along Liberty Road where activists Campbell and Wolfson live have taken thirty years to transition from all white to 80 percent African American. Deintegration appears to be just as certain today as it was fifty years ago. But the fact that it took thirty years meant that nearly two generations of children had the experience of growing up in a racially mixed neighborhood before it was thoroughly resegregated. For anyone who values integration, this is, while not a final victory, a change with practical significance. The efforts of residents like Wolfson and Campbell, coupled with the spatial characteristics of the suburbs, slowed resegregation considerably.

Nonetheless, slow transitions could also result from effective white resistance to Black efforts to enter a neighborhood or other segregationist tactics. The earliest buyers did face some opposition. In this case, however, home buyers and realtors during the central period of the transition reported that Black entry was not obstructed by residents. Black and white residents believed that slower white disappearance was beneficial to all residents because it protected property values. Over decades, the greater community cohesion of a slower transition created continuity in the community organizations that enforced maintenance standards and the middle-class social norms that residents desired. In these ways, the particularities of contemporary suburban racial transition produce outcomes that are much more beneficial to homeowners than earlier ones.

Qualified Success

African American suburbs proved to be more stable communities than earlier studies would have predicted, thanks to a combination of

activism and spatial organization. Distinctive features of postwar suburbs contributed to this outcome. Activists like Ella White Campbell
and Emily Wolfson used suburban zoning restrictions and homeowner
associations, while the available land and abundant new construction
in the suburbs also improved the prospects for new African American
home buyers.

The result was a large African American community that defied expectations that it would decline into physical decay and deteriorating
property values. Instead, the neighborhood has for decades remained
consistent, providing well-maintained homes to families of a range of
means. Yet it has done so by adopting sometimes unforgiving attitudes
about lower income residents. As we will see in subsequent chapters,
suburban African Americans' attitudes about African Americans "from
the city" shape views on a range of local political issues. Those attitudes
are certainly shaped by the exclusive culture and organization of the
suburbs, even as they reveal themselves to differ from whites' attitudes
about people moving out from the city.

Meanwhile, although local residents like Wolfson and Campbell have
maintained a remarkable degree of stability, the significance of race does
not entirely disappear in the rolling lawns of suburban subdivisions.
Comparison of home and income data in chapter 6 among white, Black,
and transitioning parts of the Baltimore suburbs shows the difference
that color still makes, measurable in dollars and cents.

From the perspective of racial justice, Randallstown demonstrates
how much work remains. But from the perspective of prospective Black
home buyers, Randallstown indicates that suburban homes can provide
families with useful tools to create a stable home and realistic chances of
establishing the markers of middle-class status, even in the larger context of dogged racial inequality.

Because the outcomes in Randallstown contradict the expectations
of urban-centric understandings of racial conflicts, their meaning is not
immediately clear. For instance, white hostility to African American efforts to move into Baltimore County were replaced almost overnight
by a substantial Black community, but this was evidence not that tolerance increased but that the opponents were bypassed. Nor is ethnic succession an adequate description for the transformation since the new
group didn't just inherit the used housing stock of their predecessors

but also gained new homes. And despite the successes of African American homeowners in moving into the suburbs, Baltimore County ultimately resegregated those who broke the county/color line. The story in Baltimore County was of a hard-won victory for integration without the defeat of segregation: African Americans succeeded in gaining access to desirable suburban communities even though whites didn't succeed in abandoning their segregationist practices. Even once African Americans were well established in the county, their work was only beginning. Political issues confronted residents, and the suburbs shaped residents' responses to political questions, some of which were age old, others brand new.

4

Growth

How Suburban Space Reshapes Black Community
Issues and Politics

Suburbs can invert racialized political issues in America. For instance, while African Americans have traditionally paid *more* for housing because of segregated markets, in the suburbs today upper-middle-class African Americans buy the exact same new luxury home on all-Black cul-de-sacs for a *lower* list price than whites pay just a few miles away (Figure 4.1). In another example, while the boundary between city and suburban school districts has been used to establish underfunded Black city schools and well-funded, de facto–segregated white suburban schools, today it's easy to find overcrowded, underperforming all-Black high schools and well-funded white schools in the *same* suburban school district. Along Liberty Road the space of the suburbs and the priorities and social organization of the middle class have reshaped both the manifestation of racial conflicts and residents' responses to them.

This chapter examines two such inversions to understand why race, although it continues to play a central role in political issues in the suburbs, manifests itself differently on the suburban landscape than in the urban settings where discrimination and inequality have most often been studied. In the first case examined here, priorities for economic development in African American suburbs differ both from cities and from predominantly white suburbs. While there are many activists in both low-income urban areas and white suburban areas who oppose the arrival of chain stores like Walmart, residents in Randallstown did not. In the second case, class and suburban location led Black residents to take the same position that racially exclusive whites long had. The county had planned changes to bus lines. Plans to cut bus lines in the city provoked protests from city residents. But plans to extend a bus line into Randallstown triggered resident opposition. White suburbanites

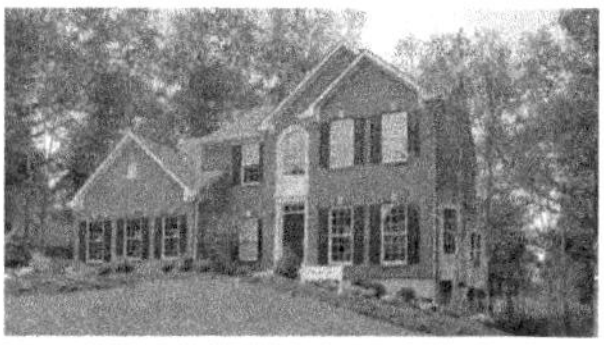

WINANDS RUN PRICE LIST

The Zachary: Designed as a non-traditional, two-story home that combines both drama and efficiency, the Zachary has become one of the best selling homes in the Ryan series. The innovative design begins with the side staircase that overlooks the two-story open foyer. One of the most unique features of the Zachary are the column and niche details that create and accentuate the angled vistas from formal to everyday living areas. The spacious kitchen features a center island, large pantry and conveniently located laundry room. Upstairs, all the rooms branch off the open hallway. The hallway is filled with light from the two-story foyer and stairway with its unique half round window. The owner's suite features double entry doors, a huge closet and dual vanities. Included in The Zachary are four bedrooms, a two-car garage and unfinished lower level. Also included is a full list of Ryan Homes included features.

Elevation A ....$386,990 **Elevation C $396,990**
Elevation B ....$389,990 **Elevation D $389,990**

GREEN VALLEY WOODS PRICE LIST

The Zachary features four bedrooms, two and one-half baths, a grand two story open foyer, and a two-car garage. The Zachary has a formal living room and dining room, which is separated by a side staircase. The spacious kitchen with center island is adjoined by a dinette area and large family room. This home represents a new design and layout and includes a full list of Ryan standard features.

Elevation A..........$599,990 **Elevation C..........$607,440**
Elevation B..........$602,490 **Elevation D..........$614,340**

(2007)

Figure 4.1. The exact same model home, the Zachary, listed for $200,000 less in an African American neighborhood than in a white neighborhood that was a fifteen-minute drive away. African American home buyers often have smaller down payments and obtain loans with higher interest rates, so the final monthly cost may not be lower. The difference gives some sense of the premium whites are willing to pay to live in a white neighborhood or near white schools. Text re-created from original.

had earlier opposed the expansion of mass transit for fear it would bring Blacks to their neighborhood. Now Black suburbanites opposed mass transit on the same grounds.

Community attitudes toward economic development and mass transit expansion demonstrate how the spatial organization of the suburbs (as well as their social and political structure) can foster conservative political perspectives. While cities are also home to middle-class residents and political conservatives, suburbs like Randallstown are organized in ways that enable the predominance of conservative political perspectives over progressive or more inclusive framings of local political issues. That said, the absence of an organized, articulated progressive position on the issues examined here suggests not that progressive politics are impossible in the suburbs but that for now much suburban terrain has effectively been ceded to conservative views. As the suburbs altered the manifestation of racialized community issues, we need new perspectives that incorporate race, class, and space to address racial inequality.

To examine economic development in Randallstown, it is worthwhile to take a brief tour along Liberty Road, which forms Randallstown's retail and economic spine. Most visitors would approach Randallstown from the Baltimore Beltway, the interstate highway that encircles Baltimore City and was built in the era when highway construction and other urban renewal projects displaced tens of thousands of African Americans in the city. From the highway, Liberty Road extends in a straight line to the northwest. Writing ethnographic field notes poses some challenges in a car-centered landscape. So as I drove the length of the street one rainy early evening in 2010 to document the businesses along the road, I balanced a video camera on my dashboard and narrated what I saw. The broad street's two lanes of traffic in each direction were separated by a turn lane. The road was busy with cars. Stoplights were spaced a quarter mile apart. Traffic moved at thirty miles an hour or more most of the time. The street was almost entirely commercial. Large parking lots and occasional sections of grass pushed the stores farther back from the road, so illuminated signs along either side of the street were the most visible marker of what was on either side. Sticking up into the sky were signs for chain pharmacies like Walgreens and Rite Aid and fast-food restaurants including the biggest chains (McDonald's, Wendy's, Burger King). Along the strip malls were the large yellow awnings of locally run fried seafood and chicken restaurants like Chick'n Trout, the Crab Shack, and Hip Hop Chicken. Nationally franchised gas stations clustered at one corner, mechanics occupied older buildings, and muffler, brake, and tire shops added to the sense that auto maintenance took up much of the real estate. Supermarkets served as anchors for the larger shopping centers along the way. One had closed in recent years but two remained, along with lower-end grocery stores that had filled in and sold canned food and soda but little fresh produce. In storefronts, single-story offices and converted houses in between the larger illuminated signs for fast-food restaurants, gas stations, banks, and pharmacies were smaller locally owned businesses that were less noticeable but probably nearly equaled them in quantity: tax preparers, medical offices, churches, dry cleaners, a liquor store, a psychic adviser, and a tattoo parlor.

Baltimore has many such commercial corridors sprawling out from the city. While driving them gave the sense of a long, unending chain of single-story retail establishments surrounded by parking lots, activity concentrated at certain intersections. One such hub was about two and a half miles out from the Beltway. Three bank branches clustered there. While there were few public institutions along Liberty Road, to the right of this intersection (not far from resident activist Emily Wolfson's house) was a shopping center that included a free-standing branch library. To the left of the intersection (near community leader Ella White Campbell's house) was a community hospital. Just beyond were spaces for two large retail stores. In the space to the left was Home Depot, the huge hardware and home goods store. To the right, behind two gas stations, was an even larger shopping center. It was almost entirely vacant. Since 2004, residents had heard of plans to turn the vacant discount department store space into a Walmart.

Beyond these two shopping centers, I had seen before that the stores thinned out considerably over the next three miles and ended as Liberty Road entered the woods, crossed a bridge over Liberty Reservoir, and left Baltimore County for Carroll County, which was more exurban and rural than suburban. Back in the commercial core of Liberty Road, to the east behind the vacant shopping centers, were a range of residential housing developments. The nearest ones were 1960s single-family one-story homes. At the top of a ridge were two-story houses built in the 1980s, which could be dated by their style and their beige or pastel vinyl siding. Further on were newer developments, the newest of which were almost mini-mansions with tall columns and large bay windows, or condominium row houses behind stone walls and hedges. Beyond them, ten minutes from Liberty Road, was Owings Mills Mall. The mall opened to great fanfare in 1986 and impressed locals with topiary in the food court, a vintage Army Jeep parked halfway through the window of a Banana Republic and, a first for the area, a tony Saks Fifth Avenue department store in addition to Macy's and a local department store. The mall was at the center of an area designated by the county for intensive development: a subway line from the city terminated relatively close to the mall (though travelers still had to walk fifteen minutes across parking lots to get from the station to the mall and there was no direct bus service from Liberty Road to the mall). Around the mall were several office towers and a growing number of restaurants like Red Lobster. Though a movie theater built near the mall was still busy on weekends, twenty years after its grand opening the mall itself had many vacancies; one section was entirely closed. The high-end stores had long since left, as had almost all of the original tenants. When the mall opened as the most high-end shopping location in the county, the area was still mostly white, with many Jews and some Blacks to the west, mostly Christian to the east. By 2010 Randallstown, to the west, was predominantly Black, and whites to the east rarely shopped at this mall, traveling farther to a newer, fancier mall in a whiter part of the county. For several decades a cycle had persisted in the county, in which the oldest area mall would struggle or shut down and a new one, either constructed on farmland or on top of the oldest, failing mall, would take the lead position as the county's most desirable shopping destination. A mall cycled through the hierarchy from the most prestigious to semivacant in about twenty-five years. By this pattern, Owings Mills Mall was due to be renovated and residents heard rumors it would be bulldozed and rebuilt.

Mass transit service in these commercial areas of Randallstown is an incomplete network that is difficult to use, known only to those who must get around without a car. A bus line runs up Liberty Road but terminates about a mile past the Home Depot. There is no bus service from Liberty Road to the nearby Owings Mills Mall. The county had recently installed an attractive new sidewalk with brick trim for much of the length of Liberty Road, and while new benches had also been installed at several of the bus stops along the walk, most had no shelter and left riders exposed to the elements while they waited for a bus. There is a subway line that radiates out from the city, parallel to Liberty Road. The subway line is almost entirely inside the Beltway, the unofficial urban/suburban division. In the city it runs along one of the main commercial arteries. Upon reaching the suburbs it moves away from that busy street, traveling between Liberty Road and another major commercial thoroughfare so that riders are far from either artery. The subway line continues three and a half miles to make only one stop outside the Beltway, at the Owings Mills Mall. (That station and the mall were built at the same time, and the station is intended, theoretically, to serve the mall, but the station is nearly half a mile away from the mall itself.)[1] A bus line that crosses Liberty Road at the commercial hub near the library does take riders to the subway line but brings them to a stop inside the Beltway, not at the suburban mall.

Thus Randallstown's commercial corridor had considerable activity but evident problems. There were a wide array of businesses, but a noticeable tendency toward downscaling. Over the years, some large national chains had closed on Liberty Road and in the mall, though there were significant exceptions (both around the Home Depot and along the ring road encircling the mall, where national chains were building new casual dining restaurants). Along Liberty Road there were few vacancies because comparatively undercapitalized businesses moved into the stores that had been vacated, often managing to stay in business but rarely expanding or renovating the properties. Mass transit was designed in a way that made the network incomplete and difficult to use. It was in this context that residents, business leaders, community activists, corporate representatives, and county planners sought to engage in economic development and community improvement as they defined it. The particularities of the suburbs' physical and social landscape shaped these actors' goals, tools, and obstacles.

Economic Development: Hello, Ruby Tuesday

Economic development remains an important issue in African American communities. Randallstown residents were working for economic development along Liberty Road. But unlike in poor urban neighborhoods, in the middle-class suburbs the goal was not better jobs for local workers, retail development as a means to combat the blight of abandoned stores and renovate the building stock, or full-service grocery stores as a means of providing healthier food options. Middle-class residents wouldn't be working in such places, vacancy rates were not high, and Randallstown already had several supermarkets. Instead, residents were frustrated that the shopping options in their neighborhood were inconsistent with the socioeconomic class in which they saw themselves. In suburban Randallstown, residents and the county used different strategies, and pursued different goals, than those active in economic development for poorer Black neighborhoods in cities like Baltimore.

In his history of African American suburbs, Wiese pointed out that commercial disinvestment or underinvestment is a systematic problem facing Black suburbs, which consequently lose lucrative business taxes to whiter areas. Strip malls in Black suburbs typically have high numbers of vacancies. Randallstown conforms partially to this pattern. A major supermarket did leave, but there were still other grocery stores in the area. One largely vacant shopping center appeared to be struggling, but it was expected to be the site of a Walmart that had languished for years in the planning stages. In general, retail along Liberty Road was lower end, less well maintained, and in somewhat more precarious shape than it appeared to be on the other radial commercial corridors of Baltimore County, but it was not characterized by widespread vacancies. As Peirce MacGill of the county Department of Economic Development described it, "What I would say has happened is the quality. You don't have your retail goods store. You have your food and your hair and service stores now as opposed to any real good stores. But from a vacancy standpoint it's more been of a change in the tenant, you know, a lot quicker turnover and how long these smaller businesses last. . . . But vacancies have never really been a problem on the west side of the county." Thus Randallstown faced economic shortcomings that were not extreme but still real. Residents who were active in the planning process were primarily interested in raising Liberty Road's retailing profile to accurately reflect their status, not to create jobs.

In sharing their opinion of Randallstown, community members frequently discussed the inadequacy of the retail strip. Leticia Martin, who lived in Randallstown and worked in the area as a realtor, explained a point of dissatisfaction she had with the neighborhood.[2] The real estate brokerage firm was near the Social Security headquarters twenty minutes from Randallstown. Speaking in the conference room of the large offices where she worked, she said, "One of the things we don't like is that there's no place to have a nice sit-down dinner. Ruby Tuesday, TGI Fridays. . . . They were getting complaints about how Randallstown has one of the highest income brackets for Baltimore County. But for dinner we have to go to Owings Mills, to Reisterstown. Now you see signs for Ruby Tuesday. They need to build. Because the people who are there don't necessarily want to get a fish platter or a chicken box." People living in half-million-dollar houses, she explained, didn't want their only dinner options to be soul food takeout, but that was the most common option along Liberty Road. Denise Murphy, the president of the Liberty Road Business Association, said she fielded this complaint frequently from residents.

There are several points to consider regarding residents' discussion of commercial development. First, most residents didn't think about developing retail stores in terms of job development since people who could afford to own homes in Randallstown made considerably more than retail jobs paid. Nor did community leaders, church leaders, or county planners frame economic development in terms of local job creation, making it less likely that residents would consider it primarily in that light. A second point to consider is that contrary to what residents suggested, they weren't far from other shopping options. For instance, there was already a Ruby Tuesday restaurant less than ten minutes away in the nearby mall, just three miles east of Liberty Road. By my count of mall patrons, 80 percent of shoppers there were Black. Thus it was part of the African American corridor in the county but did not resolve residents' desire for nationwide chains in their neighborhood. Since most residents drove everywhere they went, chain restaurants were already convenient, so there was something else that dissatisfied residents.

Residents' comments demonstrated that they didn't object to driving to the mall nearly as much as they disliked the fact that their main street didn't have the businesses catering to the middle class that the radial streets passing through comparable white communities did, like Starbucks, Barnes & Noble, big-box stores, and high-end supermarkets. Multiple residents repeated the frustration expressed by Leticia Martin who wanted a Ruby Tuesday on Liberty Road rather than a bare, minimally decorated takeout restaurant with food heated in metal trays behind glass. As it happened, I had eaten lunch at those takeout restaurants many times in the course of my research and had a favorite spot. When one resident commented that she wanted more than "chicken and fish joints," I tested her objection, mentioning that I had eaten there and liked some of them. Backing up for a moment, she, like others, conceded that the food was good, and she, like others, admitted to having her favorite place. But that didn't change residents' feeling that the preponderance of such restaurants signified a status lower than that of these residents. This resident didn't want chicken and fish joints to be her only dining option. She didn't take her family out to a restaurant with aging fast-food-style booths and plastic utensils. While she wanted it to be easier to bring her family to a chain restaurant that had spent more money on its decor, such dining options were available—and growing. (Amid the continuing economic downturn, in 2011 several new restaurants, including an Olive Garden, were under construction off the road ringing the mall.) Residents' primary desire in this regard was to have businesses on their most visible commercial strip that reflected a higher socioeconomic status. Upper-middle-class, gentrifying *urban* residents (Black and white alike) live in neighborhoods where small locally owned boutiques, stylish bars, and fashionably designed restaurants signify a status superior to that of nationwide chains. But in autocentric suburbs (particularly middle-class ones), nationwide big-box stores, restaurants, and anchor stores rank higher than local merchants' less capitalized businesses.

The result was that county planners found themselves in a very different position in Randallstown than elsewhere in the county and used different tools than they did either in the rest of the county or in African American communities outside the suburbs. One example was in the differing "theory of liquor control" used in urban Black neighborhoods and suburban Black neighborhoods, governing the use of liquor licenses to improve the community.[3]

In recent decades, residents near high-crime areas in Chicago have led the way in using licenses to restrict liquor stores. Residents have acted in the belief that *reducing* the number of corner liquor stores would reduce crime, public drunkenness, alcohol abuse, and other problems.[4]

In contrast, Baltimore County planners developed a program to *increase* the number of liquor licenses along Liberty Road specifically, as a means to attract establishments like Ruby Tuesday: in the county, a business could have only three liquor licenses. (This limit of three licenses was said to be a holdover from the restrictive laws passed after Prohibition.) Chain restaurants used these licenses to open restaurants in other, whiter parts of the county. Under the county's new rules, businesses could secure an additional liquor license for a restaurant opened along Liberty Road. County planners were quick to point out there were differences between liquor stores and restaurants. Also, the regulations required relatively high levels of investment in these restaurants, seeking to ensure that they were attractive, relatively high-end establishments. In one setting liquor licenses spawned social problems; in another context they were seen as a source of economic growth. This Black middle-class suburb embraced different economic development strategies than communities that were only either Black or middle class, but not both.

Chicago's approach of restricting licenses to reduce crime has spread to other municipalities near that city.[5] Interestingly, the Black suburb of Chicago Heights adopted a hybrid approach that showed elements of Chicago's strategy and the desires of African American suburbs. When I visited the area I found a community with nearly identical housing stock to much of Randallstown and strip malls whose vacancies showed evidence of more severe retail disinvestment. The Chicago Heights city council reduced the number of liquor licenses, as Chicago did, but stated that they would increase the number of licenses if a national chain restaurant wanted to open a store.[6] Planners suggested that a national chain was different because they invested larger amounts of money in a restaurant than a local proprietor might. Planners did not believe a chain restaurant such as TGI Fridays, Ruby Tuesday, or Applebee's would be a hot spot for crime and other problems. This likely reflects the middle-class image that these restaurants work hard to display in their advertising and marketing. In preferring national franchises, Baltimore County planners, Chicago Heights city council members, and resident activists disregarded American culture's celebration of small business. Elsewhere, local restaurants could have been imagined as a friendlier, more personal form of capitalism or a means to keep business profits in the community rather than having them siphoned off by corporate headquarters to distant locales. These suburbs put more faith in the quality of corporate standards.

Randallstown residents' support for nationwide chains was in contrast to the preference for "boutique" retailers frequently identified in studies of gentrified urban neighborhoods. Sharon Zukin, for instance, contrasted the opening of a Kmart in New York City to Greenwich Village's "bohemian reputation" for "vintage clothing stores, coffeehouses, and off-Broadway theaters," adding that "local organizations raise a constant war against tall buildings, *chain stores*, and all kinds of schlock."[7] Given the pervasive fondness for small stores among the urban upper middle class, it can be hard for people enmeshed in that culture to believe it is not universal. But Randallstown residents did not rue the opening of a new chain. To the contrary, people regularly told me of the opening of a new chain store when listing promising changes in the area. For instance, Pastor Charles T. Sembly, whose Union Bethel AME church is one of the oldest churches in Randallstown and oversees an active nonprofit organization that offers a food pantry, foreclosure prevention, and other services, described to me both the challenges and the promise of his community. In his office in Union Bethel's extended complex of church, school, and offices, he explained, "A few months ago, we shared in the groundbreaking for what will be Walmart. A few years ago, we got Home Depot. There's hopes of some franchise eateries coming in this corridor." Leronia Josey, who ran unsuccessfully for Councilman Ken Oliver's position, explained, "It's about providing a need, and there's a need for nice places to go. I mean, we don't have a Ruby Tuesday's, we don't have an Applebee's. I'm not talking about something . . . you're going to break your bank going to. . . . Just some nice places here in this area." Lenwood Johnson framed community need in terms of a restaurant to go to after church: "Traditionally in the Black community, you'd go to church on Sunday and then you'd go home where mother and grandma would have your chicken dinner and everything ready to eat. . . . Well grandma doesn't cook anymore and mom doesn't cook anymore. So right after church, people are heading for restaurants by large number and you do not have that on Liberty Road." There had been midrange restaurants like Friendly's and the International House of Pancakes near his church, but those places had closed and not been replaced over the years. Desires for new restaurants were not limited to politicians or influential community leaders; neighborhood activists and others gave similar descriptions. Residents not only did not oppose chain stores but actively sought them, saw them as positive economic indicators for the neighborhood, and did not express nostalgia for an imagined bygone era of "locally owned" stores. Residents who had known Randallstown decades ago described it not as an intimate community of a local butcher, baker, or grocer but as "gasoline alley," a multilane road of gas stations, garages, discount stores, and large parking lots. They expressed no nostalgia for that unattractive period in the area's development. Chain stores were welcome, and none more so than the largest corporation in the world, Walmart.[8]

Welcoming Walmart

Randallstown residents' preference for national chains is evident in the development of plans for a Walmart in their town. Nationwide, plans to open up a Walmart meet with community opposition so frequently that the company has stopped advanced promotion of upcoming stores, instead waiting until the last minute before announcing their impending arrival. In contrast, residents of Randallstown didn't oppose Walmart but eagerly awaited it. News spread across town that Walmart would be moving into a largely empty strip mall on Liberty Road at the northern end of Randallstown. County planners groaned that elected officials had announced Walmart sooner than they should have—a contract for the property had not even been signed yet. But planners regretted that the announcement was made so early not because it gave time for an opposition to organize but because residents then began calling, impatiently wanting to know when the store would finally open. As one planner wryly observed, "And so Towson and these other areas"—known as white, waspish, and elite—"they'll fight a Walmart, they'll fight a Home Depot; in Liberty Road they want them. So it's kind of fun for a change. Do a Walmart groundbreaking and not get people killing you."

African American suburbanites are not unaware of the status differences between retail stores and may name some sooner than others on a wish list. According to one planner, everyone, regardless of race, thinks there should be a "Starbucks and a high-end clothing boutique in their backyard." Indeed, a business leader in Randallstown was pleased that the restaurant chain "Ruby Tuesday is supposed to be coming . . . the community asks for things like Starbucks . . . the ice cream place Cold Stone or something like that which would be nice to have. . . . Because we had a Giant [supermarket] leave. So we're looking for something to come in there." But rather than opposing middle-class-oriented chains, as some communities have, African American suburbanites, even upper-middle-class ones, are still trying to get their fair share of chain-store status symbols. In this light, Walmart was a welcome addition.

Community groups did not object to the arrival of Walmart. One neighborhood association president explained that "Owings Mills Mall is about 90% empty so we need businesses in the community."[9] The Liberty Road Community Council, a coalition of community organizations, also supported the arrival of Walmart.

Even small businesses did not object to the impending arrival of Walmart, according to Denise Murphy, a financial coach and executive director of the Liberty Road Business Association. In other settings, businesses had been concerned that the low-priced behemoth would compete for their customers. Murphy said that had not been the case in Randallstown. We talked in the café of a Barnes & Noble bookstore fifteen minutes away from Randallstown—on the commercial street of the neighboring white community because Randallstown didn't have a Barnes & Noble. Murphy explained that local businesses hadn't objected. "That's what you'd think, but I haven't gotten that from the small businesses," she said. "I thought the same thing, initially, that they would have been a little *put off* by the fact that Walmart is coming. But I have not received that at all. They seem to be very excited about Walmart coming because they're thinking about the business they're going to be bringing in." Murphy pointed out that many businesses along Liberty Road were not in lines that competed with Walmart: insurance companies, lawyers, chiropractors, and restaurants sold products and goods Walmart did not. But according to Murphy, owners more broadly saw Walmart as a store that would increase traffic, not one that would draw off their own customers. There may have been differences of opinion among local business owners that Murphy did not detail. But organized opposition to Walmart's arrival was not evident.

Thus African American suburbanites' approach to economic development differed from that of both other African American communities and other suburban communities. Poorer communities often oppose Walmart as representative of the declining wages of a casualized, precarious workforce. For instance, one report warned that the expansion of Walmart into New York City would cost four thousand jobs, one hundred five business, and four million dollars in state health care programs to support Walmart employees denied insurance by their employer.[10] Nationwide, suburbanites may oppose Walmart (either for similar economic reasons or because the store embodies the aesthetics of a discount big-box store), or they might passively enjoy the store once it opens.[11] But few residents in other established suburbs speak enthusiastically about the opening of a Home Depot, Walmart, or Ruby Tuesday.

But Randallstown county councilman Ken Oliver championed Walmart. "It's been a long wait," Oliver wrote to constituents, "so it is especially gratifying to celebrate this milestone in the construction of the Randallstown Walmart."[12] While other regions had criticized Walmart for causing job loss in a community, Oliver celebrated. "The most important benefit is the 350 jobs that will be created right here in the fourth district." In contrast to Oliver's enthusiasm, at the state level Walmart was a popular political target: legislators had passed a bill that would have applied only to Walmart, requiring that the firm spend more on employee health insurance.[13]

A *Baltimore Sun* editorial called the Randallstown Walmart a "big box of hope"; a community paper termed the announcement that construction would begin on the "long-awaited Walmart" a "valentine."[14] Certainly, the *Sun* should be expected to be guarded in what it wrote about a large retailer and advertiser as important to the newspaper as Walmart: the paper had opposed legislation intended to require that the firm provide either a living wage or adequate health care. But the *Sun* had also editorialized six months before their endorsement of the Randallstown store that "the giant retailer is no friend to unions, has a destroyed much of its competition, has promoted the sale of cheaper, foreign-made goods to the detriment of U.S. manufacturers, and has provided salaries and benefits that are often relatively low even by retail standards."[15] However, they saw the opening of a Randallstown Walmart as positive for the area.

Randallstown's enthusiasm for Walmart contrasted with organized opposition in Belair, a predominantly white community in eastern Baltimore County. Consistent with community activists' responses in other locations, residents there formed the Bel Air South Community Foundation to oppose plans for a new Walmart.[16] The group gathered over four hundred signatures on a petition opposing the new store. Likewise, even preliminary plans to open a Walmart in a racially mixed part of Baltimore City quickly brought out "more than 100 people—many of them opposed to a Walmart," according to a local newspaper account. "Many of the questions and criticisms were based on negative perceptions of Walmart as a company that drives small stores out of business and underpays female workers."[17]

But in Randallstown the opening of the Walmart went ahead with no identifiable opposition. The store had been delayed by pollution from a dry cleaning business that had once been on the site. Eight years after Walmart's interest was first announced, elected officials gathered at the site to celebrate, officially, that Walmart would be opening a store in Randallstown. Though forty chairs had been set up on the parking lot in front of the construction fence, a hundred fifty people attended.[18] The store was due to open in less than a year. Meanwhile the Ruby Tuesday, whose opening had been discussed by residents for so long I had begun to think it was a myth, appeared to be on its way as well. Peirce Mac-Gill of the county's Office of Economic Development explained that the restaurant had been leasing a lot across the street from the Walmart site for years but that "they're not going to build until they see Walmart."[19]

Communities that object to Walmarts in their areas have many legitimate reasons to do so—the company's history of poverty wages, sex discrimination, harm to local merchants, and wage-cutting behavior provides plenty of reasons to oppose it. But though many would deny it, residents in whiter and more affluent communities also object to the intrusion of a Walmart because of its class implications; such residents seek to distinguish themselves from mass society and the mainstream Americans who shop at Walmart. Black suburbs like Randallstown, however, face a status threat related not only to class but to race: the commercial disinvestment that is common in African American communities constantly threatens to exclude them from that mainstream. Chain stores anchor residents' status rather than threaten it. As the *Baltimore Sun* editorialized, "It may sound odd to people in other parts of the county that residents there desperately want a Walmart and a TGI Friday's, but it's easy to scoff at big box stores and chain restaurants when you have them. Other parts of the county also don't have to wonder whether the lack of quality commercial development has anything to do with the residents' race."[20]

I should be clear that I do not intend this analysis to be a defense of Walmart or evidence that Walmarts should be seen as beneficial to any community. I found no real discussion in Randallstown about how Walmart would affect local job opportunities or wages or what it would do for low-income residents and job seekers. These issues had not been primary concerns for people who spoke up about Walmart, and there were not organized groups that had spoken for poor or working-class people on the matter.

Others have criticized Walmart on those grounds quite strongly elsewhere.[21] I needed to understand middle-class suburban residents' framing and analysis of their problems and the strategies they adopt in addressing them. To say that residents are enthusiastic to get a Walmart because racial discrimination and prejudice by retailers, white consumers, and investors has left them with inadequate options is hardly a glowing endorsement of one retail giant. It is instead a recognition that residents, community leaders, and politicians have recognized how race, class, and space converged to produce a distinctive approach to local development issues. Studies of neither urban Black communities nor white middle-class communities offer sufficient guidance in understanding the Black suburban case. A paradigm that replaces assumptions that suburban communities are white or that Black communities are urban with the recognition instead that race and suburbanization are each independent variables and interact differently in every permutation is the minimal necessary precondition to understanding economic development in African American suburbs.

Get *Off* the Bus

Though differences among African Americans (such a class) have always created divisions within Black communities, the space of the suburbs has the potential to create divisions on issues that were previously not subjects of contention.

In May 2005 the Maryland Mass Transit Administration (MTA) announced sweeping changes to bus service in the Baltimore area.[22]

According to the MTA, the goal of the Greater Baltimore Bus Initiative was to cut back on underused routes to fund expanded service where needed. As part of the proposed expansion, the bus line running up Liberty Road would be extended east along a route that led to the Owings Mills Mall.[23] At the same time, proposals were made to extend the bus routes further up Liberty Road as well.

Riders, politicians, and community members responded strongly to the proposals. In the city, coverage of the changes focused on cuts to service that would force travelers to walk longer distances to reach the bus or leave people unable to get to work or to the hospital. In Baltimore County, the response was different. Residents organized against extending the route.

Suburban opposition to mass transit is not uncommon and frequently has a racial undertone to it. So-called urban myths abound in which a bus, subway, or trolley line was extended from a city into a suburb and crime increased. One white resident said a conservative talk radio show had convinced him that a trolley line extension had increased crime at the suburban mall near the line's terminus. A study that happened to be published not long before the bus debates found no support for such tales.[24] But such stories remained pervasive. A longtime white resident who had taught in schools in Randallstown and Reisterstown gave a typical account. I asked about ways the area had changed since she moved there decades earlier. She responded, "The metro. The metro changed this area for the worse." In addition to the subway built from the city to the Owings Mills Mall, a light rail line had recently been built from the city to a terminus at the next closest mall, Hunt Valley. She explained why this was a problem. "Because there was easy access from the city out to the county. And then the buses from the Metro, brought them out. If you look at Hunt Valley, while they were there working on the Metro [and the station was closed], the shoplifting in the Walmart over there went down like 50 percent. And then they fixed the Metro and it [shoplifting] started up again. So, yeah, the transportation system definitely changed this area a lot. And then Section 8 housing. I mean, there's a Section 8 housing house down the street. And the police have been called, several times, sex in the backyard, fellatio on the front step. Oh yeah. So. . . ."

Suburbanites present these matter-of-fact accounts of transit, crime, poverty, and race as unassailable truths. But they are typically entanglements of a host of stereotypes. In this case the speaker worried about mass transit train lines that brought "them" out to the county. For suburbanites, Baltimore City is frequently coded as Black, so that discussions of "them" coming out from the city to steal is inevitably a race-coded discussion. The speaker then transitioned seamlessly from crime perpetrated by people from the city to Section 8 housing and poor people to inappropriate sex. Light rail in particular has been targeted by people living in suburbs (in Baltimore County and around other cities in the country). The train lines are potent symbols. New, expensive, high-profile projects, they have attracted criticism. But in Baltimore bus lines traveled parallel routes before trains and trolleys were introduced and continued to do so when light rail stations were temporarily closed. Of course the availability of other mass transit options merely points out the symbolic basis for such light rail discussions; in reality thieves tend to operate closer to home. Once bus lines are in place they are nearly invisible to the majority of residents who have cars. Only when there is talk of expanding new lines are they more prominent.

The conflation of trolleys, crime, the inner city, poverty, and sex highlights the racialized nature of the discussion. Communities' opposition to mass transit is a common if bizarre manifestation of white suburbanites' efforts to keep Blacks away from their neighborhoods. The hysteria embodied in the urban myths and enacted in opposition to mass transit is driven by a multilayered paranoid phantasm that mass transit users are Black, and Blacks are criminals, and Black criminals want to take buses out to the suburbs to harm white suburbanites. In Randallstown, the twist to this common story was that most of the mass transit opponents were Black.

To white community activist Emily Wolfson, the opposition to busing was a repeat of a similar battle that occurred before the racial transformation of Randallstown. As she explained, "We've been trying to get the bus out to the end of Liberty Road. We've been trying for twenty years. And when we started, little old white ladies used to say, 'We're gonna get raped in our beds and get our TVs stolen.' Now little old Black ladies say, 'We're gonna get raped in our beds and get our TVs stolen.'" Wolfson concluded, "I want to say, 'You know, *you* were the people some people were afraid of!'" From this perspective, Black residents' opposition is surprising, given that it is based on stereotypes whose damaging effects should be most apparent to middle-class African Americans.

Adrienne Jones, an African American who served as one of the area's state delegates, summarized the opposition this way: "They do not want them coming through the community. I actually had an African American woman, leader in the Randallstown area and she said she didn't want 'those people,' you know, these unsavory kinds." Jones wryly refers to this attitude as *Jefferson*ian—Jeffersonian not as used to refer to Thomas Jefferson's verdant dream of a nation of yeoman farmers but as used to refer to the TV show *The Jeffersons*, about a Black family that moved to a rich neighborhood, as George Jefferson quickly adopted the airs of his new surroundings. Jones had heard to complaints: "What people say is they'll come and rob you, take your TV." She did not agree with those residents' predictions, dismissing them out of hand at a purely practical level: "They're not gonna take TVs on the bus." Though Jones was critical of what she saw as people forgetting where they came from, opposition to buses in this context is less of a paradox than it initially seems. African Americans who live in the suburbs are simply adopting a suburban perspective that they believe will maintain the exclusivity, desirability, and dollar values of homes and neighborhoods.[25]

African American community activist Ella White Campbell described the bus proposal, which she opposed, in a way that both elaborated residents' stated objections and confirmed that nonracial objections about traffic and noise were inextricably tied up with fundamental associations of the city with crime.

> What happened was the MTA was going to change the bus lines. And they were changing the bus lines because a lot of the businesses that were further up in Randallstown were saying they were impeded from hiring because the people had to come from, I guess they were implying, *the city* in order to get to their businesses, and that was a problem because the bus didn't run out there. So they mapped out a plan where they were going to run the buses through the communities. And the communities were in opposition because they felt it was going to expose them to crime

because, in other words, people were going to ride through it and see
and the break-ins and that [would] increase. So the community fought it,
vehemently, and they stopped it.

Campbell reasoned that the current bus line served *residents* well enough
and wasn't worried about nonresidents. People in Randallstown could
walk to buses on Liberty Road without having them drive through their
neighborhood, so she saw no reason to compromise what she described
as "the serenity of the area."[26]

Denise Murphy's comments are a reminder that even in the face of
widespread opposition, "the community" was not unitary. From her perspective as executive director of the Liberty Road Business Association,
she saw "part of the community" proposing the bus extension to connect
their businesses, and part of the community opposing it because "little
old women" were afraid "we'll be mugged and all this kind of stuff, if
the buses come through." As a business organization, Murphy was in a
position to recognize that "the community" had a variety of opinions on
the matter.

Lenwood Johnson, a county planner and longtime member of the
NAACP, described how neighborhood opposition killed the bus plan.
"When the community found out about that they hit the ceiling. So they
called everybody, called their state senator . . . and . . . that was taken off
the drawing board." By August 2005, just three months after the original proposal, the MTA canceled plans to extend the bus line to Owings
Mills Mall.[27]

Incidentally, Johnson added that the mythological linkage of mass
transit to crime and African Americans was long established in the
Baltimore area. Twenty-five years earlier he had heard that "I think
the joke goes that they came out to Randallstown on the MTA and
somebody stole a BMW," and so the bus line was shortened so that it
wouldn't quite reach that part of the suburbs. Even earlier, around 1970,
another planner had explained to Johnson that the white community
opposed a new subway line because "they could get in town quickly
but so could those people in town come in, steal their twenty-five-inch
color TV and get back to town very quickly." The regular appearance
of the "color TV" in such stories suggests that the transit-race-crime
nexus may have first been articulated in the mid-twentieth century; it

was clearly in place by the 1970s and has remained a fixture of public discussions of mass transit.

It is easy to chastise opponents of the bus extension. Among other things, the case is an ironic reversal of the Birmingham bus boycott: suburban African Americans targeted the buses not because Blacks didn't have equal rights to ride the bus but because Blacks *were* riding the bus. But this case exhibited more than just the adoption of exclusive suburban attitudes by African Americans as they bought homes in the suburbs.

To better appreciate what was going on in the bus case, the diversity of the community views must be kept in mind. The proposal to extend the bus line, after all, was in response to some community members' support for the proposal and expectations that there would be significant demand for the service were it implemented, suggesting that businesses and riders constituted at least two constituencies who favored extending the bus line. The expansion plan had been well received enough in the first place to be included in the MTA's larger restructuring proposal. And while the Randallstown area's African American state senator, Dolores Kelley, ultimately came to oppose the extension plan, saying she was being responsive to her constituents,[28] opponents had evidently not convinced State Delegate Adrienne Jones or business association director Denise Murphy, among others. Thus there were constituents in favor of mass transit and local elites sympathetic to them. But proponents were not organized, nor was there an organization that encompassed business owners, current bus riders, and people who wanted to get to the shopping mall by bus. The anti-transit ideology, in contrast, was already firmly entrenched in the suburbs and was consistent with the priorities of existing community and homeowner associations. The story, then, was not that African American suburbanites pulled the drawbridge up behind them to keep out fellow African Americans from the city but that in a community of diverse opinions, institutional networks already existed to promote a position that was grounded in stereotypes, while no comparable progressive network was mobilized. The failure of the bus expansion was less a story of a universally exclusive and conservative view than a forfeit by potential progressive forces of contested issues in the suburbs.

The Promise of Progressive Politics in the Suburbs

The difference in how racial issues manifest in the contemporary sub-urbs has research and polemical implications. Sociologists have only recently begun to assess the impact of space on social relationships, and the suburban case makes a strong argument for moving the attention to space beyond the city boundaries where it has so far been concen-trated. Here, it was not only class differences but the spatial organization of the suburbs that shaped views. In the case of the new Walmart store, the comparative class homogeneity of the spatial arrangement of subur-ban developments reinforced residents' belief that retail stores should deploy at least middle-class (if not upper-middle-class) signifiers. The suburbs' use of space to create exclusive zones of relative privilege simi-larly underpinned residents' objection to expanded bus lines, which they saw as introducing poor people into neighborhoods they imagined as middle class. Studying racial issues in the suburbs highlights the need for a new progressive framing of issues faced by Black suburbanites to provide an expansive, inclusive alternative to the narrow, exclusive response encouraged by the space of the suburbs and the hegemonic political attitudes forged there. Such a progressive response would dif-fer from current approaches in that it would integrate the insights of suburban activists and differ from suburban attitudes in that it would be founded on a commitment to share broad-based improvements across society rather than the beggar-thy-neighbor politics represented by efforts to exclude others from a community. One concern voiced by residents that is relevant to such an approach is that if one section of the suburbs is welcoming, other more exclusive sections of the suburbs may benefit at their expense. Randallstown residents felt they already had a disproportionate number of Section 8 subsidized tenants, group homes for older children in the foster care system, inexperienced teachers, and bus lines. Even those who support social welfare policies worried that having more people with greater needs in the African American com-munity of Randallstown would bring greater burdens. They believed that more poor residents could make life in Randallstown more diffi-cult and reinforce whites' stereotypes that Black areas inevitably have more problems. Thus a progressive framing that challenged exclusionist opposition to things like bus lines would need to succeed countywide, not only in the African American community, if it were to avoid exacerbating, at a county level, the very exclusivity it opposed at a local level.

But there is another possibility. Despite the best efforts of the county's Department of Economic Development, local business associations, and resident boosters, new chain stores have not yet come to dominate Randallstown. For those people who dream of suburbs without chain stores, this is in some ways a historic preservation district. (Old-time residents agree that Liberty Road was never a high-end retail destination and has always been a disorganized assemblage of locally owned and low-volume businesses.) Since chain stores are not coming in large numbers, if anti-Walmart activists proposed an alternative to big-box retail that still brought status to this middle-class suburb, residents might well endorse it. In the absence of the characteristic suburban big-box retail environment, there is the opportunity to join with residents who are promoting a more community-oriented vision of the main street.

In the more conventional model of business development, targeted low-cost financing could be made available. If business owners along the Liberty Road corridor had access to sufficient capital to upgrade their stores to middle-class standards, residents' desire for a more attractive retail strip would be realized, while Black small businesses, a systematically undercapitalized component of the economy, could flourish. The unique confluence of race and economics in Randallstown creates not only the well-known challenges but also unusual opportunities—for an unusually strong main street or to foster locally owned business.

The opposition to bus service expansion presents contradictory stories of defeat and possibility. On the one hand, the exclusive priorities of suburban space led Black people to oppose bus service because it would bring Black people. Class distinctions within the Black community are nothing new, but Black adoption not only of white strategies but of white hysteria regarding the impending arrival of Blacks by mass transit has depressing implications. Nonetheless, the busing case simultaneously illustrated that there were identifiable constituencies for progressive transit policies but that they lacked a unifying organization and ideology.

While each case holds progressive political promise, it is undeniable that each case also reflected significant conservative tendencies: the continued segregationism of white residents, the classism of suburban communities, the transformation of "economic development" from better jobs to better places to shop, the rejection of mass transit by suburbanites. While even the most conservative African Americans don't embrace all the tenets of white conservatism, there are certainly plenty of sources for conservative points of view on any issue.

Yet conservatism is not the only option in the suburbs. Each of the issues in Randallstown included components that would be promising for any group that sought to frame issues faced by African Americans in the suburbs in a progressive light. These components are generally discovered only by examining social conflicts and community activism in the suburbs. From examining the history of Randallstown's racial transition and community conflicts, progressive activists might make use of new residential construction as a strategy to break open a segregated community. They could be inspired by the unity of multiracial homeowner associations that have effectively opposed white flight. They might recognize the potential for broader alliances in a suburb that is still largely free of big-box retail, perhaps between working-class advocates of economic development focused on higher-quality jobs and anti-chain-store activists working to build high-status, noncorporate retail environments. And activists could recognize the potential of the suburbs' diverse but disorganized constituencies for progressive projects like mass transit. What is needed are organizations that include these diverse constituencies in a progressive platform and beyond that a progressive ideology for the suburbs that will make sense of issues as diverse as segregation, school funding, economic development, and mass transit in ways that are expansive, equitable, diverse, and dignified.

A comprehensive progressive framing of issues like these would come only through engagement with those issues on the ground. But the cases examined here demonstrate some of the tools and opportunities activists and organizers in African American suburbs could make use of to present an alternative to the exclusive, conservative ideology that is ever accessible in the suburbs.

If the study of space is as valuable as its increasing number of proponents suggest, it cannot be ghettoized in studies of urban space. And if progressive politics are not to be marginalized, they cannot be marginalized in the suburbs, where half of America, including ten million African Americans, live. Twenty-first-century suburbs are already center stage in struggles for racial equality, and residents in those locations may already be producing innovative solutions.

5

Barriers

The Right to the City and Changing Suburban Space

Sometimes it's necessary to ask questions one already knows the answer to. I was interviewing Louis Diggs at his home, a condo in the New Town development of Owings Mills, just a few minutes from Liberty Road. After Diggs retired from the Navy, he was a substitute high school teacher. When he asked his students to write about local history and found that African Americans could find no local history about their communities, he spent years collecting oral histories from African Americans who had lived their whole lives in Baltimore County's historical African American communities and published the research in a series of books. During our interview Diggs was describing his own recent search for a home. So much had changed, he said, from when he and his wife had first looked for a home in the 1970s. Back then they found property they wanted near Winters Lane—one of the first Black communities Diggs would later write about. But it was across the street from the neighborhood, not in it. Whites responded violently. For the transgression of buying property across the street, they had the windows shot out of one of their three cars and a cross burned on the lawn of the oldest African American church in Winters Lane. But *these* days, Diggs, explained, were different. Gone was the era when where African Americans could live was determined by a road not to be crossed or limited to a small community with poor pavement and dilapidated houses. Today people were more welcoming. "They're more understanding of you as a person, you're just accepted more," he explained. "You know it's not like in the old days when they're afraid that the young Blacks are going to get the young white girls or whatever." He and his wife had moved to a well-manicured development in New Town, just between the single-family homes of Randallstown and the Owings Mills Mall. Diggs explained, "They're not moving like they used to. There used to be a time when a white would sell their house on the block [to a Black buyer] and every house would come out with a for sale sign. You don't see that anymore. That's—that's encouraging. . . . That if people have problems, they work them out, and just lick it." He sounded confident that times had changed.

I wondered aloud if new complexes like his were easier to integrate than existing neighborhoods, but Diggs disagreed.

> I think it would happen anywhere. My wife and I, before we moved here, there was a place in Carroll County, that we absolutely loved. Carroll County, most Blacks don't go, because you know, there could be problems there. And it was a new complex. Shucks, man those people were just as nice, I mean, really wanted to buy there. But it was just a little too far away for me. I mean the guys would come out, we'd be just looking around, you know—with the agent of course, and while my wife was looking at the house, I would go out and speak with them, and "Oh, say, you retired," "Oh yeah, I'm from the Navy." You sit down and enjoy talking with people. And you have the sense that this is not a bad place to move to. I think that's true all over now. . . . I believe so.

I considered Diggs's statement that so much had changed. "You said most Blacks wouldn't want to move up to Carroll County," I said. "Why is that?"

Louis Diggs didn't pause. "Klan."

Carroll County was less than six miles from his home where we sat.

Nor was he alone. Another resident described how her heart had always raced in a mix of anger and anxiety when she had to drive across the bridge from Baltimore County to Carroll County. "I used to not go to Carroll County. Oh, Lord. They used to lynch people in Carroll County when we were still here. Oh Lord, I wouldn't go across that bridge." Only after decades of avoiding the area did she start to go up regularly, to visit a store with a better flower selection for her beloved garden, and found, over time, that her anxiety eased and the drive over the reservoir bridge started to feel peaceful. Later she was able to drive there during political campaigns.

What did Louis Diggs mean when he argued that so much had changed? Clearly it had. As a man who had been confronted by racist violence, by everyday insults, by a politician's condescension when Diggs sought help confronting neglect in the Winters Lane community by absentee land-lords (if he didn't like it, the county executive wrote, he should move back to the city), Diggs was certainly correct that much had changed.

Diggs felt less constrained in where he could live. Yet just six miles down the road lay a place where most people like him would be afraid to go. In this chapter I explore the meaning of this continued sense of constraint and the ways that the contours of space and spatial boundaries continue to map out a restricted landscape for African Americans in the suburbs. I argue that these restrictions are not just an injustice in themselves but can be better understood in the context of the burgeoning right to the city movement. Despite the advances made by African American residents, professionals, and activists, Black Americans are still denied the right to the city. Thinking about the denial of a basic right sheds light on persistent questions about African American segregation. Social scientists have disproven the popular assumption that whites and Blacks live in separate communities because (as my students have suggested time and time again) it's natural that "people like to live with their own kind." Yet a structural view leaves no room for African American agency. The right to the city perspective pays attention to action taken by African Americans while still understanding the social structures that continue to impose segregation.

First we must consider what exactly is meant by the "right to the city." This chapter argues that segregation, racial profiling by police, and exclusionary school district lines and county boundaries are all profitably understood as denying African Americans the right to the city. Despite all the progress Diggs accurately described, the contemporary denial of the right to the city demonstrates historical continuity between issues suburbanites confront today and the experiences of African Americans in the Jim Crow era of rural Baltimore County. The right to the city perspective helps explain why some of these practices persist and why for most of the county features like residential racial segregation are nearly as pronounced in the absence of legal strictures as they were with them.

The Right to the City and Neoliberalism

The right to the city was first asserted by theorist Henri Lefebvre in 1968. Lefebvre's work has been popular and influential despite not being as clear as it could be. The early definition was somewhat imprecise. In discussing the right to the city Lefebvre pointed out that people have not just individual but social needs: the needs for security and access, certainty and adventure, work and play, the predictable and unpredictable, isolation and encounter, independence and communication. In addition, Lefebvre argued, people have needs that cannot reliably be met commercially or through mass culture, including types of creativity and information. Lefebvre went on to suggest that this bundle of needs is met in particular social spaces and that people therefore have a right to spaces that allow them to fulfill their basic social, creative, work, play, security, and adventurous needs. This he called the right to the city.[1]

Lefebvre showed his Marxist roots in setting out the right to the city as fundamental for the working class. As Don Mitchell points out, the right to the city required the right to *inhabit* the city, and thus the question of housing was central as well.[2] Access to housing is a very different issue for the workers Lefebvre described than for the residents of Baltimore's African American suburbs, who at least have the means to secure decent housing, if they have not always been allowed to enter the racially segregated housing market. Even if Lefebvre conceived of the right to the city as "a cry and a demand" by the working class, the concept quickly became a broader, "post-materialist" demand that included new social movements. As it was adopted by activists seeking more usable and social public spaces in their communities, the right to the city became in some ways a middle-class expectation as much as a working-class cry.[3]

David Harvey has further elaborated on the right to the city, identifying it as a common rather than an individual right. Harvey called the right to the city "the freedom to make and remake our cities and ourselves" and the power to reshape the process of urbanization.[4]

British sociologist Gareth Millington has provided one of the clearest distillations of the right to the city.[5] Drawing from several sources, Millington identifies several features of the right to the city. It is, he concurs, a right to inhabit the city (rather than owning a plot of it). While inhabiting the city, people have the right to participate in the collective social project of work, creating, benefitting, and growing. To a Marxist like Lefebvre, the city is a centralized concentration of wealth and power, and so the ability for less powerful people to come to the center is no less than the ability of the disenfranchised to assert power. To be marginalized physically is to be marginalized socially, so the right to inhabit the center city is inherently a political right of inclusion and participation in power. The right to the city thus includes participation in the political life of the city and its management and administration. The city had the potential to "overcome differences" and provide room not only for work but for play and leisure as well. Critically, Millington reminds us that Lefebvre's goal was not only to provide a bourgeois space in the city but to define, in the right to the city, the potential for a revolutionary liberation, a reclaiming of public space and of the public sphere by people who were otherwise excluded from the command and control functions of the center city.

Thus the right to the city was first formulated with a class-based analysis by Marxists (an unorthodox Marxist in the case of Lefebvre, and a more orthodox one in Harvey). As such the right to the city was initially conceived of as a challenge to the power of capitalism in the bourgeois city. However, as activists in the Global South developed a right to the city movement, they enlarged the concept to encompass not just a classically Marxist, class-based opposition to capitalism but also support for anticolonial, antiglobalization, anti-imperial movements. Activists in Brazil and elsewhere challenged the damage and depredation of imperial global capitalism directed by the United States, Europe, multinational corporations, and other components of the Global North. In this expanded framing, the right to the city underwent three changes. First, activists integrated it into the international language of human rights used by nongovernmental organizations and the United Nations. Second, by the time the World Charter for the Right to the City was introduced at the Conference for Human Rights in Brazil in 2001 (and later at NGO- and United Nations–associated meetings like the World Social Forum), the right to the city had been defined with a clearly enumerated set of elements. In the proposed charter, the right to the city meant the following: All people have the right to be free of discrimination, the right to use cities and express themselves culturally, politically, economically, and socially. People have the right to join unions. They have the right to work in decent conditions and engage in political and cultural self-determination. They have the right to exercise these earlier rights in cities. (Here, "cities" meant not only actual cities, or even small towns and villages, but individual public spaces and any socially signifi-cant social space.) In essence, the right to the city is the right to travel through, inhabit, use, and reshape the physical landscape in which we exist socially, for the purpose of securing our basic rights—including everything from work and sustenance to cultural identity and politi-cal affiliation.

In this context, the right to the city became closely tied to movements against neoliberalism. According to antiglobalization books (as well as, implicitly, the work of Harvey, who wrote widely read books about both neoliberalism and the right to the city), in cities the privatization of neoliberalism often involved the privatization of formerly public re-sources and institutions, including public space. Objections that New York's Times Square was becoming "Disneyfied," that public space was becoming privatized, that main streets were being replaced by shopping malls, that parks were being sold off, leased out, privately controlled, and reoriented toward profit-making uses all came from a critique that the growth of neoliberalism constrained the right to the city. The right to the city movement was an explicit challenge to the neoliberal city. How, then, does the right to the city in the suburban and African American context relate to neoliberalism? The relationship is revealing but differ-ent from other right to the city critiques of neoliberalism.

It is not coincidental that the World Charter for the Right to the City equated this right to citizenship, broadly defined. Because the right to the city was the right to move freely, use public space, express oneself se-curely, be free of discrimination and violence, and be able to organize po-litically, to have the right to the city meant to be a citizen.[6] Harvey made a similar point when he equated "ideals of urban identity" with "citizen-ship and belonging."[7] To have the right to the city is to be a citizen. To be denied the right to the city is to be denied full citizenship. Geographer Mark Purcell saw citizenship as a core challenge that the right to the city leveled at neoliberalism, writing that "citizenship based on the right to the city radically challenges and reimagines the capitalist world order."[8] African American struggles are likewise linked to the notion of the right to the city since the United States throughout its history has used race, perhaps preeminently, as a visible marker of citizenship. To have the right to the city is to have citizenship, and US citizenship and race have been enmeshed since well before the 1790 Naturalization Act that explicitly defined those eligible for citizenship as "free white persons."

In its development, the concept of the right to the city successfully expanded beyond its original definition. The right began as a Marxist and thus strictly class-based concept. With its adaptation by global movements against corporate globalization, it grew to include the concerns of people disenfranchised not just by class but by nationality, ethnicity, culture, and race, becoming a *human right*. But it had not yet made a final critical transformation. In the United States, race-based discrimination is addressed as a matter of civil rights. Malcolm X, toward the end of his life, sought to tie the struggle of Black Americans to global struggles for freedom and justice, arguing that Black issues were properly seen not as national-level civil rights but as universal human rights.[9] But that framing has not been dominant, and African American social movements continue to be described in terms of "civil rights" rather than human rights. Whether this difference is strictly semantic or not, it means that concepts from the global human rights movement are often not integrated into the US civil rights movements. This chapter draws in the concept of the right to the city—and the denial of that right in the United States today—to the larger investigation of the effect of neoliberalism on African American suburbs, to better understand the contemporary African American suburban experience.

For a book on suburbs, it is worth reiterating that the "city" in "right to the city" does not mean the legally bound city—say, Baltimore City as opposed to Baltimore County. In the formulation of Lefebvre, Harvey, the activists in Brazil, and everyone after them, the right to the *city* means the right to exist and use the social space around us, be it urban, suburban, or small town.

Considering the right to the city makes clear the historical continuities between the experiences of contemporary African American middle-class suburbanites and the denial of rights experienced by African Americans in the same places a century or more before. African Americans have not had the free right to travel across the landscape. They have not had the right to live where they want. Whites have partitioned the landscape and denied power and access by establishing barriers and boundaries.

Segregation and the Right to the City

Americans often consider segregation inevitable. According to sociologist Eduardo Bonilla-Silva, white Americans in particular "naturalize" segregation, so that the virtually all-white neighborhoods many of them live in appear to be the norm and not the product of racist, segregationist activity.[10] The work of Douglas Massey and Nancy Denton does more than any other source I know to demolish this myth. To upend the assumption that segregation is inevitable, they make several important points.

First, the researchers point out that high levels of segregation are not natural or universal but particular to African Americans. African Americans (and whites, it should be noted) live in far more segregated neighborhoods than any other ethnic or racial group. "Even at the height of their segregation early in this century, European ethnic groups did not experience a particularly high degree of isolation from American society."[11] By Massey and Denton's measures, the *highest* levels of segregation for groups such as Italians, Russians, and Jews were below the lowest levels typically experienced by African Americans in major cities by the mid-twentieth century.

Second, the United States was not always characterized by the highly racially segregated neighborhoods it has today. As Massey and Denton point out, in 1900 African Americans lived in small communities that were racially mixed, in close proximity with other groups. The "ghetto," that is, large neighborhoods in a city, where almost everyone was Black and where almost all Blacks lived, was produced through violence. In the 1920s, as African Americans moved from the rural South to the urban Northeast and Midwest and urban Black populations grew and sought integration into the industrial economy, there was a nationwide wave of race riots in which African Americans were assaulted and killed, often with the help or at least complacency of law enforcement. In Tulsa, Oklahoma, days of rioting by whites killed three hundred African Americans and left ten thousand people homeless, yet the atrocity was almost entirely forgotten by history but has regained some of its much deserved notoriety recently. Eyewitnesses reported that the government used aircraft to drop incendiary devices on blocks of homes in Black neighborhoods.

The gruesome Tulsa riots were but one incident in a wave of such attacks. In their aftermath, African Americans realized that they were not safe. They did not return to the small enclaves and mixed-race areas where they had lived but concentrated instead in larger, almost entirely African American neighborhoods. As the Great Migration continued to increase the number of Blacks living in cities, particularly in the North and Midwest, those neighborhoods grew, as did white animus toward the newcomers, and likewise African Americans' need for collective defense against the possibility of white-led assaults.

Few people, white or Black, even remember that those race riots took place, and thus few people know how segregated African American communities were created, or why almost all African Americans in any given metropolitan area live in such communities.

Though it is useful in understanding the initial creation of urban ghettos almost a hundred years ago, this history would not normally be taken as an explanation for why such high levels of segregation persist. The assumption has often been that such segregation is a holdover, a remnant of an earlier age, the product, to use the term common to civil rights adjudication, of "past discrimination." Given that new suburban communities develop with levels of discrimination only modestly lower than the virtually complete segregation of older center-city ghettoes, the choice of the term "past" seems politically expedient rather than empirically justified.

Massey and Denton point out that discrimination is not in the past but continues in two forms. First, African Americans may be reluctant to enter a white neighborhood. "Although the level of anti-Black violence has declined since the 1970s, Black apprehension about entering white neighborhoods are by no means unfounded," they wrote in 1993, citing the high number of reported hate crimes.[12] The authors point out that "Blacks express considerable reluctance about entering all-white neighborhoods." But given that this is the result of reasonable fears of hostility, they conclude that "the high degree of segregation Blacks experience in urban America is not voluntary."[13] The lion's share of the chapter on "The Continuing Causes of Segregation" studies discriminatory behavior by real estate brokers and rental agents in the housing market. Steering by realtors and unequal treatment of home seekers happens, by their conservative measures, in one-third of all visits to a realtor or rental agent.[14] The chapter's focus is understandable from a policy perspective, since the authors seek to demonstrate that the Fair Housing Act is inadequate—that even when fair housing groups "have pushed private fair housing enforcement to the legal limit, they have produced *essentially no change* in the degree of racial segregation within [an] urban area."[15]

Massey and Denton and others focus on practices of refusing to show homes and apartments to Black home seekers, steering them to Black neighborhoods, and establishing more demanding credit checks on African American than on white home seekers. Yet discrimination by people in the real estate industry has nothing to do with the "reasonable fears" many Blacks experience at the prospect of moving into a white neighborhood. According to Baltimore-area realtors, most often African American home buyers come to them looking for houses in areas that already have meaningful African American populations—not in the majority of the county that is overwhelmingly white. The role of discriminatory real estate agents is preempted when most African Americans don't want to look in white areas in the first place. Middle-class suburban African Americans' decision to move to already Black neighborhoods and avoid white areas—avoid not only living there but in some cases traveling there—casts the persistence of residential segregation in a different light. Segregation is not a historic artifact, nor simply an outdated barrier imposed by self-appointed racial deputies in real estate offices and banks, but the result of threats to personal safety that are rarely discussed as policy matters.

Historical African American Communities

Like many other suburbs, Baltimore County was never all white. The county's northern border is the Mason-Dixon Line—the traditional boundary between North and South that divides Maryland from Pennsylvania. As the county is located so close to the Mason-Dixon Line, escape was closer for Baltimore slaves than for most people. Perhaps because of that or perhaps because this particular area of the Chesapeake Bay was ill suited for the tobacco farming that created huge slave plantations, by the census immediately before the Civil War and Emancipation there were more free Blacks than slaves in Baltimore County.[16] African

Americans formed at least forty small Black communities throughout Baltimore County, including in Randallstown, that predated the Civil War and in most cases exist today. Most often the communities are composed of a small number of houses on a country road, often including an AME church.[17]

After these original Black communities, the next significant addition to Black Baltimore County came, as it did in other suburban areas, with industrialization. As early as 1891, African Americans from Virginia and the Carolinas (along with other groups of workers), growing to nine thousand in number in the 1950s, moved to Turner Station and Sparrows Point in the southeast corner of the county to work in the steel mills.[18] Historian Louis Diggs notes that while the rest of Baltimore County's African American communities tended to be home to Methodist churches (like the AME Church, founded just to the north in Philadelphia in 1787), Turner Station had a concentration of Baptist churches, reflecting the predominance of the Baptist church among African Americans who came from farther south. While there was only incidental interaction among the historic settlements, which were scattered throughout the rural county, and Sparrows Point, which was relatively isolated on the waterfront, both the rural and industrial communities established and institutionalized African American communities in Baltimore County.

Life in the small rural African American communities could be isolated. The church in a community in Randallstown would frequently organize outings in which the residents of one area would travel together to visit those in an adjoining African American community such as Chatsworth. Young adults in the communities often married spouses from nearby communities.

The relatively isolated rural communities survived after Emancipation even though it appears that, at least at times, life for African Americans would have been safer in the city. For instance, in the 1930s, when authorities wanted to protect an African American from being lynched, they brought the individuals who were in danger to Baltimore City. City newspapers, columnist H. L. Mencken in the lead, deplored lynchings (the most recent one recorded in Maryland occurred in 1933), while county newspapers, particularly those on the eastern shore, implicitly condoned lynchings by deploring lawlessness but defending local "prompt justice."[19] Protection in Baltimore may have been thin at best since many white Baltimoreans apparently approved of lynchings. But the city was also home to an African American community that numbered in the tens of thousands rather than in the dozens, so it provided safety in numbers at least.

The continued existence of rural communities after Emancipation tells an interesting spatial story, with relevance to the present day. As Halle, Gedeon, and Beveridge point out, evidence indicates that extreme segregation is maintained through violence.[20] While the denial of African Americans' right to the city can today be most readily conceived of in terms of widespread racial segregation as detailed in Massey and Denton, whites' abrogation of this right has manifested itself differently in different historical periods, as the decades after Emancipation make clear. From his extensive oral history interviews with residents of the historic settlements, Diggs explained why African Americans remained in small communities in the country. There were, of course, family ties, property ownership, and other considerations, but there was another necessary concern. The residents of the community of Chattolanee in Baltimore County, for instance, were initially slaves. Residents there continued working after Emancipation for wages. But as Diggs pointed out, "They knew they could not go into Baltimore, for safety reasons— that's where the bulk of the Blacks were. But they knew they couldn't come back and forth to work, so that's when they founded either tenant houses or they were able to buy a little piece of property to build a home, so they could continue to work." Diggs found that model typical in the communities he studied.

In this way the historic African American settlements show that there are at least two different ways in which the right to the city can be denied. People may feel unsafe in their own small communities, in which case they will move together for the protection a larger community affords. This is the explanation that Massey and Denton give for the growth of large Black ghettoes in the early twentieth century after widespread anti-Black riots exposed African American vulnerability in small communities like the historic settlements. But the explanation Diggs developed through his research for the persistence of isolated Black settlements in rural Baltimore County points out an earlier denial of the right to the city: African Americans felt more unsafe traveling outside of their communities, so they needed to live close to their workplace. The right to the city requires both the right to be safe in the public spaces of one's own community and the right to travel freely through other public spaces outside one's community.

Through the mid-twentieth century, Blacks were not allowed to attend white high schools in the county, which provided no Black high schools. So students who wanted to go to high school had to travel daily to Baltimore. The county already severely restricted the number of African American students it allowed to attend school in the city, but the need to travel, alone, through unfriendly territory no doubt further reduced the chances of some students to get a high school diploma.

In the nineteenth century and early twentieth, two of the ways that the right to the city was denied were by making the landscape unsafe and unfriendly to African Americans outside their own communities and by denying the possibility of free and safe travel throughout the metro area. When people needed to travel, they often did so in groups: visiting another community was a special and collective social occasion. Insecurity in the metro landscape and the denial of free passage continue today.

Contemporary Suburbs and the Right to the City

African Americans' lack of a sense of safety in areas that are not predominantly Black continues. It is evident in Louis Diggs's comment about Carroll County. On closer inspection, his comments reveal even more uncertainty about the county. When I first reviewed the transcript, I took his statement that "I think it would happen anywhere" to mean that the welcoming reception he got could happen anywhere. But I had asked if it was easier to integrate new complexes (as other evidence had suggested to me). Diggs said it could happen anywhere, then told a story of going to a *new complex* in Carroll County and initially being uncomfortable. I wonder now whether he meant that what could happen anywhere, whether a new or old development, was the "problems" that could happen in Carroll County. After all, when he said that he was "just looking around," he quickly added that he was "with the agent of course," to clarify that he wouldn't have been walking around the condo complex without a real estate agent to explain his presence.

Other Baltimore County residents had the same trepidation about other parts of their own county. When Leronia Josey was running for the position of Orphans' Court judge, she needed to campaign county-wide.[21] She didn't have a lot of success on the east side, which county residents associate with working-class whites from the now-shuttered steel mills, shipyards, and auto plants, and which has a reputation as an unreconstructed racist place. "I got some votes on the east side," insisted Josey, "but I didn't really get a lot because they didn't know me." When she went to campaign on the east side, she said, "I used to tell my friends, 'God, there are no Black people over here. If I don't come home, you all know they lynched me.' I mean, we would go to these little American Legion Halls, and all that, but the people were really nice, but I says, nobody Black in there but me, not even the people cleaning up are Black." Like Diggs, Josey insisted that people were nice, even that "they listened, I sat down with them, you know." But it was still an environment where she felt pressed to look to the cleaning staff to find fellowship in another Black face. (Interestingly, both Jewish and African American residents felt the west side of the county was different, even different enough for them to identify an eastern accent that was distinct from that of the western side of the county.)

In the nineteenth century, African Americans were safe only in certain neighborhoods and could not necessarily travel from one area to another in safety. Residents described the same conditions in the contemporary suburbs. Residents did not feel that they could reliably travel securely on public roads and streets.

During my interview with Patricia Ferguson, her nineteen-year-old son came by, and she took the opportunity to point out what she had taught him as a young Black man. "What do I tell you?" she asked. He obligingly ran down a list of instructions his mother gave him to follow while driving, all to reduce the chances he'd be pulled over: Wear a seatbelt. No loud music. No leaning back (riding with the driver's seat tilted back, which was the "cool" way to drive at the time). Ferguson continued: "And I also say try not to have no more than how many people in the car?" "No more than two or three." She turned back to me. "But don't think it's not a day that goes by that if you're an African American female with sons in Baltimore County that you do not tell your children be careful . . . Don't give them any reason to stop you." The son insisted he obeyed all his mother's instructions, so that the police didn't have a reason to pull him over. But she still saw risks. "But if he's walking in their neighborhood or around that way at night, he's in trouble. Or if something happened, hasn't there been times you all have been stopped because of other incidents?" Her son agreed: "Like they'll just pull the car around. They'll be on the opposite of the road and just turn around, make a U-turn just for no apparent reason. I don't know, maybe it's just a quota."

In fact, when Ferguson listed the problems that racism caused, a disproportionate number of her examples had to do with profiling and freedom of movement. Without preparation, she delivered a laundry list with a firm, poetic cadence. Drawing directly from her experience at the NAACP, she quickly listed these examples:

> Racism is when . . . you've moved to certain parts of Owings Mills or White Marsh and you're driving home in this neighborhood at night and you're stopped and asked, "What are you doing here?" "I live here." So that's still happening a lot.
>
> Racism is when you're stopped at two o'clock in the morning and you just did overtime at your job but you shouldn't be driving your car at two in the morning if you're African American. Otherwise, maybe you just robbed something or you just came from somewhere. That's happening on Route 40 West. It's happening on Security Boulevard. How about racism in Catonsville. You are a student and you're taking classes all the way over by Essex so by the time you get home, you're catching buses and you're walking through Catonsville, up Winters Lane so that you can go home. But you have dreads and you're stopped and someone says, "You must be selling drugs. Why are you out here?" And when you try to explain that you're a student and you're coming home late, no because that is an area that's known for drugs on certain corners so therefore if you're walking that way at night, you're either going to buy drugs or you're selling drugs. How dare you say that you were coming from school. These are the cases that we get in Baltimore County. . . .
>
> Racism is going in to the mall and because you're with two people or three people, they watch you from the time you come in the door until the time you go out and are constantly moving as you move and asking you "Can I help you?" "No, you can't. I'm looking." When other groups of two or three come into the store and nothing is said.

Racism is when you go into a store to purchase something and they're telling you, "I don't think you can afford it."

Racism is if you feel you have done nothing wrong and you are telling the officer, "I haven't done anything wrong, why are you harassing me?" And the officer tells you to shut up or the officer says something that the officer shouldn't, and then you say something that you shouldn't have said to the officer. And you get ready to go or move—how come the officer always wants to say, and we have many cases—"Oh you assaulted me or you touched me." We have a lot of cases like that that finally get thrown out.

Why is it that every time there's a case, this is racism, you send it to internal affairs and you have the police policing the police and I don't care what the case is, it always comes back that the officer did nothing wrong even when you have pictures of black eyes. Even when you have pictures where they sic the dogs on someone even after they were handcuffed. . . .

Racism is you don't like me because someone says if I have braids and I have baggy pants and I'm driving a Lexus, I'm selling drugs. Can't be that my parents have money. It cannot be because you are working two jobs. You have to be doing something else.

Nearly half of the twenty-five examples Ferguson listed when she began "racism is . . ." dealt with denial of the right to the city, such as police profiling and mistreatment in public spaces. Given that racism takes a myriad of forms (and that we were not talking about the right to the city or profiling at the time), the preponderance of the right to the city in Ferguson's list gives some indication of its significance in contemporary racism.

Accounts of being pulled over by police for no reason came up spontaneously and frequently in my interviews, particularly for men. Leronia Josey described the experiences of her husband and pointed out the tension inherent in wanting to save money by moving out to the more affordable suburbs.

I didn't want to spend all of our money on housing where we would have never had an investment in that. I wanted good schools for my son. I wanted peace and quiet in the neighborhood, you know what I mean, and reasonably nice surroundings and stuff. It had nothing to do with wanting to come to an area that was 80-some percent white. We didn't even know it when we moved out here. We found that when my husband kept getting—the police were stopping him every night when he was coming in, because he would go like, from Aberdeen to the church, because we have a real active church, and he was singing in two or three choirs, and headed a men's organization, and all of that.

This occurred around 1978–1980, when they first moved out to the county. "African American man at night coming here, and police would say, 'Where are you going?' And he would say, 'I'm going home.' And they would say, 'Home?' And then they would follow him here. It was illegal."

Pastor Emmett Burns had similar stories from his parishioners, and of interceding with the police to try to resolve problems that had arisen for his members when the police interacted inappropriately with them.

Much changed since the residents of Chattolanee lived close to work because they couldn't travel safely in the county. But the continuing denial of the right to the city explained a great deal about continuing segregation. Most Africans lived in mostly African American neighborhoods not because of past discrimination, but because in the present, they themselves felt unsafe (or at a minimum, uneasy, less welcomed, or less certain they would be treated respectfully on the road, in stores, and at restaurants) in all-white neighborhoods. Louis Diggs and Leronia Josey asked rhetorically whether their fears of whiter parts of the state were really accurate. Diggs simultaneously expressed the wisdom of collective experiences and a consideration of reasons for optimism: "I have relatives up there. I mean the Klan was always active. I don't know where I got it from. I've always been skeptical of Carroll County. Yeah, I've never had any problems, I've been up to Carroll Community College, Western Maryland College, speaking, very well accepted. I've never had any problems. I think I'm just letting some of my old biases come into play." Diggs moved back and forth between conviction that the Klan was a problem and the suggestion that his fear was just an outdated stereotype. Likewise, Leronia Josey said she warned her friends about her trips to the east side in a half joking way and concluded that the people there listened to what she had to say. African Americans moved into large Black communities because they felt unsafe out on their own. And the interviews suggest that even for financially stable African American suburbanites looking for a home in the county, feeling safe is not a given, is not dependent solely on the standard crime statistics, and explains a good deal of why high levels of African American segregation persists. This is quite different from saying that people naturally tend toward homogenous communities. It allows room for African American agency while simultaneously opening a structural discussion even larger than that about the FHA and housing discrimination by realtors and apartment brokers. Home seekers make choices about neighborhoods and do so in a climate in which moving outside of existing African Americans neighborhoods carries risks—even considering the structural disadvantages of underinvestment, poorly supported schools, and related problems. If we need to tackle discriminatory lending and real estate practices to overcome segregation, we certainly need to address the real fears Black Americans experience when considering moving out of Black neighborhoods. That's not preference, it's pressure.

Boundaries: Spatial Strategies Reinforcing Racial Inequality

Spatially oriented strategies delineated the unequal conditions between Black and white neighborhoods in the suburbs, and those strategies affected the culture of the suburban Black middle class. *Boundaries* came up many times in my interviews and identified important ways residents related to their community and the county at large.

First, African Americans were aware that borders were being drawn around them. Hebert Lindsay pointed out that the county had resisted development of low-income housing (and had proposed zoning laws that would permit only single-family housing rather than apartments or row houses) because low-income housing led low-income people, imagined to be Black, to come into Baltimore County.

Just as the borders of the city were once boundaries that kept African Americans out of the county in large numbers, boundaries were drawn around predominantly Black schools to separate Blacks from the largely white areas around them. Roxanne Umphries-Lucas commented that there were elementary schools that had been predominantly white and fed into predominantly white middle and high schools. As those elementary schools became predominantly Black, students were increasingly being fed into predominantly Black high schools. Boundaries, it seemed, had changed. "And I'm going to tell you that some of this is very racially driven," said Umphries-Lucas. "I honestly believe that."

Patricia Ferguson of the county NAACP made a similar observation. Ferguson found school trajectory shifted as the race of different schools shifted. Several people believed that New Town had been anticipated to be predominantly white and was districted with nearby white schools. But as New Town proved to quickly become an African American suburb, residents said students started ending up in predominantly Black high schools in the area.

Just as new boundaries could appear just in time to cut African Americans out, when there was no longer a difference between two areas, the boundaries dividing them could be merged. Thus Umphries-Lucas observed that "the trend that we're seeing now, blending, is the north end of Randallstown blending more with the south end of Owings Mills." As both became predominantly Black, students from those elementary schools could feed into the same middle and high schools.

African Americans came to expect boundaries to change. "They could always, the County Council could change . . . the boundaries and shift the residents," said Patricia Ferguson of school boundaries. More than that, "It seems like they sit down and draw lines when it's convenient." Other residents spoke of other boundaries as if expecting them to change, just as the areas had changed racially.

But African Americans were not just witnesses to boundary changes, but agents of change. True to the trend of using the tools of the suburbs to their own ends, residents used boundaries to try to establish a stronger presence for the African American parts of the county. The county NAACP, for instance, was involved in a long and ultimately successful effort to get "Black" districts for state elected representatives. Boundaries were redrawn so that the Black areas in the southwestern part of the county made up large enough parts of the districts that African Americans were elected as three state delegates and a state senator. The four were the only Baltimore County members of the Maryland Black Caucus.

Another way in which residents noticed how boundaries were being crossed gave them pause. Residents talked about city residents—conceived of as Black—using a friend's or relative's address in the county to get their children into a suburban county high school. Roxanne Umphries-Lucas evocatively called the students "boundary jumpers."

She explained, "So you see that moving into the Woodlawn and Randallstown area every day. And we definitely see it on the outskirt schools because there are a lot of boundary jumpers: children that live in the city, but have an address or a residence of some sort in the County. That is normally a type of Randallstown kind of, Woodlawn activity." Many people, like Leronia Josey, were sympathetic to the situation city parents found themselves in, even as they observed the boundary transgression. Josey explained, "So let's say there's somebody who's really concerned about their child's education in the city. And they would say, 'Listen, can I use your address?' And so that's what happens." People who moved from the city to the county (or used an address to allow their child to attend school in the county) were pursuing the same thing that white and Black county residents had. But African American residents were more likely to have a mixed assessment of such actions: they believed that such students were more likely to bring problems to suburban schools, but they recognized that the children's parents were seeking the same thing they sought for their kids. White county residents were less likely to acknowledge this commonality.

In other contexts residents rejected the meaningfulness of boundaries. When social ills happened from within the boundaries, residents sought to redefine boundaries to preserve their moral meaningfulness. One resident talked about two boys who were involved in a shooting. They were "from Baltimore," the way she saw it, but they actually did live in the county. They were "legally living with a family member . . . displaced from a violent home. So you know, the statistics [saying that the perpetrator was from the county not the city] were correct. What are you gonna do?" This resident knew that the offender lived in the county. Where they actually lived was something of a technicality to her because where they were *from*, the location she used to understand their violent behavior, was somewhere else.

Boundaries influenced not only schools but also churches. Just as synagogues had moved up Liberty Road from the city to the county as Jewish residents suburbanized, so African American churches had begun relocating to the suburbs or opening second churches there. This could be a boon for the church, but it caused conflict in the suburbs. Such moves could challenge residents' sense that the city was on one side of a boundary, the suburbs on another.

Some residents were concerned about traffic from large churches. For others, church expansions contradicted the divide between county and city. As an attorney, Leronia Josey for years had represented a church that was trying to get approvals to construct a building on an essentially rural parcel a few minutes off of Liberty Road. But neighbors objected. Neighborhood concerns didn't surprise her, but their tenacity did. "A fifteen-year battle against a church is a little bit hard for me to understand." During that time, she had dutifully represented the church, and so she focused on the details: traffic reports, environmental reports, neighbors' worries. As we discussed it, though, Josey reassessed. The objections, she concluded, were not all about traffic. "I think for some people, it was a race thing. And for some of the middle-class people who live in those homes that are almost a million dollars," she continued, "I think it was a class thing."

Leronia Josey reflected, "I think that some of those people who opposed this, and who were themselves African American, I think they identified Bethel as a city church, bringing in the drug addiction program, bringing in the Alcoholics Anonymous, bringing in unemployed people. I think it was, and I don't mean to disparage people's values." Josey was sympathetic. She could appreciate residents' objections: "That they had moved to the suburban area, wanting sort of all the suburban things." But she also wanted her client, the church, to be able to build a new location for their congregation.

The discussion about the roots of residents' opposition to the church brought Josey to a type of racial, intraracial, and class conflict that she had not put words to before. This was the first time that she had said that this issue was a "racial thing" and a "class thing." In the midst of the negotiations for the church, she couldn't consider the bigger picture, about why residents endlessly objected to a church. At this later juncture, she could look back and think more fully about the race and class motivations to the extended development process. "You can't call it, you can't name it. Do you know what I'm saying? And for years, until you just asked me, because I've never named it. Because if I named it, that would have interfered with my ability to represent my client. So I said, 'No, that's not it.'"

Once again, being in the suburbs was not enough to be suburban. An institution that had an association with the other side of the county-city boundary was suspect and at times unwanted. Other residents described similar conflicts, even between neighboring churches, in what one observer called a "Black on Black" issue. Such a church "might attract people from outside of the community" including "some people in the city." In each case, residents quietly marveled at the opposition, even as they understood where their resistant suburban neighbors were coming from.

Perhaps as a result of the capricious manner in which boundaries were employed, African Americans seemed in their everyday conversation and in their informal maps of their communities to give less credence to the unofficial neighborhood boundaries that whites found useful. In particular, whites spoke about and used a whole host of informal neighborhood names. Typically these were names that had been given by a developer: Courtleigh, Villanova, Kings Park, Granite, Chartley, Lochearn, Campfield Gardens. In part this may have been because whites were often the original owners and had purchased the homes when developers were handing out flyers with the development name or lived in the area as those original developments were being built. Since the homes in such an area were built at one time by one developer, different names could evoke very subtle distinctions in class, depending on the value or newness of the homes. In conversations with African Americans, such informal area names were rarely used. Residents might talk about the "Randallstown area" or "Liberty Road" or distinguish different areas by other qualities—"that's expensive"—but less often by name. Contrary to gentrifying urban areas, in which real estate brokers often anoint tiny areas with new trendy-sounding names, a process of consolidation in the suburbs subsumed micro-level names under more general categories.

James Crockett believed neighborhood names didn't matter to African Americans because they weren't looking for a *neighborhood*: "Baltimore consists of a number of neighborhoods. And these neighborhoods mean something to white people," he pointed out, listing prestigious old neighborhoods in Baltimore: "Roland Park . . . Gilford. Homeland. All in the same area. . . . The lines of demarcation say, this is Roland Park, this is Gilford, and you couldn't tell when you leave one neighborhood and come into another neighborhood. Okay? So they mean something to white people. Financially, socially, religiously, and everything." Crockett found his Black clients had a different approach. "But blacks look for housing. So, when you're going out Liberty Road . . . you enter Baltimore County. Further up Liberty Road, that's called Lochearn. And as you go further up, it's called Randallstown. Because these areas' designations were there. But to Blacks, it doesn't make a difference. . . . You see that wasn't called Randallstown. . . . It might be Old Court, or something. So the designations didn't mean anything to Blacks but it meant something to whites."

Crockett concluded that Blacks were looking for housing. But why wouldn't they want the prestige and symbolism—financially, socially, religiously—that neighborhood names gave white people? In my interviews, it was not clear that neighborhoods provided African Americans living in the suburbs with a sense of status. This is unexpected, and it is unclear how broadly this is the case. As Lawrence Jackson shows in his memoir of being a teenager in Baltimore, young people made distinctions between neighborhoods in endless turf battles and also saw peers from the county as fundamentally different from those from the city.[22] But for adult suburban homeowners, the micro neighborhoods faded in significance. From Crockett's suggestion, it may be that neighborhoods didn't project status, but individual houses did. Also, since most developments in these suburbs had not been built with brick signs at the entrance announcing the name of the community, the name was known only as long as original residents who had seen it on promotional materials used it in conversation enough to convey it to newcomers. The disappearance of those unofficial names may therefore point to a break in communication between the earlier white residents and the newer African American ones. If the two groups had few interactions, then this small bit of local culture would disappear with the relocation of white residents. Boundaries that had conveyed subtle class meanings no longer existed.

Negrophobia and the Loss of the Right to the City

Although suburbs were designed by whites with the intention, among other things, of keeping Blacks out, whites too lost elements of the right to the city. This loss, it could be argued, was an exclusion of their own making.

What was the nature of whites' aversion to living with African Americans? Certainly the term "racism" could define a wide range of the activities already detailed in the history of suburban exclusion, segregation, and discrimination. But the term is not all-encompassing: fleeing blocks just because Blacks had moved in seems different than hostility and provides unclear benefits for the people who sold and ran. Whites often showed anxiety at the prospect that their children would mingle with African Americans in any way. In Baltimore County a battle raged for years to integrate a small, local amusement park named Gwynn Oak Park, just off Liberty Road. Older African Americans often referenced that prolonged struggle.[23] (The park was eventually convinced to allow African Americans to visit in 1963 but was destroyed by Hurricane Agnes only ten years later.)

In seeking to understand white attitudes in my research, I often found it useful to conceive of their views as *Negrophobia*. The term borrows explicitly on the formulation of homophobia from the gay rights movement. Given that the root "phobia" means fear, homophobia was always a brilliant tactical redefinition by gay rights groups: people who were opposed to gays and lesbians, or to lesbian, gay, bisexual, and transgender equality, didn't *hate* gays but were *afraid* of them. Fear can still be a dangerous emotion, but it changed the footing of the discussion from the antipathy the homophobes directed at gay people to the anxiety, insecurity, and fear they felt triggered in themselves by the visibility of LGBTQIA people and organizations. Likewise, Negrophobia focuses not on hatred but on fear. Negrophobia describes non-Blacks' discomfort, anxiety, and fear around Blacks at the micro level. That fear can be transmogrified into hatred at the macro level, as when politicians exploit white fear and anxiety into campaigns and policies of real hostility, violence, and damage to whole Black communities.

The term "Negrophobia" has occasionally surfaced in discussion of white/Black interactions. The most thorough exploration of the concept comes in an over-the-top novel called *Negrophobia: An Urban Parable*, by Darius James.[24] James does less to define and specify Negrophobia than to present it in its most feverish, hallucinatory manifestations, painting grotesqueries of a white teen's distorted imaginations of a world of stereotypical Black figures. One point James's book makes clearly is that Negrophobia has an implicitly physical component to it, not a fear of Blacks abstractly but a fear almost always connected in some way to a fear of Black bodies physically. It is perhaps for this reason that

Negrophobia starts at the micro level, then aggregates further up the social food chain.

Previously, even public parks, streets, and retail establishments were "white spaces." In Baltimore, African Americans were not allowed in department stores. They were not served in restaurants. Amusement parks and other vacation destinations were segregated. Arrest under vague "vagrancy laws" (ruled unconstitutionally selective in 1972) showed Black men and others the public spaces, parks, and street corners they were not allowed to inhabit and the boundaries of the segregated public spaces to which they were effectively confined.

With the Great Migration and the civil rights movement, by the mid-twentieth century African Americans were occupying public spaces that they had not before. Whites interpreted this change as a breakdown in the social ordering of public space and retreated.

Negrophobia contributed to the retreat by whites from public space in the mid-twentieth century. It also played a role in the construction of a new physical environment in the suburbs that lacked public space. If public space was now "disorganized," the solution was to have no public space. Whites were more comfortable in private than in public spaces—better the backyard, shopping mall, and movie theater than the front stoop, main street, or performance in a public park.

This approach and the effective elimination of public space meant not only that Blacks were further cut off from whites and vice versa, but that anyone living in the suburban landscape missed out on many of the functions of public spaces: People meet others they know. They come to have some understanding of others they don't know. They develop a collective identity and strengthen networks through informal meetings. They have a means to communicate political views to others through posters, flyers, protests, and speeches. A bumper sticker is a meager substitute for public space.

Negrophobia can certainly describe some of the motivation for whites moving out of, or not moving into, a racially transitioning neighborhood. Negrophobia can also account for an array of micro-level interactions between whites and Blacks that otherwise just seem weird. One is the uncertainty whites sometimes exhibit in otherwise banal social interactions, when they involve African Americans. There is, for instance, the "Zelig" phenomenon, in which whites sometimes take on Black speech, or even have trouble speaking, when conversing with African Americans.[25] White clerks or customers sometimes have trouble carrying out everyday transactions: when buying something or making change at the cash register, Americans tend to put coins in each other's hands, the fingertips of the person giving the change barely touching the palm of the receiver. In Baltimore County I have occasionally witnessed a white person stumble in this exchange with an African American, suddenly unable to figure out how to complete this normally rote action. The problem is in the touching and physical intimacy with Black skin, which they somewhat unconsciously cannot process as a normal part of a normal interaction. The white person will hesitate, change in hand, and then sometimes put the money on the counter. Likewise, in public space whites sometimes have greater difficulty navigating through close quarters around Black bodies than around white bodies.

In a more stark example, realtor Mal Sherman remembered meeting fellow realtor James Crockett for lunch at a diner in Baltimore, sometime before 1966. As Sherman recalled it, the person behind the lunch counter refused to serve Crockett. Sherman said he "put up a kick" until Crockett was served. But as they left, the employee threw Crockett's dishes and silverware into the trash rather than wash them and serve another customer with plates that had been used by a Black man. It is perfectly reasonable to describe his actions as racist, which they certainly were, and his emotion as hatred or hostility. But the server's actions can also be described as Negrophobia—a fear of Blackness, of Black skin, of Black bodies.

The effects of Negrophobia are seen throughout this book. But in terms of the right to the city, Negrophobia has unintended consequences for whites. For Lefebvre, the city represents the center, and one component of the right to the city is access to the geographical, social, political and economic center. That is, the right to the city is the right to participate in the decision making that happens at the heart of power. While suburbanizing whites were granted privileges upon their arrival in the suburban periphery, their Negrophobia, their unwillingness to enter the center that was now associated with African Americans, meant that they were willing to marginalize themselves from the political and social interaction that requires a central, public location.

In this way, while it is clear that whites' Negrophobia shaped the suburbs that African Americans soon made their own, shaping a landscape of racial exclusion and inequality, Negrophobia exhibited an influence over the experiences and lives of whites as well. Wittingly and not, in different degrees and measures, Negrophobia frustrated the right to the city for Blacks and for whites.

Suburban Exclusion of the Right to the City

Segregation is not simply a manifestation of "past discrimination" and discriminatory real estate practices that keep African Americans out of white areas. African Americans are denied the right to the city in that they have not secured the freedom to inhabit any part of the suburbs or the freedom to move, without harassment, from any one part to another. Given adversarial relations with the police, even suburban professionals do not believe they can rely on the state to properly defend their interests during disagreements with white neighbors, and police profiling while they patrol highways and side streets alike makes clear that even mundane travel is fraught with risk.

There are other ways the right to the city is impaired in the suburbs. The design of space influences the possibilities of social interactions. A thousand-year-old village with pedestrian streets too small for cars to pass exhibits a kind of social interaction that is not possible when the main commercial street in a suburb is a six-lane road. Social interactions require certain types of social relations, of course, but they are facilitated by certain types of spatial organization.

In these ways, an African American community demonstrates that the right to the city is abrogated not only by the latest depredations of neoliberalism but by a set of much older strictures rooted in US racial inequality.

In the United States, suburbs were built to a significant degree as manifestations of white flight from the cities as African Americans moved in during the Great Migration and overturned Jim Crow at the height of civil rights activism. Elsewhere I have described the "suburban strategy" of separating privilege from disadvantage with distance. In addition to spatial segregation, Negrophobia drove the creation of suburbs characterized by a lack of public space.[26] There were rarely large parks, and they were not heavily used. Streets were places for cars to travel, not for people to see each other and interact. Town squares disappeared from these new towns, and even the commercial main street soon disappeared, replaced by a privately owned mall that was built exclusively by for-profit interests committed to maximizing sales revenue, not developing a multipurpose public space. Although other things factored into the disappearance of public space, such as calculations by the developers of these new suburbs that building a "public square" provided an inadequate return on their investment, race played a role. To whites, public spaces in the city had become associated with a social world that was no longer racially ordered in a dependable, rigid hierarchy. Instead, the presence of people of color in public spaces marked, to whites, a breakdown in the order they had been raised to recognize. When suburbs were built, they were built without such public spaces.

As African Americans made their claim on the suburbs, then, they inherited a space that had been dramatically denuded of public spaces and organized in forms to keep them out. The irony is that once African Americans were in the suburbs, a suburban form that reacted against a Black presence was obsolete, constructed of obstacles designed to keep out the very people who were now there. Yet the peculiarly concrete nature of space as an institution of social reproduction means that it remains in place after the social function that gave it rise has faded. While African Americans can (and sometimes do) use the spatial and political organization of the suburbs to keep poorer people out, it continues to deny inhabitants the right to the city.

In fact, the form and social organization of the suburbs further disenfranchise people of any race of the right to the city. The kind of public space Lefebvre presumed would allow for occupation of the center city is lacking. Access to the center is missing. The center still represents a significant concentration of power. The community along Randallstown has worked hard to organize politically, develop African American districts for state elected office, and develop organizations, like the county chapter of the NAACP, socially involved churches, business improvement associations, and school organizations, that provide the kind of local political power that suburbs preserve for the middle class. In this respect they have been largely successful, notwithstanding the ongoing political difficulties of securing adequate resources for African

American communities. But after this degree of political organization, the right to the city is still elusive. People are still kept at the margins. African American suburbanites experience a double denial of the right to the city, on account of their race and on account of their physical location in the suburbs.

6

Foreclosure

Punctuated Equilibrium

Contrary to the old blockbusting model, racial transition in Randallstown since 1970 has been the outcome of two competing forces—civil rights activism and neoliberalism. The outcome of these two forces is not the precipitous decline expected in "blockbusting" but a process of long periods of relative stability interrupted by acute moments of crisis. Borrowing from Stephen Jay Gould and Niles Eldredge, I call this process of stability and crisis "punctuated equilibrium." Under punctuated equilibrium, African American middle-class suburbs experience decades of stability—as measured, for instance, by household income and home values. However, the underlying contradictions between the collective demands of civil rights and the individualized prescriptions of neoliberalism can erupt in periodic crises that disrupt that equilibrium. The housing collapse that began around 2008 is an example of one such crisis.

This chapter tells the story of punctuated equilibrium. I use forty years of census data to compare the development of three different suburban communities—one Black, one white, and one mixed.[1] This comparative, longitudinal study demonstrates how much white and Black neighborhoods diverge or remain the same over several decades. The data also demonstrate subtle threats that challenge neighborhood stability, particularly in African American communities. Then I look at how an acute crisis—the nationwide wave of foreclosures—threatened an African American community more dramatically than predominantly white suburbs. Interviews with foreclosure prevention specialists demonstrate the efforts of people to mitigate these threats and maintain neighborhood stability. Those efforts, however, have been in opposition to systemic neoliberal threats to neighborhoods' stability. It is hard to know what the long-term effects of the bursting of that bubble will be on African American communities. But this analysis indicates that neo-liberalism's individual-level approaches are ill suited to resolving African Americans' ongoing quest for quality housing and stable communities. Punctuated equilibrium provides a more accurate understanding of how residents' efforts and structural racial and economic pressures can produce long periods of stability *and* measurable inequality. In the suburbs, we can recognize that racial inequality is still real without predicting that everything will immediately come crashing down.

Racial Divergence: Randallstown, Reisterstown, Bel Air

I compare three neighboring parts of Baltimore County. Moving west to east across the county, the first is the Liberty Road corridor (including Randallstown and some surrounding census tracts, all of which became predominantly African American). The second is the Reisterstown Road corridor (which transitioned from almost all white to 30 percent African American). Third is the Belair Road corridor (which remained overwhelmingly white).[2] Through this comparison I gain an understanding of how housing price appreciation affected African American and white suburban communities differently. I analyzed the three areas in terms of household median property values and median household income. While they were all predominantly white in the 1950s, their racial compositions have diverged significantly since the 1970s, so comparisons among the three highlight the impact of changes in the racial composition on suburban communities. Research on these three areas demonstrates considerable differences between recent events and the traditional model of racial transition that expected precipitous decline.

It made sense to compare the three areas, which had so much in common except their later racial composition.

Suburbanization occurred at a relatively even pace across the county, so the three areas grew up at around the same time, moving up along commercial routes that radiated out from Baltimore City. This radial pattern of development resulted in communities that were very similar in terms of median property values and median household income (as well as in age and style of housing stock, geographical size, distance from the city, retail amenities, and other features) but that varied in racial composition after the 1970s.

In 2010 the three communities were very similar in outward appearances: behind the main four-lane road with strip malls and supermarkets were postwar suburban houses, some townhouses, and garden apartments. The housing was of similar styles, often by the same builders. Virtually all the homes had been built between 1950 and 2010, with similar styles representing each decade in each of the three communities. County planners had designated two zones for more intensive commercial and residential development. One was near Belair Road, and one was fitted between Liberty and Reisterstown roads. James Rouse's development company had built shopping malls in each of the areas of intensive commercial development. The two malls opened in the 1980s, so there was a major regional mall within five or ten minutes of each of the three main streets. Eventually those malls were surrounded by more big-box stores, chain restaurants, office buildings, and other businesses, providing both an economic engine for the three areas and a shopping destination.

I delineated the three areas using a combination of census and county-level boundaries. In Baltimore County, suburban communities typically cluster around commercial roads that radiate out from the center city. Suburbanization in Baltimore County has a technical outer boundary called the Urban-Rural Demarcation Line, beyond which public water and sewer pipes are generally not provided, preventing construction of large-scale exurban housing developments and restricting sprawl.[3] I defined the three corridors to be studied by including all the census tracts adjacent to each of the three commercial streets, from the city line out to the Urban-Rural Demarcation Line.

In 1970 Liberty Road was the largest of the three study areas, with a population of about 42,000, reflecting a slightly earlier and more rapid suburbanization along the Liberty Road corridor, followed by Reisterstown Road, with a population of about 34,000, and Belair Road, 23,000. By 2010, the three suburban areas were closer in population, with 59,000 in Liberty Road, 58,000 in Reisterstown Road, and 54,000 in Belair Road.

In 1970 Baltimore County, like the three study areas, was predominantly white. The entire county was only 3.1 percent African American. Over the next forty years, from 1970 to 2010, however, the three areas diverged, most notably by race rather than by median property values

TABLE 6.1. Percentage of African American residents. These three suburban areas were predominantly white in 1970. Over the next forty years, Randallstown became 83 percent African American. The Reisterstown Road corridor represented a middle case, becoming 30 percent African American. Belair Road remained almost all white.

	1970	1980	1990	2000	2005–2010 ACS
Belair Road	1.10%	1%	3%	6%	13%
Liberty Road / Randallstown	5.46%	37%	60%	78%	83%
Reisterstown Road	3.79%	10%	13%	21%	30%

Source: National Historical Geographic Information System.

or median household incomes. According to the 2006–2010 American Community Survey (ACS), Belair Road had changed the least in terms of the proportion of African Americans: only 13 percent of its residents were Black in 2010 (up from 1.10 percent in 1970). Liberty Road had become 83 percent African American by that year (up from 5.46 percent in 1970). Nearby Reisterstown Road was in the middle, at 30 percent African American in 2010 (up from 3.79 percent in 1970). Liberty Road's racial transition had begun soon after 1970 but had progressed slowly. The number of African Americans in the Reisterstown Road area increased after Liberty Road's transition had started and experienced a similarly gradual increase.

Because the three areas are similar in terms of median property values and median household income but dissimilar in terms of racial composition, we can examine the difference that race makes for these three suburban study communities and identify how much neoliberalism's detrimental effects are disproportionately borne by African Americans. In an earlier chapter we saw how neighborhood activists like Ella White Campbell and Emily Wolfson worked to maintain the middle-class character of their neighborhoods. Descriptive analyses of ACS 2006–2010 data and examination of the foreclosure crisis indicate the limits of such strategies.

Race and Property Values

Homeownership is one of the primary strategies middle-class Americans use to accumulate wealth. It is also a primary strategy of class reproduction, when older parents give or bequeath some of that equity to their children, who often use it for down payments on homes of their own. Thus the ability of African Americans to securely join the ranks of the middle class depends to a significant degree on their ability to use this strategy to build equity and wealth. The record over two decades in this suburban county suggests that homeownership does build wealth for middle-class African Americans but that they are penalized for their race. Homeownership is a useful strategy for African Americans to consider, even while the outcomes demonstrate that homeownership is not as beneficial to Blacks as to whites. Home values have remained close to those in white parts of the county, but the difference that the race of a neighborhood makes is clear—and crucial.

Figure 6.1 shows the degree of similarity in the shifts in median property values in the three study communities from 1970 to 2010 (all values provided in 2010 dollars).[4] From a common starting point around $20,000 in 1970 (equivalent to $100,000–$117,000 in 2010 dollars), median property values increased and decreased roughly in tandem through the inflationary 1970s, the bearish 1990s, and the bullish 2000s. Rising median home values reflect both the appreciation of existing homes and the construction of more expensive new homes in each area. Despite the increase in its African American racial proportion, the first story the graph tells is that property values in Liberty Road roughly kept pace with the other two study communities.

When considering nominal dollars, homeowners in all three areas probably would have been largely pleased. Because of inflation, home values in nominal dollars (not shown in Figure 6.1) jumped in all three areas from $20,000 in 1970 to $50,000 in 1980, $100,000 in 1990, $120,000 in 2000, and $250,000 around 2010. Values were going up, and everyone was a winner.

However, on closer inspection important differences emerge, particularly when accounting for inflation by using the constant dollar values. First of all, Liberty Road did much less well relative to other areas, particularly all-white Belair. Liberty Road began with homes valued 14 percent higher than Belair's, but finished the forty-year period with homes worth almost 9 percent *less* than Belair.

The 2010 data still reflect some of the overvaluation from the housing bubble, and for that reason those elevated values are ephemeral and

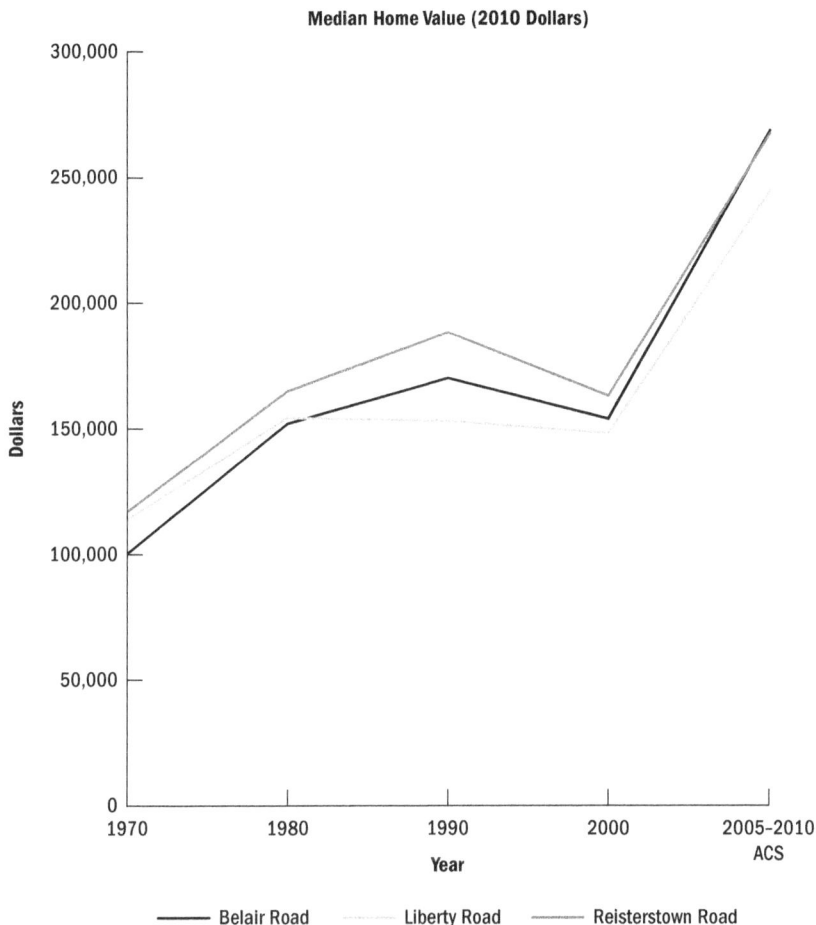

Median Home Value (2010 Dollars)

Figure 6.1. Median property values of single-family owner-occupied homes in Liberty Road, Belair Road, and Reisterstown Road, 1970 to 2010 (in 2010 dollars). Randallstown was not characterized by the sharp decline in property values associated with urban blockbusting. From 1980 to 2000, the whitest area appreciated 1 percent, while Randallstown's values fell 4 percent. The small percentages amounted to tens of thousands of dollars.

Source: Longitudinal Tract Data Base, Spatial Structures in the Social Sciences, Brown University.

not entirely reliable. Consider therefore home appreciation from 1970 to 2000. Over thirty years, residents in Randallstown saw their homes appreciate 30 percent.

Thus homes in Randallstown appreciated by 1 percent per year (even compounding annually). This may be surprising because Americans are told to expect homes to appreciate more than this. But outside of more volatile metropolitan areas, studies have shown homes to be investments that grow very modestly. (One notable longitudinal study in the Netherlands found that over four hundred years home values in one middle-class area had essentially stayed flat, just keeping pace with inflation. Homes are often safe investments that appreciate little if at all in aggregate.)[5] To the extent that homes create wealth for the middle class, they do so by accumulating some percentage of homeowners' mortgage payments and by keeping pace with inflation. They are a constant-dollar, forced savings plan more than an investment that will add wealth through real appreciation (as investors hope stocks will) or revenue generation (as rental properties do). That minimal appreciation is probably a good thing overall, for while individual homeowners would like their homes to increase in value, if the cost of the average house increased by 5 percent per year in real dollars, housing would get more expensive for subsequent generations and eventually be unaffordable to almost everyone.

Whatever the benefits of stable home prices to society at large, rising prices benefit owners. While homes along the Liberty Road corridor appreciated 30 percent in three decades, homes in transitioning Reisterstown appreciated by 39 percent, and the white Belair corridor saw prices go up a particularly strong 53 percent. (Incidentally, Belair's astronomical rise came from an annualized increase of just 1.43 percent, testifying to the power of small growth over long periods of time, as emphasized by economist Thomas Piketty.)[6]

If we consider home values in a slightly narrower period—from 1980 until the very beginning of the bubble inflation—Liberty Road's median property values fell. From 1980 to 2000 median home values along Liberty Road dropped from $154,320 to $148,051, a 4 percent drop, while the other two, whiter areas saw price changes of less than 1 percent in any direction. Liberty Road, which had become predominantly African American by 1990, lost ground, slipping from a middle spot in 1970 to the lowest median property value of the three study communities in 1990, where it has remained since.

These statistics tell two stories. First, it is true that for many (though not all) residents in the predominantly Black Liberty Road area, buying a home created wealth—as much as 30 percent over the long term. But in other time periods homes did not appreciate. Particularly considered in terms of the effect on intergenerational transfers of wealth, the gap in growth rates between white and Black areas would continue to significantly impair African American homeowners' wealth acquisition strategies. This lower rate of appreciation adds to other obstacles that frustrate African American efforts to invest in homes or build economic stability for their families. Coupled with challenges African American home buyers systematically face such as higher cost loans and lower down payments, the success of home buying as a strategy for wealth acquisition varies considerably depending on the race of the buyers. That homes in Black neighborhoods are leakier vessels for investment denies the African American middle class much-needed capital. The result is a challenge for the promise of equality and prosperity: the primary means of wealth accumulation used by the US middle class is significantly less effective for middle-class Blacks than for middle-class whites.

There is apparently more to the story, however, than that home buyers in African American neighborhoods experience slower appreciation (or none at all). In fact, there is suggestive evidence here that rapid appreciation goes along with at least some presence of African Americans.

Randallstown's home values peaked in the decade when the area was between 6 and 37 percent African American and declined in relative (and often absolute) terms since then. The case of Reisterstown Road, between Black Liberty Road and white Belair Road both geographically and in racial composition, is also instructive. Reisterstown's values, relative to the other areas, peaked in 1990 when it had grown to 13 percent African American. But white Belair Road was closing the gap, and by 2010 the median home value in Belair was slightly higher than that in Reisterstown, making it the highest priced of the three areas in the county. In 2010 Belair was 13 percent African American.

There is an intriguing observation to be made about home values and race in all three areas. From these three cases, being all white is not optimal for an area's home values. In fact, all three areas studied here saw their highest home values when they were about 13 percent African American. The United States was roughly 13 percent African American during this whole period. In the decade when each of these three communities' racial composition reflected the national averaged, their home values were about 10 percent higher than the other areas. Whether African Americans increase home values or appreciating real estate investments attract African American buyers, these three cases suggest that strict segregation is not the most profitable strategy to pursue.

Despite that rise, once African Americans came to make up 30 percent of local residents, the appreciation of home prices cooled. At 30 percent Black, both Liberty Road and Reisterstown began losing ground to whiter areas.

The intent of this account of home values is not to valorize rising home prices as an unalloyed good. A slower run-up during the housing bubble could have led to a less catastrophic decline.

Housing prices are related to local government budgets and school equity: the inequality in schools' budgets comes substantially from the differing amounts rich and poor local governments can contribute to their school systems. A municipality with high property values has more money to spend on education than a less wealthy government, so that racially inequitable home values and local school funding are key means by which wealthier, whiter districts have better-funded schools and segregated communities can deprive people of color of fair funding.[7] This happened not to be the case for Liberty Road because schools from Black Randallstown to white Belair were all part of the same Baltimore County school system, so any neighborhood-level differences in tax receipts did not influence funding, which was collected across a county of 832,000 people (ten times the size of Randallstown) and distributed at the countywide level. Elsewhere, however, lower property values can be tied to issues such as school funding inequity.

Irrespective of whether rising real estate values have more benefits than disadvantages, they are, in these three cases, tied to the racial composition of the areas. Consistent with the first characteristic of punctuated equilibrium, home values in the African American suburbs along Liberty Road (and later along Reisterstown Road) did not decline in value but continued to appreciate over several decades. However, race still mattered, as African Americans were highly likely to live in increasingly African American neighborhoods. After an initial boost to areas with modest numbers of African Americans, home values in increasingly Black neighborhoods had trouble keeping up with increases in whiter sections of the same suburban county.

Median Household Incomes

The racial transition of a neighborhood from primarily white to African American is often associated with declining median household incomes.[8] In her nuanced study of West Philadelphia, Woldoff found that incomes often declined not because of the arrival of the first generation of African American "pioneers" but because of the subsequent second generation, who are less financially secure and have greater difficulty paying for their homes.[9]

Comparing inflation-adjusted median household incomes by race within the three study communities, African Americans moving to Liberty Road were anything but poor. Table 6.2 illustrates that African Americans in Liberty Road had the highest median household incomes of any group in 1980 and 1990.

Consistent with Woldoff's hypothesis of a "second wave," however, median household incomes of African Americans in Liberty Road fell after 1990. By 2010 the median had decline 12 percent compared to 1990, although the incomes of African Americans in Liberty Road did not fall nearly as much as the incomes of white residents in this community, which declined by 17 percent. The white decrease may be attributed in part to the increasing proportion of retirees in the community since new (younger and working) white home seekers were not moving into the Liberty Road area.

In the same period, median household incomes in Reisterstown Road, the study community that had an African American population of 10 percent in 1980, 21 percent in 2000, and 30 percent in 2010, were increasing for both whites and African Americans from 1980 to 2000. However, this growth was reversed in 2010, when the median household income for whites was $61,907, below the level in 1980 ($63,854), and the median household income for African Americans was $56,040, slightly below 2000.

TABLE 6.2. Median household incomes in Liberty Road, Belair Road, and Reisterstown Road, 1970 to 2010 (inflation adjusted). Median income fell in predominantly Black Randallstown—for whites and Blacks. Likewise, median income was high in overwhelmingly white Belair, for whites and Blacks alike. Reisterstown, whose African American population was smaller than Randallstown's but was growing, experienced greater fluctuations.

	1970	1980	1990	2000	2010
Liberty Road-All	71,194	60,388	64,904	62,123	60,098
Liberty Road-White		66,897	62,332	55,894	55,526
Liberty Road-Black		67,489	68,639	63,787	60,367
Reisterstown-All	62,642	52,650	63,941	64,221	59,149
Reisterstown-White		63,854	67,683	68,629	61,907
Reisterstown-Black		42,400	50,586	56,504	56,040
Bel Air-All	63,583	60,689	66,610	65,724	68,086
Bel Air-White		66,823	67,960	66,759	66,793
Bel Air-Black		43,643	67,500	55,600	70,305

Source: Longitudinal Tract Data Base, Spatial Structures in the Social Sciences, Brown University, 2012.

Whites and Blacks fared differently in the three areas. Along Liberty Road, African Americans began in 1980 with similar incomes to whites and afterward always had median incomes that were higher than those of their white neighbors. Along Reisterstown Road, in contrast, whites' incomes were always considerably higher than nearby Blacks' median incomes. White Reisterstown residents earned about the same as Black Liberty Road residents. The Belair case is difficult to examine by race since for decades there were so few African Americans in the area that incomes could fluctuate wildly with changes in the incomes of a small number of residents. (In 1980, for instance, there were only 500 African Americans in a community of 35,000 people.) Recently, as the Black population along the Belair Road Corridor has grown to 7,000 people out of 55,000 total residents, African American median incomes in mostly white Belair have actually been higher than white median incomes. It is too early to tell whether this is part of a longer trend or another example of the rapidly fluctuating data from Belair Road.

Overall, however, the data are not strongly positive. In each of the three areas African Americans had either high incomes or rising incomes, but not both. African Americans along mostly Black Liberty Road were roughly on par with white earners, in a group at the top of the income distribution. But their incomes fell considerably from 1990 to 2000. In Reisterstown African American median incomes shot up by a third from 1980 to 2000 and have not declined. But those incomes remained 9 percent lower than the median incomes of whites in the area. Until recently the Black population along Belair Road has been too small to show a consistent pattern, exhibiting stark rises and falls. At present African American median incomes exceed white incomes in Belair, though that may or may not be a long-term trend.

Changes in median incomes are certainly the result of many factors, including changes in the age distribution of an area's population and changes in the percentages of retirees, young workers, and midcareer workers. Other factors at play reflect the role of neoliberalism and racial discrimination: long-term stagnant or declining incomes and increased unemployment and underemployment rates for African Americans, and a second generation of in-movers with lower incomes than initial Black "pioneers." The trend, however, is that while African Americans in each of the areas generally did not experience collective reversals of fortune—such as plummeting wages—African Americans, whether in suburbs that are largely Black, somewhat Black, or largely white—are unlikely to be able to make their income both grow *and* achieve parity with their white neighbors. Most often the Black community either sees their incomes grow but still lag behind whites, only occasionally surpassing them, or sees their fortunes slowly drift downward in tandem with the white community. In terms of incomes, punctuated equilibrium means that African Americans can and do move toward middle-class status. But in most times and places studied here, it is difficult to achieve and maintain that status, as wages of one's Black neighbors do not keep up over the decades or whites remain firmly situated in a higher income bracket.

Foreclosure Mitigation

The longtime evolution of home values and median incomes in Baltimore County was interrupted there, as elsewhere around the country,

Baltimore, Maryland, Metropolitan Area House Prices

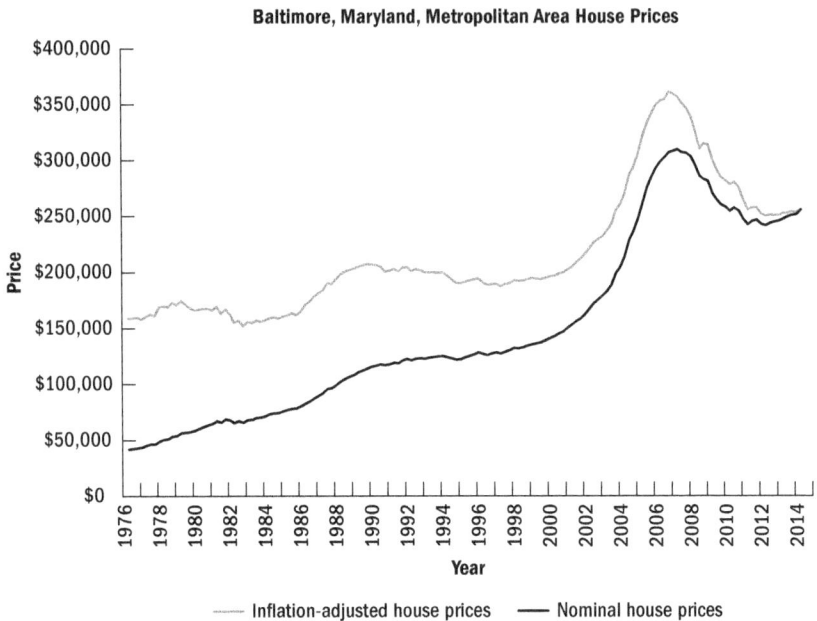

Figure 6.2. The housing bubble in the Baltimore metro area involved a long run-up and a deflation to historical levels that, as late as 2014, may not have been complete.
Source: Data courtesy of http://www.jparsons.net/housingbubble/baltimore.html.

by the bursting of the housing bubble, beginning in 2007. Home values had shot up in the previous ten years, both in Baltimore and elsewhere, as loans were readily made available and buyers were told they could afford ever more expensive homes. Home loans were being repackaged and resold as investments to large speculators, leading to a frenzy to create as many new mortgages as possible—even when the loans were made with payments that the borrowers would have great difficulty making. As the housing bubble progressed, increasing numbers of subprime loans—with high interest rates, ballooning payments, and little documentation of borrowers' financial stability—were made, particularly in African American neighborhoods. As investors finally became wary of buying investments with poor prospects of repayment, loans dried up, home values fell, homeowners could not make payments, and lenders began retaking, or foreclosing, the houses their loans had helped buy (see Figure 6.2).

The foreclosure crisis itself was a dramatic example of the effect of neoliberalism on a community like Randallstown. Several of neoliberalism's defining features laid the groundwork for the speculative mortgage bubble that crashed and initiated the 2007 downturn that is sometimes called the Great Recession. For instance, mortgage market speculation required deregulation of the mortgage industry, overreliance on market mechanisms, and expanded financialization of an array of activities. Finally, as Saegert, Fields, and Libman astutely point out, neoliberalism normalized citizens putting themselves at greater financial risk to manage their finances.[10] Once the crisis began, a typically neoliberal response exacerbated matter. The federal government provided $700 billion to bail out financial institutions that had made reckless investments in the secondary mortgage market. But while that bailout included provisions to allow the money to be used in foreclosure prevention, the US Treasury declined to do so, and financial industry bailouts dwarfed money eventually provided to aid homeowners. The destruction was considerable, and little was done to mitigate the damage wrought by big banks.

Decennial census data are measured too rarely to perfectly capture the run-up in home values during the bubble. But they offer a sense of the scale. Home values along Liberty, Reisterstown, and Belair roads had increased at least 65 to 75 percent, and probably more at the very height of the bubble. Data for the Baltimore metro area showed that since the first quarter of 2007 median home prices had dropped by 30 percent.[11] Data as late as 2012 showed no real consistent sign that prices had stopped dropping.

Home prices dropped nationwide as the bubble burst, bringing with them a wave of foreclosures as homeowners, who had bought homes at inflated prices, could not make payments and began being foreclosed on by banks. The foreclosure crisis was a nationwide problem, but it did not affect all areas equally. Instead, foreclosures in many cities were heavily concentrated in Black, or Black and Latino, neighborhoods.

Baltimore and Baltimore County were no exceptions. Figure 6.3a–b shows the correlation starkly: the map on the left indicates where middle-income African American households live in Baltimore County and Baltimore City.[12] The map on the right shows where high-cost loans were concentrated early in the foreclosure crisis.[13] (As the crisis broke, there were no local-level foreclosure data. The US Department of

Middle Class African American Households
in Baltimore City and County

Estimated High-Cost Loan Rates
in Baltimore City and County

Legend

1 Dot = 5 African American
households earning an income
equal to or above $75,000

Source: U.S. Census 2000

Legend

Baltimore

Estimated High-Cost Loan Rate

0 - 16.00%
16.01 - 32.00%
32.01 - 48.00%
48.01 - 64.00%
64.01 - 80.00%

Source: HUD, U.S. Census 2000

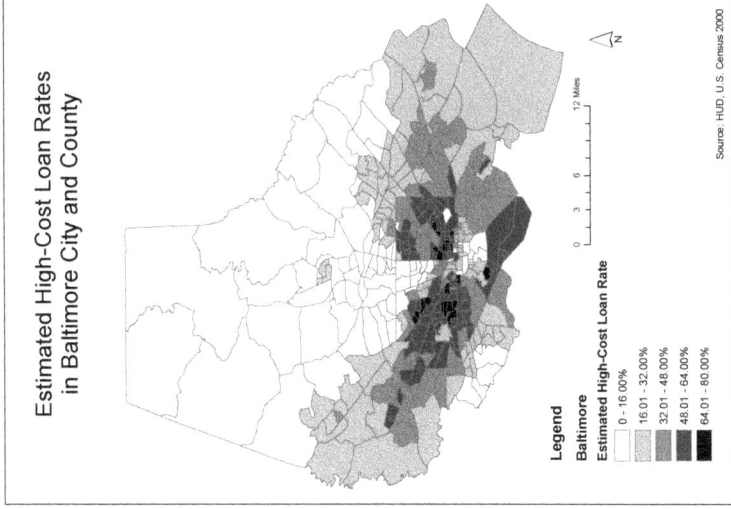

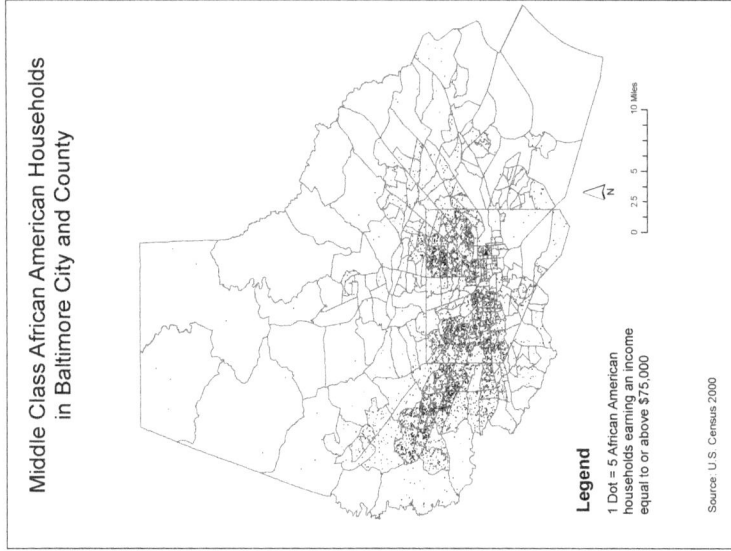

Figure 6.3a–b. Race and subprime mortgages correlate closely.
Source: Maps by Tess Brustein.

Housing and Urban Development had only state-level foreclosure data. To estimate local foreclosure rates, they compiled a list of indicators at the level of the census tract, including vacancy rates and how many people were behind on their mortgages. The high-cost loan data shown on the map correlated with the estimated foreclosure rate but had the benefit of being a concrete measure rather than an estimate.) The two maps seem to be mapping almost the same data—where there are African Americans there are high-cost loans and high risks of foreclosure, and vice versa. The pattern held for both the city and the suburban county surrounding it. The only exception is in the very southeastern corner of Baltimore County, the deindustrialized white working-class enclave that was home to few African Americans in the middle-income range but a noticeable number of foreclosures.

The foreclosure crisis quickly threatened to cause serious damage to African American neighborhoods. Disclosures uprooted families, created vacancies and unmaintained buildings, reduced home values, and destroyed home equity for families that remained. Displacement by foreclosure forced children to change schools, imperiling their academic progress, and large numbers of vacant, bank-owned buildings became magnets for vandalism, crime, and other local-level problems. As one community activist explained, foreclosure was a threat to anyone who might lose their home. But beyond that, "foreclosure can destroy a neighborhood like *that*. Something as simple as, you know, even the president of a community association, if they're in foreclosure, that community association could actually go away, thus a lot of strength and a lot of leadership are gone."

Strategies were needed to address the foreclosure crisis that confronted Baltimore County and the nation. In the Baltimore metro area as in the rest of the country, foreclosure was higher in African American neighborhoods than in white areas. Lenders made more high-cost or subprime loans in Black neighborhoods.[14] My interviews with counselors and directors at nonprofit foreclosure counseling organizations illustrated how foreclosure had become a serious problem in African American communities like Randallstown, how the problem was and was not framed in neoliberal terms, and what African American communities were doing to address the crisis.

I visited and interviewed directors or counselors at three agencies. The first, We Are Family, was a community service nonprofit founded by Union Bethel AME Church, the oldest African American church in Randallstown. The second was the Maryland Housing Counselor Network office in Baltimore County. The third was the seventy-year-old nonprofit Citizens Planning and Housing Association (CPHA).

During the foreclosure crisis the groups scrambled to provide much-needed services in different ways. We Are Family added foreclosure counseling to its menu of services. Former mortgage lenders became foreclosure counselors. And venerable community groups that had worked on neighborhood preservation did increasing amounts of work on foreclosure as the issue became more prominent.

Joyce Coleman, a foreclosure specialist at the Housing Counselors Network, was in a unique position to understand how the foreclosure crisis had come into being and why it was concentrated in African American communities.[15] For fifteen years she had worked in the mortgage industry for lenders in Baltimore and North Carolina. She was a mortgage originator at several firms that specialized in subprime mortgages.

When the financing dried up she could no longer find work selling mortgages and switched sides. She heard about a position as a housing counselor, which felt, she said, like "a natural transition." Sitting in a windowless office upstairs from a sleepy shopping mall in a deindustrialized white working-class area on the east side of the county, she reflected on her new job. She knew many people who had switched from lending to counseling; though the money wasn't as good, it provided a paycheck. She enjoyed the work she was doing but was still looking for ways to restart her career in real estate.

Though Coleman denied she sold risky mortgages or added hidden fees to increase her profits, she had been an enthusiastic proponent of homeownership. In North Carolina Coleman, who was African American, had hosted a radio program called "Possess the Land," borrowing its name from a passage in the Bible's first chapter of Joshua. It was a call-in show on a Christian radio station, and Coleman interwove biblical imagery and housing advice. She would tell them, "Don't be afraid, you may have obstacles, you may have giants in the land, but you can conquer these giants. And I'm going to help you. We will get your credit ready. If you need money for down payment we will help you to possess your piece of the land." Twice a week she told callers about finance options, no-money-down mortgages, and grants for down payments.

The "whole goal" was to get buyers into a house. Coleman would give customers an adjustable rate mortgage, or ARM. A few years later when their credit improved, she would explain, they could refinance at a lower rate. Coleman said she didn't expect what actually happened. "I would coach them through that year: 'keep your mortgage paid.' But then what would happen after the two years—I don't know why I just didn't think this—after two years, you go back to the people, their credit is worse than what it was before! And so they couldn't refinance to get into the prime rate." In my interview with her, Coleman conveyed surprise at that outcome. Looking back after the mortgage collapse had revealed the peril of such reckless lending, that surprise seems hard to believe. But at the time Coleman's employers, along with television commentators, enthusiastic economists, and others, all insisted that the housing markets' upward momentum would have no end. Perhaps she failed to carefully consider the overly optimistic claims of the company that had trained and employed her. Or she may have found it easier to do her job by adopting unquestioning optimism rather than dangerous skepticism. Others in the industry adopted a brutal cynicism about their actions. Whether Coleman could foresee or was willfully unaware of the consequences of the mortgages she gave to customers with "scarred credit," the consequences were the same.

Coleman did have firsthand knowledge of lenders' tactics for targeting homeowners for subprime second mortgages. First, mortgage lenders would get mailing lists of people with 30 percent home equity, and credit scores of five or six hundred. One lender would send out ten thousand mailers every month, offering a tempting "bogus" low rate on a second mortgage, specifying that the rate was available only to people with a credit score of seven hundred or more. When the customers called, they were told their credit score didn't qualify for the low rate—but another loan was available.

Coleman explained how she was taught to sell such second mortgages, despite the higher interest rate. She said she would tell borrowers, "'You don't qualify for that rate, but you can get this rate. . . . You will be able to have $10,000 cash in a month.' And people hear that, and they're like, 'Oh wow! I can get 10,000? Great! I can pay off all my bills.' And that's how they taught us to sell: sell the benefits, don't worry about the interest rate. Don't worry about the loan amount, sell the benefits." She told prospective clients, "Your payments are going to be reduced—I don't even know how that's going to happen—you're going to save a hundred bucks a month."

According to Coleman, "Lenders, especially up here in Maryland, when they would send out mailers they would target African American people." She went on: "I worked in some places and seen some things that just turned my head, like I can't believe you guys are charging so much for a client. And they would target minorities. . . . The mailers would target minority people." Lenders were looking for people with equity, debt, and poor credit. Subprime lenders didn't want to deal with "'A' paper," people with good credit scores. Such people would "nickel and dime you, they're going to shop around, they're going to look for options, they're not going to be hung on your every word. That is why some loan officers stay away from those types of people. But I actually enjoyed that [people with good credit]. . . . That was a good type of loan that we had . . . I did okay doing that."

The practices Coleman observed were not isolated: nationwide, while subprime loans made up only 20 percent of mortgages made to whites, they constituted nearly half (49 percent) of loans made to African Americans. Although most subprime loans, in raw numbers, were made to whites (because whites make up a larger share of the population), African Americans were still twice as likely to have subprime loans. And while more subprimes overall were made to whites, foreclosure rates were still typically 50 percent higher than expected for African American homeowners—even among high-income homeowners.[16]

A counselor at We Are Family agreed that predatory lending targeted people of color. "It's also targeted by community. . . . I mean you target neighborhoods by race. People don't want to say that." From their perspective, steering toward unaffordable homes and mortgages began with realtors and continued through several layers of the homebuying industry.

By 2006 or 2007 the market in North Carolina changed, and Joyce Coleman was no longer able to sell products to callers on her radio show. "The banking industry changed and, it was about mid like 2006 beginning of 2007. And I remember because I [had been] able to get people into products where they didn't have to put a lot of money down. And those banks that would come to our office that were able to help people just closed down, and they were gone. So the clientele that I had I wasn't able to service as much anymore. Couldn't get them mortgages."

Coleman knew lenders were targeting people with debt and equity. "Those are the people that are going to need to refinance, because those are the people that have a bunch of credit card bills that they can't pay." But she wasn't in a position to identify why lenders targeted African Americans to find those kinds of customers. Community groups that had worked in African American communities had seen more of the causes of financial stress.

We Are Family had already been providing emergency community services—they were known as a place to go when residents were at risk for eviction or having their utilities turned off. I first sat down to talk to leaders of the organization after the ribbon cutting for their new offices. Located in a single-story business park, the new space gave We Are Family room for the wide range of community services they conducted. Beyond the reception desk was a glass wall revealing a large meeting area. Behind that was a neatly arranged, garage-like space used for the group's food pantry, where residents could schedule appointments (rather than wait in lines) to pick up bags of food. In offices on either side counselors helped people with emergency assistance. Once a month, the group also held first-time home buyer classes, even while it helped other homeowners facing foreclosure.

At the grand opening Reverend Charles Sembly, pastor of the church that had founded We Are Family, introduced me to the director, Reverend Linda Mouzon. I sat down at a large table with her and Delegate Adrienne Jones, who was also a member of the church, along with staff of We Are Family.

While Joyce Coleman could only speculate as to why African Americans were targeted in the search for distressed homeowners, We Are Family's broader experience with community assistance gave the staff concrete understanding of the factors that put people, disproportionately African Americans, in situations of financial distress. Rather than articulate what made people attractive targets for subprime mortgages, they listed these features in explaining how people ended up at risk for

foreclosure. For one thing, African Americans were traditionally less secure. "Last hired, first fired," said Mouzon, citing an African American
adage regarding employment insecurity. In addition, many people who
sought the group's assistance were older workers who had been laid off
and hadn't been able to find a job that paid what they had made before.
Other people worked in financial companies or technology companies.
While many had found new jobs, they were earning less money and
were having trouble making ends meet and paying bills. Other members
of the group highlighted the role of predatory lending. "A lot of people
bought a bag of goods that wasn't there." While some clients were se-
niors, "most of them are families."

Other clients had faced crises in their lives.[17] "We'll hear about
somebody who died," explained Mouzon, recalling clients who explained their financial stress by saying, "'I had to plan for a funeral.'"
An unexpected medical bill could push people into debt they were unable to get out of. While such events could befall anyone, interviews I
completed with African Americans, Latinos, and whites indicated that
African Americans were much more likely to experience such crises
and acute downward economic mobility than members of other racial
groups.

Mel Freeman, director of CPHA, gave a similar assessment of the causes
of financial distress for homeowners, calling it "the four Ds": death, disability, divorce, and debt. Whatever the myriad causes, neighborhoods
across the country, particularly African American neighborhoods, were
imperiled by the threat of widespread foreclosures. In Randallstown,
there were certainly vacant houses for sale. When I sought out empty
houses for sale in 2010, they were not difficult to find. But the houses
were in good repair. Lawns were mowed (whether by the owner or by
neighbors), and the homes were generally not in physical disrepair,
although some needed minor outside maintenance after a period of
vacancy.

Public policies that addressed the foreclosure crisis were inadequate. While some national and state programs were implemented,
all three organizations I interviewed pointed to state programs that
had been useful until, as the leaders of We Are Family explained, "the
money dried up."

In some respects the neoliberal philosophy of individual responsibility has hampered the development of sufficient programs. Some counselors would chastise an abstract home buyer for using their house "like an ATM" from which equity could be irresponsibly withdrawn, even while their specific stories were of clients who needed money to pay legitimate debts. Others criticized home buyers, concluding that "the issue is you really can't afford the home anyway." That criticism ignored counselors' intimate familiar with the chain of manipulations from realtor to lender that led people into houses whose prices had been inflated. Blaming individuals also bypassed counselors' knowledge that the people who were moving into homes they "really can't afford" were concentrated in particular neighborhoods and racial groups.

In a related vein, education was widely seen as the key, particularly in the form of first-time home buyer programs. While such an approach seems unobjectionable, other researchers have noted the way that education-based remedies relocate the source of the problem from a widespread social structural issue to an individual-level trouble.[18] Such neoliberal explanations and solutions have hindered addressing the foreclosure crisis at the local and national levels.

People in communities hard hit by foreclosure have thus been left to assemble ad hoc responses out of the irregular programs they have found or fashioned themselves. Thus while all three groups made use of state or federal programs when they were available, others in the community sought to do more. Congressman Elijah Cummings, who represented parts of Randallstown and other areas with high foreclosure rates, regularly organized events for people facing foreclosure. The congressman used his influence to demand attendance from representatives of the major lenders, so that people could sit down "face-to-face" with people and try to resolve their problems. All three groups gave this program high praise. It is not coincidental that Cummings is African American, as were all of the housing counselors I spoke with.[19] Foreclosure reflects the racialization of neoliberalism: First, the damage of neoliberalism's financialization, speculation, and deregulation targeted and fell more heavily on Blacks than on whites. Then there was inadequate political motivation to provide adequate solutions to problems that disproportionately affected African Americans.

Skepticism of Institutions

African Americans were more likely to face such financial difficulties and were targeted by lenders for subprime loan products. In addition, some of the foreclosure experts suggested that lenders had exploited their status and relationships with clients. Freeman noted that maps of foreclosure had shown that the same brokers and lenders appeared multiple times on the same block. He attributed this to neighbors' tendency to talk to each other and recommend a broker. But Coleman had suggested a different explanation. "I think that African Americans are 'relational,' and I think that if we found somebody we liked, we trusted them. You know, you have a nice face, you look like, you're a Caucasian, you're a nice guy, I can trust you, you're not going to steer me wrong." Consistent with this thesis, other counselors suggested that while whites were more likely to get loans from banks, African Americans were more likely to get loans from people they already knew in their communities. Social networks could be exploited to get more business from people who weren't shopping around.

Such an explanation for the concentration of subprime mortgages among African Americans can skirt close to a reductionist, culturalist syllogism. But Coleman elaborated in a way that suggested a different explanation. The problem was whom to trust: according to her, African Americans "will go to this loan officer they feel comfortable with and go back next year and refinance next year, with them again. It's like their financial person, [even though] this guy is just after what you can get out of them." African Americans, she concluded, built relationships with individuals they trusted, while white customers were likely to shop around among institutions and have less connection to individuals. But the difference that Coleman proposed is likely not an idiopathic cultural difference but a reflection of systematically different experiences whites and Blacks have with major institutions.

In satellite research I conducted in African American neighborhoods in Chicago and its suburbs at the same time as my research on Liberty Road, I found a wide range of examples of how financial institutions behave much more predatorily toward Black (and Latino) customers than they do toward middle-class whites. The array of institutions African American respondents cited was striking.

The high interest rates of even conventional credit cards can make them look like a scam and can quickly lead people deep into debt. But several African Americans and Latinos had experiences with more dubious credit cards. Tanya Jackson had studied sociology in college, was active in her community, and worked for a congressman. But she was drawn in by a credit card that promised no annual fees, only to find that it was deducting money from her bank account. Eventually, she was able to get her money back from the out-of-state bank that had taken it. But it left here wary of all credit cards. Alma Perez was embarrassed that when she had bought her last two cars she had needed a cosigner for the car loan because she had no credit history. So, consistent with conventional financial advice, she had signed up for a credit card and planned to pay her cell phone bill with it to develop a strong credit history. But she instantly had a balance to pay off because the card required a "security and deposit" that was almost the size of her credit limit (meaning that the card company never extended her more "credit" than the amount of her cash it was holding, simply lending her her own money). Such cards appear to be marketed much as Joyce Coleman described the marketing of subprime mortgages that she witnessed: issuers targeted people with bad credit and focused their mailings on neighborhoods with high minority populations.

Even banal institutions like the post office were not exempt. Complaining about the post office is as tired a pastime as discussing the weather. But in one large African American community just inside Chicago it altered residents' financial transactions. Residents referred to one post office branch by name: "McGee." They had so many stories of stolen checks, lost mail, and other disruptions that most had long since stopped paying bills by mail.[20] It was a primary reason they gave for paying everything from utility to cable bills at check cashing establishments and drove others to pay bills online. At first, after I had heard repeated explanations by residents of why they wouldn't pay bills by mail, I had thought Chicago residents in general were especially distrustful of the Postal Service. But then one African American respondent said casually that she paid bills by mail. I asked if she was afraid they'd be lost, and she explained to me, "Oh no, we have a normal post office here. I don't live near McGee." Tanya Jackson said of McGee, "There's some corruption in that post office." She avoided using the post office at all cost. Other

African Americans in virtually all-Black neighborhoods had similar stories of extreme unreliability of mail service: a credit union had sent a check to Kristin Foreman *three times* and she still didn't receive it. Only when she was able to get a postal inspector to investigate was the check found. In contrast, far away on the north side of the city, in another zip code with few African Americans, Guadeloupe Del Rio wondered if the post office might be "a little shady," but it didn't stop her from paying her bills by mail.

Although McGee offered evidence that disparate behavior of institutions correlated with race, respondents suggested that class influenced the responsiveness of institutions as well. Jamey Del Rio discussed the effects of gentrification. Regarding his local post office, he said, "The neighborhood's changing, so everything's on time," adding, "so when power goes out, it's back on in an hour. You make one phone call." As Massey and Denton have pointed out, even inequality based on poverty will hit African Americans particularly hard since poor people of other races are rarely so segregated and concentrated. While class can play a role, the most dramatic disparities in institutional behavior were attributable to race.

Just as residents avoided credit cards and post offices, people sometimes avoided banks. This tendency was more common among working-class people than the middle class. But it helped shed light on why African American home buyers would not have gone as naturally to banks to apply for mortgages as others did.

Clearly, James Crockett's accounts in the previous chapter recall that for a long time banks were institutions that were hostile to African Americans in every way they could be. African Americans and Latinos still recounted discomfort in banks. Jaime Bernard, a community activist whose family was from Puerto Rico, described raising money for a member of his community group, whose son had been arrested in Florida. (Bernard believed he was innocent.) Bernard collected five thousand dollars from other members of the group and went to a bank branch to transfer it to Florida. The teller said casually, "Oh, that's a lot of money, what are you sending that for?" He already felt somewhat out of place at the bank, and being asked what the money was being sent for, particularly since it was for bail money, made him feel more awkward and as if his privacy was being intruded upon. Having to stand before the teller as a Latino sending bail money was humiliating because he felt he was playing into a stereotype. For that reason he preferred sending money via a wire service at a check cashing storefront: the service was quick, and no one asked questions about what the money was for.

Blacks described similar interactions. The authors of *How Race Is Lived in America* recount the experiences of a young African American man buying a six-thousand-dollar certificate of deposit with lottery winnings. The teller looked puzzled, he recalled, and said, "This is different. Your kind likes to spend the money, not save it." After that experience he stopped using a checking account.[21]

No one likes standing in line at the post office or at the bank, and credit card interest rates are high for everyone. Yet middle-class whites generally use these institutions and express puzzlement as to why others do not: Why don't subprime borrowers go to a regular bank? Why do some people cash checks and pay bills at check cashing facilities? Why don't others have checking accounts at banks? Of course millions of African Americans and Latinos use all of these institutions. But experiences with each of them make such places seem anything but neutral. For people of color, choosing "responsible" financial institutions thus simultaneously becomes more difficult and requires consideration of additional factors.

As Joyce Coleman suggested in Maryland, in banking and other interactions whites frequently received the impression that they could trust "reputable" institutions. (It is irresistible to note that, after the financial crisis, whites' confidence in big banks seems even more misplaced than the relationships African American borrowers built with purveyors of subprime loans.) While for whites "mainstream" institutions (like banks, post offices, and conventional credit) appear unquestionably more reliable and respectable than their more marginal competitors (like check cashing storefronts, wire services, and scam credit cards), African American respondents often found all of those mainstream institutions to be highly unreliable—at least where they and other Black people lived. White home buyers might have less attachment to an individual and feel confident shopping around because they believe they can trust reputable institutions such as mainstream banks. But African Americans have had less positive experiences with respected institutions (such as police, the judicial system, the labor market, and mainstream banks themselves, all of which have documented patterns of mistreating African Americans). With experiences that auger against trusting even mainline institutions, they must seek out individuals to trust, with less weight given to institutions than whites, since even venerated institutions regularly have histories of discriminatory treatment. Particularistic relationships create stronger ties and obligations and reduce the ease with which someone can cut ties and shop around. In the end everyone must put their trust somewhere. As Coleman explained, the attitude of buyers she worked with toward lenders was, "It's like a professional in your life. They are the expert in mortgages—I'm not the expert, I don't know anything about this stuff, so there's no way you can go out there and rip me off, because you're licensed, you have a legitimate office." In the run-up to the home mortgage crisis, everyone's trust was misplaced.

Punctuated Equilibrium and the Future of the Suburbs

African American suburbs ringing Baltimore have defied the patterns that earlier racially transitioning neighborhoods in Baltimore and elsewhere followed. They did not experience "precipitous decline." Instead, residents and activists sought and worked to maintain stability while the deregulated, neoliberal market sowed the seeds of crisis. The outcome of the conflict between these two opposing interests is best described as one of punctuated equilibrium.

Over the past four decades, while African Americans have maintained the status quo in African American suburban communities in Baltimore County, residents have been remarkably successful at altering the traditional story of racial transition from white to African American that was thought to result in decreasing property values and median household incomes. Residents used neighborhood-level strategies and the momentum of the civil rights movement to desegregate parts of Baltimore County. Activists like Emily Wolfson and Ella White Campbell, who were described in chapter 3, worked to preserve the status and value of their neighborhoods.

However, there are inherent contradictions in this process. Maintaining property values while household incomes gradually declined was partly dependent on easy access to mortgages.[22] However, the foreclosure crisis, the lending freeze, and the silent housing affordability crisis made maintaining property values more challenging. African Americans are typically less able than whites to muster political support for effective responses to crises that disproportionately affect African American communities. Congressman Cummings's approach was an exception to this pattern.

Punctuated equilibrium is produced not only by the threats a neighborhood faces but also by the mitigating influence of residents and other actors. The force of the events that punctuated the area's relative equilibrium appears unprecedented in these quite recently constructed suburbs. But other examples of punctuation—deindustrialization, war, political repression, race riots—can and do disrupt communities that had also enjoyed periods of stability.

The long-term outcome of such crises will depend not only on responses at the national and state levels but on the response of residents and community activists. However, the data on income examined in this chapter give some indication of the limitation of local strategies: although counselors worked to aid residents facing foreclosure and activists worked hard to maintain the middle-class status of their Randallstown neighborhoods as the areas became increasingly African American, their success was measured. The neighborhoods did maintain middle-class norms, and property values held. But foreclosures swept the area. Incomes were much more volatile and often declined or continued to lag behind those of others, particularly whites, nearby and in other parts of the county. As neoliberal crisis shook neighborhoods like Randallstown, punctuated equilibrium imposed a deceptive rhythm on African American life.

7

Conservative Politics

Left and Right or Black and White?

One of the first interviews I conducted, early in my research in Randallstown, was of the Revered Emmett Burns. I turned off Liberty Road and drove a few minutes down a slightly winding lane lined with single-family suburban houses. The church was a relatively modern, brick-fronted building with a white steeple at the top and two crosses out front. I entered, nervous.

My regular uncertainty about whether to address Protestant clergy as "reverend" or "pastor" was compounded by the fact that Burns was also a Maryland state delegate. I asked for Reverend Burns and was shown in. The office was an expansive room. Burns sat behind an imposing wooden desk.

Burns's biography was an intimidating roster of civil rights, political, and community commitments. He was born in Jackson, Mississippi, and said that growing up, it felt like the *Dred Scott* decision was still in effect: "Blacks had no rights. If you were intertwined or got tangled up with a white person, you lose. Simple as that." Burns explained that his introduction to civil rights came early. When he was thirteen years old the civil rights activist Medgar Evers moved to Jackson. Burns was a paper boy, and in order to have enough copies of important news stories (in the era before photocopiers) Evers bought five or six copies of each day's paper. When Burns was in college Evers suggested Burns, who was already active in the NAACP, pursue civil rights activism full-time.

Burns last saw Evers in April 1963 and remembers him waving as he drove off, telling him to be careful. Two months later Burns heard a radio announcer say, "Death has hit again in Mississippi. The prominent civil rights. . . ." There seemed to be an agonizing pause, while Burns asked himself desperately, "What's the name? What's the name?—I knew all of them." The radio announcer finished, "Medgar Evers was assassinated." "When I heard that on the radio, I resolved that I would go back to Mississippi and work for civil rights." He succeeded Medgar's brother Charles Evers as field director. Burns later named one of his sons Medgar Evers.[1]

Reverend Burns opened our conversation with the story of meeting Medgar Evers when Burns was just thirteen. There was another violent landmark in civil rights history that he did not bring up, and I did not ask about. Two days after Burns's fifteenth birthday, a fourteen-year-old with the same first name, Emmett Till, was murdered by whites who wanted to make an example of him.[2] Historians have considered Till's murder "the catalyst for the modern civil-rights movement."[3] Till's lynching took place about a hundred miles from Emmett Burns's hometown.

Burns's involvement with the NAACP led him to its headquarters in Baltimore. He sought to be appointed director but was not chosen, and his involvement in that organization waned. As a minister and elected official, however, he remained constantly involved in civil rights issues. Often the matters were immediate: a few months before I interviewed him a woman had been pulled over by police and mistreated; Burns applied pressure to the police, held a press conference, and threatened a lawsuit; the charges against the woman were thrown out.

Other times the issues were deliciously symbolic, and Burn's response was a joy to observe. The Baltimore-Washington area had three airports: Dulles (named after John Foster Dulles, secretary of state under Republican Dwight Eisenhower), National Airport, and Baltimore-Washington International Airport, or BWI. Republicans had begun a misplaced campaign to canonize Ronald Reagan: they wanted to replace the portrait on the dime, of the great liberal founder of the modern US social welfare system Franklin Roosevelt, with Ronald Reagan. They wanted to name buildings after him. And they wanted to name an airport after him.

Reagan is venerated by Republicans, but his attacks on welfare were stained with racism. Reagan gave his first speech as a presidential candidate near Philadelphia, Mississippi, where the civil rights workers Goodman, Chaney, and Schwerner were murdered by police. In the speech, a hundred miles east of Burns's hometown, Regan supported "states' rights," a term used by white supremacists to oppose federal civil rights legislation. He spread the myth of an imaginary "Cadillac Queen" who collected welfare but drove a fancy car, feeding into resentful whites' fantasy that welfare programs enriched African Americans.

In 1998 the US Congress, led by Republicans, renamed National Airport for Reagan. Burns noticed that while Congress had the right to rename Ronald Reagan Washington National Airport, the Maryland State legislature, in which he was a delegate, had the right to rename Baltimore-Washington International Airport. In a fitting response, Burns garnered the support necessary to christen Thurgood Marshall BWI Airport, after the Baltimore-born civil rights lawyer and Supreme Court justice.

Just as Marshall was not a man to mince words unnecessarily over the reality of race,[4] Burns was not one to sit by and do nothing. Burns was a fighter and, it seemed, had no doubts about which side was right.[5]

Given Burns's decades of dedication to the cause of civil rights, it was all the more painful to hear him discuss gay rights. Burns dismissed claims that civil rights for gays and lesbians were analogous to civil rights for African Americans. "If you want to call it discrimination—I don't. . . . You can hide it! But can I hide this?" he asked, referring to his skin color. "So don't come here and tell me that we're in the same plight." Burns believed that schools were teaching that being gay or lesbian was "all right, it's acceptable, it's permissible. The homosexual family is just like a heterosexual family." Such views were "being pushed by the gay and lesbian agenda."

He even alleged that because people were teaching students that being gay or lesbian was acceptable, "one school has a heavy population in high school of gays." I asked which school that was, but he demurred. "I'll just say one of the high schools. One person from that high school said, 'Hey, the whole tenth grade class is gay.' And they will admit it. It's an acceptable lifestyle. And it's being pushed by the gay and lesbian agenda."

As Eduardo Bonilla-Silva has pointed out in his research, there are prejudices that are widely held but are incompatible with the conventions of public discourse. In such cases speakers often make paradoxical concessions. For instance, in his rhetoric against gay rights Burns still felt he should pay lip service to norms of tolerance. Even Burns, whose homophobia was on the surface, still had to couch it, at least superficially, in terms of individual liberty. "Whatever floats your boat that's fine with me," he began, tipping his hat toward an ideal of individual liberty rooted in American political ideology and even embraced in conservative talking points. But he continued, "But don't push it off on children, don't equate it with my skin, don't equate it with the family unit."

His gesture toward tolerance—"whatever floats your boat"—seemed insincere, particularly in light of his response to a campaign for gay marriage in Maryland in 2012. Two months before a gay marriage initiative was to be put before voters in the general election, Baltimore Ravens linebacker Brendon Ayanbadejo spoke out publicly in support of the initiative. Burns then wrote a letter to the Ravens football team management to silence Ayanbadejo.[6] Burns argued that Ayanbadejo should not be "allowed" to speak his mind on the gay marriage initiative. Burns's argument did not make a lot of sense—he argued that Ayanbadejo should not voice his opinion on a political matter because his employer was in the "entertainment" industry. Furthermore (and contrary to the ideal of individualism) Burns suggested that Ayanbadejo should not speak out in support of gay marriage simply because many of the team's fans might hold opposing views. Burns was roundly excoriated not only for his opposition to a gay marriage ballot measure in Maryland but for his effort, while an elected official, to censor the speech of a citizen. (In an expletive-laced letter, Minnesota Vikings kicker Chris Kluwe argued in support of Ayanbadejo that Burns's letter violated the First Amendment's prohibition on government infringement on free speech.)[7] In the end, as documented in the film *The New Black*, Maryland voters approved the measure in November 2012, legalizing same-sex marriage in Maryland.[8]

In chapter 4 I suggested ways that suburban political issues could be reframed in progressive ways. In this chapter I offer several observations about progressive and conservative political views in Randallstown and the African American middle class. In particular there is the longstanding question of what direction the Black middle class will take politically. Answers to this question often depend on whom an analyst believes middle-class African Americans will ally themselves with: the larger Black community, the Black urban poor, middle-class whites, or fellow suburbanites. Among other things, E. Franklin Frazier's work on the Black bourgeoisie implied that the Black middle class were not the agents of history and that in their political irrelevance they could live in a world of make believe in political as well as social terms. More recently, Michael Dawson has suggested that the political future of the Black middle class will depend on whether rising or falling prospects of economic and racial equality tie them to a rising middle class or an imperiled African American community. I argue that there are concrete reasons the politics of the Black suburbs are distinct from any of these groups. This independence carries a particular risk: without obvious alliances with other larger or more powerful groups, members of the Black middle class experience greater political power than poorer African Americans but still lack the collective political power of the middle class to securely protect and advance their interests.

First, it is worthwhile to spell out some of the complexity of political views among the suburban African American middle class. Burns's positions on civil rights encapsulate centrally important points about politics and political beliefs in African American suburbs. First, the residents and community leaders I interviewed, as politically complex individuals, typically held beliefs that included both progressive and conservative elements. Black voters may be the most reliably Democratic bloc in current elections, but the political diversity of African Americans is obvious.

Certainly there were strong progressive themes among interviewees. People active in the NAACP spoke concretely of racism and current campaigns to fight it. Veterans of the midcentury civil rights movement and the war on poverty had strong views about justice. Politicians and local government officials took explicitly inclusionary views toward development, mass transit, and housing. Even residents who were concerned about poorer people (often coded as Black) moving from the city to the suburbs conditioned their views with concern and compassion for the struggles poor people have to go through.

At the same time, in virtually every interview a respondent articulated some position—often a culturally conservative position—that would have been consistent with Republican Party views: another minister up the road from Burns blamed Black students' academic failings on their affiliation to Black culture (e.g., wearing baggy jeans). Residents opposed public buses because they would let poor Black people into the neighborhood. People spoke proudly of how they had succeeded through hard work and determination. The African American leader of the local business association was a business-oriented conservative in plenty of ways.

That said, Burns's views highlight a second important observation: that taken individually, his positions are not unique to African Americans. There are a large number of white pastors, for instance, who hold progressive views on race and class, and retrograde and homophobic views on gender and sexuality.[9]

However, African Americans with conservative tendencies are structurally precluded from adopting the simplistic take-no-prisoners political views that have been popular for the past several decades in conservative political discourse. Among pundits and the public, conservative defenses of capitalism often find it more consistent to embrace capitalism without moderation. Those who dislike one aspect of government interference believe there should be none; those who dislike paying taxes think there should be no taxes. This form of simplification in pursuit of moral consistency and the greater ease of defending extreme ideological positions is largely unavailable to African Americans with a conservative stripe, forcing them to maintain positions with more nuance, distinction, or contradiction. The way race matters is that unlike whites, African Americans can almost never identify themselves as Republicans. The racist foundation of the Republican Party's platform for the past fifty years all but precludes African Americans from voicing their conservative views with a Republican Party affiliation.

Thus political heterogeneity does not find expression in the two-party system. This is related to a difference between the perspectives of African Americans and whites. Even African Americans with a large number of conservative views still recognized that racism and discrimination were real. For instance, in the course of our wide-ranging conversation, Pastor Burns articulated a wide range of views consistent with the positions of white cultural conservatives: Like cultural conservatives, Burns worried, for instance, that some people might make public assistance part of "their lifestyle," concluding, "I cannot accept that: people who will not seek to better themselves." But he also insisted that there were people in the county who needed help from programs like Section 8 housing assistance, and he worked to keep the programs available.

Yet Burns's perspective as an African American meant that those views were joined to other views that contradicted those of white conservatives. Burns complained that one problem in schools was "the big old pants and the big old sloppy shirts, the hat on sideways—the thug culture. If a school system permits that culture to keep going, it disrupts the learning process. In a meeting we're asking for the school board to issue a policy for the dress code. You can't wear that stuff to school." But while Burns was willing to blame hip-hop fashion for low grade point averages, he also saw racial bias in teacher hiring, a shortage of Black teachers, and a failure to meet the needs of African American students. Most often, whites' objection to loud people from the city, baggy jeans, or welfare would be accompanied by a blanket denial that racism mattered anymore or that racial discrimination caused inequality. Burns and others in Randallstown cut a finer distinction, claiming that people's own behaviors contributed to the structurally difficult positions they were locked into, while still identifying the real effects of racism and the real need for society to address the poverty that remained concentrated among African Americans. This bifurcated blame is consistent with the findings of researcher Eduardo Bonilla-Silva's surveys that while whites embraced a color-blind narrative that pretended discrimination had ended, Blacks readily explained that discrimination remained a real and present problem.[10] The mere recognition of the reality of racism meant that even Blacks with a collection of conservative views had a comparatively radical view on race compared to even moderate whites.

Despite their simultaneous embrace of both a "culture of poverty" and structural racism as the causes of poor African Americans' disadvantaged positions, African American respondents' position as suburban homeowners could at times obscure the more progressive beliefs that set them apart from white suburbanites. For instance, Burns discussed his congregants' objection to an annual party at a suburban swim club in the residential neighborhood where his church was located. His objections sounded similar to those of suburban whites: for the party, "people would come out here from the city and from all over, half-naked, urinating on the walls, blocking their driveways, taking drugs, cussing folk out." He blamed "rap artists" for problems at the event. Congregants and other residents protested, and the swim club stopped hosting the event. I asked Burns how this objection to "people from the city" was different from suburban whites' objections to Blacks from the city. Burns answered that the difference was that whites lumped all Blacks together.

He made distinctions *among* Blacks: "I think whites see the problem of the Black community based solely on race. . . . They make no distinction. I view it differently. My views is . . . if you go and act differently, and not hold the standards that ought to be held, that's a moral problem, not a skin problem. That's how I deal with it." When whites saw African Americans at a loud, disruptive party, Burns argued, they attributed that behavior to *all* Blacks. That is, after all, the very root of stereotyping, and Burns did not do so. It is worth noting that while interviewees did make these distinctions in their conversations with me, it was not clear that they maintained such distinctions in daily life. Too often it was not clear that African American suburbanites were treating everyone as an individual, and it could seem instead that residents had simply made those generalizations one degree finer and somewhat less hostile: a resident might argue that the problem at a party was not Blacks but Blacks *from the city*. Crime wasn't caused by all Blacks, only those who rode out to the suburbs by bus. In discussing social problems, suburban African Americans had a balancing act to accomplish between the conservative suburban desire to blame non-middle-class values and behaviors and recognizing that structural racism remained a significant force. In conversations people were not always successful at maintaining that distinction, though with further elaboration it would normally come out.

Despite the fact that people often risked upending the balance between middle-class values that blamed the poor and, on the other side, their own African American recognition of real inequality, conservative views did not change solid Democratic Party affiliation. Either a fundamental commitment to racial justice or even a mere softening qualification that recognized some people truly faced problems and needed society's help put respondents outside the rhetorical range of contemporary Republican discourse. (When Burns said "I am for Obama, 100 percent," he meant compared to the other Democratic contender Hilary Clinton. Republican candidates' names didn't come up.) Even African Americans for whom some conservative ideas were very important could rarely imagine voting Republican. And for good reason. But the history of African American support for the Democratic Party is different than it is normally described and its future less certain than generally assumed.

I do not desire or recommend the defection of large numbers of African Americans to the Republican Party. But asking whether the growth of an African American suburban middle class has political implications is essentially asking whether there will be a change from the current arrangement. Currently, African Americans of all classes are highly likely to vote Democratic. It is possible there will be no change and that pattern will continue. Any possibility that there will be political change in America's Black suburbs implies some kind of political realignment. Thus to consider the effects of race, class, and place on African American middle-class suburban politics, I consider the potential not only for voters to change alliances but also for the parties to alter their orientation. Shifts among voters and parties create the possibility that representatives of the suburban African American middle class might someday connect to different political allies.

History of Black Voting in Baltimore and Beyond

Republicans will on occasion roll out the old chestnut that their party is (or should be) the Party of Lincoln, meaning that the Republicans *should* have African American support (for which the speaker desires that either the party or African American voters change somehow). After all, the reasoning goes, the Republican Party oversaw the end of slavery, and African Americans had strong Republican loyalty for many decades after (and not blind loyalty, for in many of those years Republicans indeed remained comparative defenders of civil rights, in the face of concerted attacks by Democrats). When George McMechen won the nomination to run for Baltimore's city council in 1915, for instance, he was on the Republican ticket.[11] Today, however, African American politicians and voters are strongly connected to the Democratic Party.

When did African American voters leave the Republicans for the Democrats? The answer is more complicated than prevailing wisdom suggests. Baltimore provides a particularly revealing answer.

The most common answer focuses on pull factors that drew Black voters to the Democrats. Often Blacks' shift toward the Democratic Party is attributed to Franklin Delano Roosevelt's Depression-era economic relief and modest social outreach or the popularity of John F. Kennedy, who, despite his less-than-aggressive support of civil rights issues, was popular enough that his portrait sometimes hung beside Martin Luther King's in mid-twentieth-century African American households.

But pull factors were not sufficient: even in 1932 amidst the Depression, most African Americans actually voted against Roosevelt and for Hoover. FDR was a Democrat who could have brought back the southern reign to Washington (as in the dark days of segregationist Woodrow Wilson), and if Roosevelt's ill health overcame him, he would be replaced by Vice President John Nance Garner, a conservative from Texas. Granted, Roosevelt's policies during the Depression and he and his wife Eleanor's comparatively open attitude toward African Americans (inviting some Black visitors to White House, while African Americans developed some influence in the party) led to greater support. Over the course of his presidency, African American support for Roosevelt did grow.

In Maryland, Democrats were a white southern party. Thus as late as 1956, 55 percent of Baltimore African Americans voted Republican in the presidential election. Black Republicanism is hardly surprising in Maryland, as the alternative was to vote for southern-style Jim Crow Democrats. As late as 1966, for instance, the Democratic candidate for governor of Maryland voiced his opposition to civil rights fair housing laws (and support for gun ownership) with the campaign slogan "Your Home Is Your Castle—Protect It." In an extreme climate where segregationists like George Wallace did well in Maryland elections, the Republican opponent sounded like a moderate. The former Baltimore county executive Spiro Agnew, a Republican, would later be Richard Nixon's vice president but had to resign for accepting kickbacks from cronies in Baltimore County. As county executive, he did oppose open housing but claimed to follow a "middle course"—albeit a middle course he charted between explicit segregationists and open housing laws, which he characterized as "the unreasonable ultimatums of power-crazed integrationist leaders."[12] While Maryland Republicans offered very little to African American voters, Democratic candidates' explicit hostility meant that the pull of liberal Democrats on the national stage, from FDR forward, was not sufficient, on its own, to attract a majority of African American voters.

In addition to the pull of Democrats, though, there were push factors. John Hope Franklin wrote that African American disillusionment with the Republicans began as early as 1928, when the party tried to build strength in the South and replaced African American party officials with whites.[13] (This was, in essence, the Republicans' first Southern Strategy of alienating African Americans to attract southern whites, but at the time it had limited success.) At the same time, rival parties made promises of nondiscrimination, and Black movement away from the Republicans began.

A more forceful push factor is often overlooked. In this sense Franklin Roosevelt's counterpart is Barry Goldwater. While the role of FDR in shifting Black party alliances is often given prominent consideration, the role of Barry Goldwater is not. Prior to Goldwater, Republican support in Black areas in Baltimore continued. As late as the 1960 election of John F. Kennedy, 28 percent of voters in Black districts voted Republican. But by 1964 Republican support had collapsed. In that election Barry Goldwater ran on the Republican ticket under the Confederate buzzword of states' rights and opposed the 1964 Civil Rights Act. Goldwater's hostility to African American equality made Black Republicanism virtually impossible, while Johnson's presidency strengthened Democratic association with the civil rights agenda. Republican support in Black districts of Baltimore fell to 7 percent.[14]

Goldwater had inherited his father's Phoenix, Arizona, department store. He entered politics as a probusiness candidate who opposed FDR's New Deal economic policies. Early in his run for president polls showed that the majority of voters were strongly opposed to his antiunion views and the threat he posed to Social Security. But white voters were anxious about President Johnson's endorsement of civil rights and of local efforts to desegregate schools through busing. In response Goldwater's campaign emphasized his anti-civil-rights positions and claims of a culture war. His neoliberal economic positions were neatly sutured to the politics of racial backlash.[15]

Goldwater's moves led him to electoral success among whites in the Deep South, and while Goldwater was soundly defeated in the 1964 presidential election, his strategy set the template for future Republican campaigns that fostered white resentment of Black civil rights activism.

It is appropriate that the data on Black voting in Baltimore come from Kevin Phillips's *The Emerging Republican Majority* because in that book

Phillips, a former speechwriter for Richard Nixon, observed the Goldwater campaign and laid out the infamous Southern Strategy by which Republicans would achieve electoral dominance for the next forty years and into the present day. Republicans' goal was to build a coalition to win presidential elections by drawing off white Democratic voters. Republicans would foster their racial resentment, marrying Republican opposition to government intervention in business to reactionary whites' opposition to government intervention in civil rights. The strategy and its explicitly racist core were laid out frankly by Lee Atwater. After securing reelection for segregationist senator Strom Thurmond of South Carolina in 1980, Atwater moved to President Ronald Reagan's political staff. After he oversaw George Bush Sr.'s successful 1988 presidential election campaign, he was chair of the Republican National Committee. Atwater explained the Southern Strategy this way:

> You start out in 1954 by saying, "Nigger, nigger, nigger." By 1968 you can't say "nigger"—that hurts you. Backfires. So you say stuff like forced busing, states' rights and all that stuff. You're getting so abstract now [that] you're talking about cutting taxes, and all these things you're talking about are totally economic things and a byproduct of them is [that] blacks get hurt worse than whites. And subconsciously maybe that is part of it. I'm not saying that. But I'm saying that if it is getting that abstract, and that coded, that we are doing away with the racial problem one way or the other. You follow me—because obviously sitting around saying, "We want to cut this," is much more abstract than even the busing thing, and a hell of a lot more abstract than "Nigger, nigger."[16]

People like Phillips and Atwater, who used the Southern Strategy, understood explicitly that the Republican neoliberal economic agenda was married strategically and ideologically to a politics of racist resentment. As long as that is the case, there are two corollaries. First, as is evident in a range of ways explored in this book, neoliberalism is a project of both racial and economic reaction; in the United States neoliberalism has been a racial project since its first appearance in the political arena. Second, African Americans will find it very difficult to use the current Republican Party as an avenue through which to express conservative political views they may hold.

The success of the Southern Strategy has been considerable, remaking the map of the political landscape. For decades southern politicians were white Democrats. As far north as Maryland, Democratic primaries for local and statewide races received more attention than the general election because the winner of the Democratic nomination was assumed to be the winner of the office. The Southern Strategy changed that. As of 2012 southern states had only one representative in all of Congress who was a white Democrat. Otherwise, in the South Republicans universally represented whites and Democrats represented only districts with large numbers of African American voters. Historian Matthew Lassiter has made an interesting argument that the Southern Strategy in fact did not work, that it failed to paper over material differences between elite and working-class whites. Indeed, Lassiter marshals an impressive array of examples in which well-to-do whites were insulated from school desegregation, integration, and other features of federal civil rights law, while Republicans abandoned working-class whites, who knew they had been left out to dry. As Lassiter points out, the early applications of the Southern Strategy, including the Goldwater campaign, were notable for their spectacular failure.[17] But after such initial shortfalls, and despite the inherent contradictions of the coalitions brought together by the Southern Strategy, for decades the politics of racial backlash has encouraged whites to elect Republicans in large numbers.

That divisive racial strategy has been so successful that people assume it's unbreakable. But both the previous coalitions and the current one are so highly contradictory that they cannot be considered permanent. The original Party of Lincoln was a contradiction, a party of business (then as now) and the champion of the rights of African Americans, of the very people most exploited by that same capitalist system. In the mid-twentieth century there was an equally unsustainable contradiction in the Democratic Party when it created an electoral majority by combining southern whites and urban nonwhites and white ethnics.

In each case, though in different ways, each contradictory alliance has come undone. The first time around, power overcame principle and the Republican alliance unraveled during the contested Tilden-Hayes election of 1876, in which Republicans agreed to abandon African Americans to resurgent southern white elites in exchange for a presidential victory. More recently, two sides of the Democratic Party became thoroughly incompatible, as urban northern African Americans and liberal civil rights supporters could no longer conscience an alliance with southern white supremacists. Republicans eagerly and successfully cultivated racist southern voters—despite the fact that the Party of Lincoln could hardly have had a lower reputation among white southerners with an unresolved nostalgia for the pre–Civil War South.

Those contradictions and their outcomes suggest there is no less volatility to the current arrangement. After all, who would have thought the Party of Lincoln would dominate the white South electorally despite southerners' memory of Republican domination by military occupation the last time around? Today, the Republican Party's coalition is no less a contradiction: working-class whites and the very ruling-class bosses who have immiserated them.[18] The Democratic Party is also a coalition of business owners (more concentrated in tech than Republicans' extractive industries) and workers. The historical examples suggest that the current alliances are less likely to be disrupted by white southerners' sudden embrace of a left-wing, working-class-based politics, than that changing circumstances will make the compromises required of the more powerful partner in the coalition (in this case the business wing of the Republicans) intolerable to them. In 2013 the political ascendance of the scorched-earth politics of the Tea Party wing of Republicans, which temporarily shut down the federal government in a budget dispute, occurred despite great frustration by the business wing of the Republican Party with such a disruption. Studies at that time identified racial intolerance as one of the strongest predictors of Tea Party sympathies.[19] Given that correlation, the Tea Party can be thought of as the Southern Strategy wing, the collection of Republican voters drawn to the party because of the racial resentment party strategists have nurtured and made politically salient. Business Republicans' considerable frustration at the actions of their Tea Party colleagues demonstrate the potential for the two contingents to one day find their interests no longer compatible.

The election of Donald Trump brought the contrasts between those two wings into still sharper relief, as some business Republicans became "never Trumpers" and Trump supporters turned against probusiness Republican politicians who were insufficiently supportive of the resentment wing of the party.

Political alignments can change dramatically. In one striking example, Louis Menand points out that before the Civil War "Union!" was a rallying cry for *apologists* in the North who prioritized keeping the country united above liberation for African Americans and therefore refused to fight slavery for fear it would lead the South to secede. Abolitionists, in contrast, wanted slavery ended and therefore dismissed "union": if ending slavery led to dissolution, so be it. But when the South did secede and attacked Fort Sumter, the North responded with military force, asserting it would both emancipate the slaves and preserve the country. "Union!" became the battle cry of abolitionists. By the end of the Civil War political positions had been thoroughly rearranged: abolitionists were unionists, idealists were disillusioned pragmatists after witnessing the arbitrary brutality of war.[20] In the course of a few decades, southern whites were powerful, disenfranchised, and powerful again, Blacks were denied political citizenship, then gained it, then lost it again. Clearly cataclysms like the Civil War fracture and realign established political loyalties. But the history of twentieth-century African American political affiliation demonstrates that substantial shifts take place over the course of peacetime political maneuvers as well.

Black Suburb, White Nationalist President

The election of Donald Trump as president in 2016 felt like a reversal of the Democratic, multiracial years of the Obama presidency. In Baltimore's suburb, residents responded with a mixture of savvy and outrage. While they didn't hold back in their criticism of Trump, they did not want to appear naïve about the potential for racial backlash in America.

Respondents began with a clear and unambiguous condemnation of Trump, his politics, his views, and his racism. Charles Sydnor III, a Democratic who had been elected to the Maryland House of Delegates in 2014 and represented part of Liberty Road, began his assessment by saying, "I think Trump is a bigoted racist. He actually might be a white nationalist." Leronia Josey said that when she first heard Trump malign Mexican immigrants, she harkened back to the governor of Virginia in her childhood, John Battle, who had only condescending things to say about "negras." She readily associated his anti-immigrant rhetoric with anti-Black racism. People criticized Trump for attacking ethnic and racial groups. People felt he made such a bad impression on the rest of the world that one political aide called him a "buffoon."

These critiques were all the more pointed because respondents, even Democratic officeholders, were not so critical of all Republicans. While Democrats outnumbered Republicans two to one in Maryland, two of the last four governors had been Republicans, Robert Ehrlich and Larry Hogan.[21] According to Sydnor, Hogan had distanced himself from Trump-style Republicanism (and, he said, was a shrewd enough politician to take credit for policies that were initiated in the Democratic legislature).

Nor did voter support for Republicans in Maryland come only from whites. Delegate Sydnor believed that Hogan had "a lot of Black support!" Others said that a member of a prominent Black political family had supported the Republican, Hogan, for governor over the former president of the NAACP, Ben Jealous. Josey had supported Democrats but said she showed Ehrlich around to area Black churches in a gesture of crossing-the-aisle generosity, explaining that she had worked with Ehrlich's wife and that "I think there ought to be strong parties."

The distinctions Black suburbanites made regarding Maryland Republicans made their unequivocal condemnation of Trump only that much more meaningful.

There were different views of the effect Trump's ascendancy had at the local level. An African American high school teacher from the county described how disturbing it had been right after the election to see giant "Trump/Pence" signs on suburban lawns in white areas. "I really see those signs as the modern Confederate flag," she said. Neighborhoods thick with Trump signs felt newly hostile to her. The feeling was particularly acute near Carroll County, the exurban and rural county beyond Randallstown, which was also Maryland's largest Republican stronghold. Another resident described leaving a community political meeting soon after Trump's victory and having a white man unleash his dog, walk inside his home, and leave the dog to harass him. While the dog stopped at his property line, the speaker felt the action reflected a newly open hostility to African Americans.

More often, however, residents said they did not feel Trump's presidency made Baltimore County, which was still largely white, with twice as many Democrats as Republicans, feel more hostile. The woman who described alarm at the Trump signs, for instance, felt it most sharply immediately after the election. Many concluded the county was not aggressively pro-Trump country. People thought about what the views of people around them might be when they spoke, especially if the people were white, but residents said that the change in administration, whatever it heralded at the national level, did not feel, in this suburban county, like a shift in the political climate. Just as Maryland African Americans had shifted from the Party of Lincoln to the Democrats more slowly than the national story would have it, people felt Trump's election, no matter how upsetting on a national stage, had not changed the local landscape as dramatically. If this were another moment of political realignment, it was not felt yet in a mostly white but mixed-race, mostly Democratic-leaning county.

The Future of Polarized Politics

Observers have already suggested that the demise of the success of the Southern Strategy is within view. For one thing, it depends on a sizeable white-identified electorate that can be repeatedly convinced that one of their primary political commitments is to the reversal of African American civil rights gains. As others have observed, the demographic base of the Southern Strategy is weakening. As older white voters die and become a smaller electoral interest, Republicans will need to either expand their reach beyond whites or expand the boundaries of who adopts the politics of the Southern Strategy and votes against nonwhite scapegoats.

As an example of those demographic changes, North Carolina was reliably Republican when Bill Clinton lost the state in the 1990s. But the state's electorate changed quickly from 76 percent white in 1990 to 65 percent white in 2001. Hispanics now make up 9 percent of the state, and African Americans have moved to North Carolina as part of "reverse migration." In addition, technology companies have attracted educated professionals whose schooling and industry rely on government investment in research and education, portending their tendency to vote Democratic. By one observer's account, Obama's victory in North Carolina in 2008 was "ahead of schedule" but reflected significant changes that would affect future elections there and elsewhere.[22] In 2020 Trump won North Carolina with a scant 50.1 percent, but the wins by Democrats Joe Biden and Kamala Harris in nearby Virginia and Georgia underline the shifts happening in the once solidly Republican South.

A political realignment that followed from Republicans' effort to move away from the strategy of racial resentment would be difficult and incomplete. It might give at least some African Americans license to explore Republican candidates. Still, it is unlikely that a great change would happen quickly. It would be a hard sell for Republicans, and many people would not buy it. They would likely conclude, as Black voters do now, that the blame the victim strategy puts them in real danger. While a move away from race baiting and scapegoating seems at odds with the approach of President Trump, which residents discussed, the Republican strategy will inevitably change, expanding its reach or reducing its success. While not all voters would be moved by a new message, some would. Electoral history shows such shifts can be substantial and rapid.

Republicans and Neoliberalism

The full alienation of African American voters from the Republican Party (relatively recent since it occurred when Randallstown residents' grandparents were voting) is fundamentally tied up with the neoliberal threats that face suburbs like Randallstown.

The first real implementation of the Republicans' Southern Strategy occurred around the time Phillips's book came out in 1969. (Phillips is frequently credited with coining the term "silent majority," which Nixon used in 1969 to implicitly contrast his supporters with loud, "minority" and countercultural voices protesting for civil rights and against the war in Vietnam.) Nixon's choice of Baltimore County politician (and Maryland governor) Spiro Agnew as his running mate was in part an effort to attract white southern voters.

Thus the Southern Strategy was adopted in the same era that neoliberals sought to reverse the momentum of unions and civil rights organizations and reassert elites' class power, which led to the policies that have imperiled the American middle class decades later.

Because of this, the race-baiting Southern Strategy was a vital source of strength for the imposition of the neoliberalism agenda. The Republican Party, which became the standard bearer of neoliberal policies in the United States (although Democrats actively imposed neoliberal revisions as well), gained the votes it needed to win power by attracting white working-class votes with its racially divisive politics. As a result, those whites came to vote according to race rather than economic interest in a dramatic way, supporting a party whose neoliberal policies undermined their very economic position.

While it is broadly true that the Republican Party definitively alienated African American voters from the party by making them the scapegoats of the Southern Strategy and put African Americans in the crosshairs of neoliberalism, three qualifications to this political history must be offered: First, Republicans' adoptions of the Southern Strategy and of neoliberalism were not exactly simultaneous. Nixon used the Southern Strategy during his successful 1968 campaign for the presidency (which was the inspiration for Phillips, who worked on the campaign, to write *The Emerging Republican Majority*). But it is not indisputable that Nixon was a neoliberal. For instance, he imposed nationwide wage and price controls to fight inflation, a degree of government control of the economy not only at odds with what would become neoliberal orthodoxy but unimaginable to either party thirty years later. He established the Environmental Protection Agency, whose regulations would later be frequent targets of neoliberal polemicists seeking to improve corporate profitability by reducing government regulation. And his assistant secretary of labor for employment standards, African American conservative Arthur Fletcher, oversaw creation of the federal government's affirmative action hiring program to create employment opportunities for African Americans.[23]

These examples of policies implemented by Nixon that sound more liberal than neoliberal are not intended to alter his historical reputation as a conservative. Some of the policies, after all, appeared to be political calculations, as when Democrats proposed price and wage freezes and Nixon actually imposed them, stealing from Democrats a policy they could champion at his expense. But in other cases Nixon's interventionist policies seemed sincere. On the affirmative action plan, Nixon wrote in his biography that it was "both necessary and right." The policy may have allowed advocates to take aim at (all-white) building trades unions that opposed affirmative action as a threat to their insular prerogative in union membership. But the Nixon administration was forced to testify multiple times in Congress about the reality of racial discrimination and the need for government programs to create some fairness in the labor market.

The second qualification to the narrative of Black scapegoating providing the necessary electoral base for the election of neoliberal politicians is that neoliberal policies were also implemented in countries without the United States' distinctive racial structure. Harvey identifies British prime minister Margaret Thatcher as a neoliberal figure of equal importance to Ronald Reagan, for instance, but Thatcher's party's success was based on foundations other than American-style racial resentment.

Third, the neoliberal objectives were so sweeping that they crossed party affiliation. Democrats as well as Republicans forwarded the neoliberal agenda. President Clinton, after all, signed landmark neoliberal legislation such as the North American Free Trade Agreement (NAFTA) and welfare "reform" that championed the neoliberal theme of "personal responsibility."

But these three caveats do not overturn the close association of electoral racist resentment with the imposition of neoliberalism. The Southern Strategy was adopted by Republicans before they became the most fervent evangelists of neoliberalism, but the success of the latter would not have been possible without the votes provided by the former. British conservatives may have needed a different strategy to garner majoritarian support for neoliberal policies from a working-class nation, but the politics of resentment were still central, if tuned slightly differently in each country. And while in the 1990s Democrats were nearly as enthusiastic neoliberals as Republicans, Clinton's welfare reform bill is just one example of how racist scapegoating of African Americans remained central to the successful promotion of neoliberal initiatives, and neoliberalism remained fundamentally racist.

New Alliances or Isolation

Political scientist Michael Dawson has spent much of his career studying political attitudes and behavior among Blacks and whites. In his book *Behind the Mule: Race and Class in African-American Politics*, Dawson proposed four possible political futures for middle-class African Americans, depending on changes in the economic and racial climate

TABLE 7.1. Michael Dawson proposed four political futures for the African American middle class depending on improving or deteriorating racial and economic conditions.

	Economic conditions improve	Economic conditions decline
Racial conditions improve	Pluralist dream	Unite and fight
Racial conditions deteriorate	Two Black movements	Politics of isolation

(see Figure 7.1).[24] His scenarios depended on whether racial conditions improved or deteriorated and whether economic conditions improved or deteriorated. The best outcome of course was improving conditions in both racial and economic terms, Dawson's "pluralist dream." The second was one in which racial conditions improved but economic prospects got worse. Under these conditions, Dawson saw the possibility of "unite and fight," in which whites and Blacks, no longer so divided by race, united to fight their shared economic precarity. Dawson called the alternative, in which economic conditions improved but racial conditions got worse, the "least predictable scenario." He imagined that the Black middle class would still embrace a Black political identity and support civil rights but would be averse to economic redistribution. Such conditions could give rise to "Two Black Movements," one for the small Black middle class and another for the larger Black community. Finally, if racial and economic conditions both declined, Dawson saw the possibility of the "Politics of Isolation." In this scenario Black inner cities and inner suburbs would become impoverished and would be "politically powerless and physically isolated from the rest of American society." Such conditions might foster radicalism among the bourgeoisie, but their prospects for success would depend on finding other allies.

It is not easy to assess which of the futures we now live in. For one thing, economic or racial improvement or deterioration is not a single variable: the election of the United States' first African American president can be contrasted with the sharp drop in African Americans' wealth during President Obama's two terms. African American suburbs have grown, but the Black/white wealth gap has stagnated and grew sharply during the recession. Have conditions improved or declined? Fortunately it is not necessary to choose a single outcome because the four possible futures Dawson presented are not mutually exclusive. Instead elements of several can be seen in the African American suburbs that have grown substantially in the twenty years since he laid out these possibilities. The punctuated equilibrium characterizing the suburban experience, which intersperses shocks with stability and even modest progress, likely accounts for the presence of elements of both decline and improvement. Likewise, not everyone's experiences have been the same: even among suburban homeowners, some have experienced upward mobility in their lifetimes (particularly the postwar generation), while many others are more precariously perched and economically vulnerable than ever.

A useful starting place for understanding the contemporary suburbs is Dawson's scenario of the "politics of isolation," which Dawson foresaw if both economic and racial conditions got worse. The politics of isolation capture a great deal of the suburban experience. Dawson suggested that the African American middle class "would be politically powerless and physically isolated from the rest of American society" as Black neighborhoods remained highly segregated and slid into poverty. Whether or not such a double decline is taking place, isolation does capture the underlying political moment in African American suburbs, perhaps even more drastically than suggested in *Behind the Mule*. Despite a strong caucus of Black elected officials from the Randallstown area, at the national level reversals of affirmative action, voting rights laws, and other protections reveal African Americans' isolation from the larger electorate. Dawson implied that this isolation would take place as the larger (white) society turned its back on racial equality or Black progress. Middle-class and lower-income African Americans would presumably then have common issues to organize around, even culminating, Dawson proposed, in an independent Black political party. But my research indicates Black suburban political isolation has the potential to be even more profound than that. At present, African Americans are separated from white suburbanites not only due to a lack of compassion by whites, but because Black suburbanites experience different issues than white suburban homeowners. At the same time, while Black suburbanites are explicit in their compassion for less fortunate African Americans, residents do not always make common cause with urban African Americans, at least on local issues. African Americans may be politically isolated in the sense of not being fully integrated into the larger polity. But the other reason for isolation is that African American suburbanites simply face different political issues (and take different positions) than white suburbanites or Black urbanites. As the cases here demonstrate, Randallstown residents faced issues—like the failure of corporate retailers to invest in the neighborhood—that comparable white neighborhoods did not face. They often opposed the citing of "nuisance" facilities like group homes for foster children that they believed were being shunted onto their community specifically because they were Black. Their political position was different from those of both whites (who Blacks expected could deflect these facilities from their communities) and poorer Blacks (who might benefit from some of the social service facilities that the middle class opposed). Whether the economic and racial conditions Dawson considered had improved or not, the fact that middle-class African Americans were facing political issues that other potential allies were not facing meant that they would be isolated.

African American suburbs may thus experience a more profound version of the political isolation identified by Dawson. In his scenario, however, Dawson imagined that "all but a few" African Americans would remain in Black ghettoes and that the increasing poverty of inner cities and suburbs would be what isolated them from "the rest of American society."[25] Instead, a large percentage of African Americans have moved to the suburbs, and it is less the economic conditions of African Americans in the suburbs that have kept them isolated than the continuing racial residential segregation (which Dawson correctly imagined) and ongoing political isolation. One way out of this isolation is to redefine the leading local political issues. That is, local leaders could identify issues that do not leave them isolated—across-the-board increased school funding, to take one possible example, would open the possibility for many alliances across race and class lines. Alternatively, existing issues need to be reframed in ways that do not isolate Liberty Road. Mass transit could be reframed as an environmental issue. The expansion of bus lines could also be part of a more ambitious proposal to create a robust network across the city and all parts of the county (not just Randallstown), so that advocates and opponents might be drawn from both the white suburbs and the predominantly Black city. My purpose is not to highlight school funding or transit expansion specifically but to point out that isolation is in part a product of how issues and solutions are framed. Political isolation can therefore be reduced by reframing issues so that they do not divide along the same race and class lines that have isolated African American middle-class suburbanites in the past.

Given the troubling developments in racial politics on the national stage, these policy examples highlight that state- and county-level politics may be different. Politics of racial resentment can be activated at the local level too (this is the land of Spiro Agnew, after all). But retrograde national politics do not preclude local areas from following a variety of the outcomes Dawson envisions. The election of Donald Trump sharpened the question, but his long-term influence on politics afterward remains to be seen.

The second most pessimistic future among Dawson's scenarios is probably that in which race deteriorates and economic conditions improve. Unlike racial improvement, which at least led to a multiracial "unite and fight" future, Dawson proposed in this future "two black movements," one of bourgeois Blacks and one of more radical, poorer African Americans. He pointed out that this is the "least predictable scenario," and indeed, to the degree that there has been divergence in this fashion, the outcome is the least certain. African American suburbanites have, as Dawson imagined in this situation, become more averse to radical politics of redistribution, even while outward racial hostility still means that "Black" is a meaningful political category. Suburban residents' simultaneous recognition of the common oppression all African Americans do face and their desire to eschew some of the radicalism of the poor and working class leave people uncertain of what solutions to propose. Drawn to a bootstraps ideology while personally aware of social inequality, Black suburbanites cannot embrace the radical individualism of white Republican-tinted suburbs. But they wish to identify, as suburbanites, with beliefs that suggest that society, in some measure, can work. To the extent people conclude that middle-class success is distributed by privilege and not effort, it upends the logic of the entire middle-class project. The paradox of the "two Black movements" is that to the extent that poor African Americans still politically identify racial barriers to their success, middle-class African Americans are premature in believing they can downplay those radical demands in favor of bourgeois political moderation. The very existence of African American suburbs—isolated from white suburbs and available only to a lucky minority of the larger African American community—testifies to the continued necessity of policies that actively and creatively contest racial and economic inequalities.

Punctuated Equilibrium and a Plurality of Black Suburban Politics

There is no single answer to the question of whether African American suburbs are success stories or stories of crisis. The pattern of punctuated equilibrium indicates that there are often simultaneous indicators of stability (the neatly trimmed front yard) and disruption (beyond the yard, the house in foreclosure). Residents defend a moral worldview that promises hard work brings rewards even while it is more and more difficult for their own hard work to secure the suburban dream. As a result, African American suburbs are fertile ground for political responses to any range of conditions. It is not difficult to imagine, for instance, the existence of mobilized radical and conservative perspectives within the same community. There is certainly the potential to frame issues like student underperformance or affordable housing proposals in terms of either structural inequality faced by Black America or alleged cultural shortcomings of youth or poor people.

Political alliances are highly contextual. Behind the apparent calm of African American suburbs is a shifting political landscape, from the early period of activist-led efforts to push into the white suburbs, through the NAACP's consolidation of the newly Black suburbs' political power with majority-Black electoral districts, to the current era when African American politicians have challenged the first generation and reshaped Randallstown-area coalitions. (That third period is characterized by disputes between Burns and more liberal members of the caucus, the redrawing of political boundaries, and successful efforts by a diverse group of African American political hopefuls to replace an African American county councilman after charges of campaign violations.) The pattern of activism, consolidation, and reorganization may be a narrative of growing strength. But elected officials representing Randallstown still find too little support from their colleagues in other districts when addressing the needs of their African American suburban constituents.

The suburbs were built on explicitly conservative principles. Trump's election and rhetoric demonstrate that racism continues to conjure unique power in American politics. But the current configuration of the Southern Strategy that capitalized on that power is aging out of demographic effectiveness. The uncertainty of punctuated equilibrium spills over into the political arena, with a range of volatile issues that could reshape the alliances of African American middle-class voters and political organizations. The threat of new alliances is that they could be divisive, pitting one faction of the Black middle class against another. The promise is that a strategic, shifting array of alliances by the Black middle class with other groups—with their fellow county residents on one issue, with the city's African American community on the other—could integrate them more tightly and more centrally into politics.

Conclusion

The Future of the Black Middle Class and Suburbia

As I concluded research for this book, African American suburbanization neared the end of Liberty Road—figuratively and perhaps literally. Newly constructed developments spread over farmland to the very edge of Baltimore County's Urban-Rural Demarcation Line. Beyond that, Liberty Road entered a woodland that protected a reservoir. Through that barrier, Liberty Road left Baltimore County, gained elevation, and entered the highlands of Carroll County, the exurban redoubt whose reputation for rural intolerance had given Louis Diggs pause when he ventured there. The African American community might continue to grow, but it would be a different story: it might continue into Carroll County, writing a new chapter of home seekers determined to find the promised land that the suburban ideal always places just a little farther outside the central city. More likely, African American neighborhoods could spread out in other directions within Baltimore County, either westward past the Social Security headquarter, or eastward beyond the shopping mall (that became increasingly vacant until it was fully reconstructed) toward the already-transitioning neighborhoods along Reisterstown Road. The population of Baltimore City continued to fall while that of the metro region grew, suggesting that African Americans will continue to be drawn toward the growing opportunities in the Baltimore-Washington corridor and that their stories will increasingly be suburban ones.

Liberty Road symbolizes people's mobilization to achieve a modest if stable middle-class suburban home. The growth, around the country, of African American suburbs like Liberty Road pushes us to reconfigure our understanding of race and space. The story of the suburbs cannot be told well with the frameworks and perspectives of studies of urban racial inequality. Race still matters, but we must reconsider how the people, issues, and larger forces shape life in such suburbs. First, we need to pay closer attention to the actions and decisions of African American themselves—residents, realtors, religious leaders, politicians, activists. Segregation and desegregation are not unfortunate, impersonal processes, but the outcome of determined action by a range of people in communities like Liberty Road. Second, we see in Liberty Road that the issues in which race manifests itself, and the positions people take on these issues, are different from those familiar from studies of city politics. Churches are not just anchors in the community but expanding ventures that suburbanites (white and Black) may oppose. For suburban residents, neighborhood economic development is less an opportunity to make money than to spend money. (Office parks and warehouses are physically distant from residences, so the most local projects are largely about retail.) Since large-scale workplaces are considered incompatible with the residential suburban ideal, local economic development focuses on improving retail opportunities in the area.

This book has looked at Black suburbanization as the outcome of a collision on the suburban landscape of everyday activists' efforts to secure better housing and the neoliberal movement to claw back the gains of the civil rights activists and working Americans who built a more secure middle class. Just as that activism had to happen on every level, neoliberalism happened at every level as well. Activism involved mortgage lenders, heads of federal agencies, realtors, and home seekers. Neoliberalism unleashed global markets in mortgage securities that poured money into unsustainable mortgages during the housing bubble and created greater financial and employment insecurity.

There is reason to think that the neoliberal era could be drawing to a close, or at least changing in significant ways. The features of whatever might develop in the wake of neoliberalism are not yet clear and remain contradictory. Some features point to greater inequality, others to greater security. The first indications (of both continuation and interruption of the neoliberal program) are visible at the national level.

On the more pessimistic side, economist Thomas Piketty argues convincingly that the global economy is moving the balance of power between labor and capital back to a period when the importance of capital, and the return on investments by capitalists, will grow to the levels of the Victorian era.[1] Granted, tax rates and other government policies influence whether we are headed for a return of gilded age princes and paupers. But if, as Piketty argues, capital will be more powerful than it was in the mid-twentieth century when a mass middle class was ascendant in the United States, there will inevitably be changes on the suburban landscape. Indeed, after the foreclosure crisis, in Randallstown as in many other communities, many homes that had been owner-occupied during the housing bubble became, typically for the first time, owned by real estate investors who sought to profit by renting them out. Homeownership rates deceptively rose to their highest levels during the housing bubble, then fell to their pre-bubble level. Homeownership rates among African Americans dropped from 46 percent in 2009 to 43.2 percent in the end of 2013, and continued declining to 41.7 percent in 2018, consistently the lowest rate for any racial group. (After a dozen years of decline, the national homeownership rate in 2018 was 64.4 percent, but for whites it was 73.1 percent.)[2] The presence of more investment capital in the real estate market would mean that more people will have to rent rather than buy (because when seeking a home to buy they cannot beat the prices offered by investors with more cash). Given that African Americans already have lower levels of wealth than whites, they are likely to be hit earliest and hardest by a market that raises barriers to buying a home and thus accumulating a nest egg of wealth to pass on to subsequent generations.

At the same time, there were rosier indications that the insecurity of the neoliberal age was being diminished. Most notably, the Affordable Care Act moved to provide health insurance to thirty million formerly uninsured people. As a result of more widely available health care, people were not as wholly dependent on their employers for health insurance.

Then-president Barack Obama made other moves that raised the possibility of a retreat from the most aggressive aspects of the neoliberal agenda. For nearly thirty years the Federal Reserve was chaired by avowed neoliberals like Alan Greenspan. In 2014 Obama appointed Janet Yellen, whose views on politics were notably more liberal and Keynesian than neoliberal.[3] Perhaps the global financial crisis derailed neoliberal ambitions. The election of Donald Trump, his assaults on the Affordable Care Act, and his replacement of academics like Yellen and Ben Bernanke at the Federal Reserve with Wall Street–trained bankers disrupted those reforms to neoliberalism, but his policies carried elements of nationalism and protectionism that were not neoliberal themselves. The global coronavirus pandemic required exceptional deficits and spending, so that it is not clear whether the outcome will be a new orientation toward equitable growth or an eventual return to neoliberal austerity.

The Trump administration threatened to not only reverse several of those corrections to neoliberal insecurity but also destabilize the foundation on which a middle-class existence is predicated, particularly for African Americans. The notion that African Americans are enfranchised enough to participate in the middle class is thrown into question. As Ta-Nehisi Coates argued, Trump activated American racist tendencies on the public political stage. "Whereas his forebears carried whiteness like an ancestral talisman," Coates wrote of earlier white presidents, "Trump cracked the glowing amulet open, releasing its eldritch energies."[4] Race and scapegoating portended new possibilities of punctuations to the suburban efforts toward equilibrium.

At the most extreme, the rise in the United States and other countries of nationalist politics and opposition to neoliberal touchstones like free trade could spell the end of the neoliberal and liberal projects, introducing a "postliberal" era. Neoliberalism was a racially framed political backlash against popular gains in income and equality, promoting financialization, free trade, and selective deregulation. Perhaps the political moment has moved beyond that project. It is possible a postliberal age seeks no longer to expand markets, reduce regulation, and cut social safety nets but to reestablish trade barriers and further dial up the contrast between "us" and scapegoated "them," rallying loyalists under a politics of scarcity. It may also be that the momentum for racial justice, equity, and government engagement with inequality that grew visibly during the COVID-19 crisis will effectively challenge some of the stark social neglect that was central to neoliberal orthodoxy.

The outcome of these opposing trends—greater inequality and policies poised to mitigate insecurity—is thus far unclear. But they increase the possibility, discussed in chapter 7, that macro-level shifts could lead to another one of the periodic political realignments that make new bedfellows out of erstwhile political opponents. Did the Great Recession sufficiently damage the reputation of signature policies of neoliberalism like deregulation, deunionization, and dismantling of the social safety net as to create the political support for policies that reduce inequality? Or has neoliberalism entered another phase in which, having indeed dismantled the major components of the more egalitarian mid-twentieth century, those actors now accumulate more profit, buying up ever larger sections of suburban homes to rent them to people who used to own them? Before the 1940s, most Americans paid rent to a landlord rather than made mortgage payments on an investment that was supposed to bring them some measure of stability and security. The rise of more progressive Democrats simultaneous with the revanchist policies of the Trump Republicans suggests both those visions are being promoted, with the outcome of that contest unpredictable at this moment. Both sides offer evidence, however, that such a realignment is under way, as the free trade ideology that was bipartisan when NAFTA was signed has been roundly rejected and the prohibition on explicitly social democratic policies is lifted by a new generation of Democratic progressives.

If we are at the cusp of a revised set of macro-level economic relations, African American suburbs are a useful place to develop the tools and perspectives necessary to get a handle on them. Such settings combine the political agency of the middle class with the continued isolation of Black Americans, even middle-class Black Americans. Suburbs themselves remain the center stage of American domestic political discourse, the kinds of places politicians must consider carefully when crafting new policies. For these purposes, punctuated equilibrium offers the advantage of being able to make sense of stability and crisis, recognizing long periods when public policy preserves the middle class, and the crisis moments that put the middle class in peril. The expectations of the punctuated equilibrium model are also a warning that, as we assess the differential losses from the coronavirus epidemic, we must insist that policies meant to address that damage work as well for Black communities as for white ones.

Economic and political outcomes may be different at the local and national levels. In Baltimore, there are reasons to emphasize stability in the punctuated equilibrium model. Foremost among them is government employment: as a suburb of Washington, DC, the Baltimore area has higher than average government employment, which tends to pay steady if not extraordinary salaries and better withstands economic ups and downs. The most recent census data indicate that in 2019 Randall-stown (defined by the census around the outer half of Liberty Road in the county) was 81 percent Black and had a median income of $83,226, which was higher than the median in the county, state, or country. Its poverty rate (6.8 percent) was lower.[5]

At the national level, however, there are reasons to expect more set-backs. The middle class continues to shrink. Judicial reversals of civil rights gains (like the Supreme Court's erosion of the Voting Rights Act, affirmative action, and the school desegregation rulings of the twen-tieth century) seem to considerably outnumber gains. And while the Great Recession may have revealed the instability of poorly regulated neoliberal financial systems, little has been done to restructure them. All of these conditions create a situation in which a financially pre-carious, politically disempowered African American middle class could face new crises with little ability to gain adequate assistance through the political sphere.

While it is a certainty that African American residents and local ac-tivists will continue to push for greater access and a better quality of life, what the outcome of those efforts will look like is far from certain. Greater equality and prosperity are possible, but the suburban landscape has been shaped physically, politically, and culturally in ways that do not make such outcomes inevitable or even the most likely. Forces in the larger economy clearly play a huge role in what will happen, and they put African Americans at disproportionate risk. But with tools honed from research in suburbs like Randallstown, we can better understand what people's efforts can deliver.

Suburbs Can Be Black: Can They Be Green?

My conclusions regarding the promises and perils of African American middle-class suburbs are wrapped up in my own ambivalence about sub-urbs as a social and spatial form. There are considerable problems with suburbs (Black or white) as environmentally unsustainable spaces, as communities based on exclusion, and as low-density areas with limited public spaces that leave people spatially isolated and reliant on automo-biles. Low-density, autocentric spaces have pernicious effects on people, reliant as we are on social interaction.

Suburbs' autocentricity renders them environmentally unsustainable. Suburbs are dependent on automobiles for transportation. In the event of escalating energy prices (if we switch to cleaner but costlier energy sources or experience the "peak oil" projection of petroleum prices), US suburbs could be economically unsustainable if transportation costs rise too high. (Ironically, high fuel costs make construction projects more expensive too, so a period of high gas prices would be a difficult one in which to retrofit communities with mass transit networks like train lines.) Drought certainly threatens the traditional green suburban yard, but communities in the Southwest such as Las Vegas have demonstrated that suburban yards can be redesigned as "xeriscapes" that embrace desert plants and require little water. Seasonal temperatures may make homes more expensive to cool in the summer or more costly to heat if snowfall and winter weather grows more intense in some localities. If that occurred in tandem with rising fuel prices, the increased costs could be difficult for many people to bear.

There is also the question of social sustainability. The physical shape of postwar suburbs was influenced not only by the ideal of single-family houses and green yards but by the convenience of developers who mass produced housing (avoiding the expense of creating many public amenities) and the acceleration of drivers seeking to exit urban traffic. The result was low-density housing with historically low opportunities to connect face-to-face with other people. The result, I argue elsewhere, was a setting that did not provide people with adequate opportunities to socialize.[6] Their lack of pedestrian design, coupled with the popularity of exclusive attitudes (evident in African American suburbs as well as white ones), produces a paucity of public spaces and a proliferation of communities that are literally or attitudinally gated.[7] Postwar suburbs were unsustainable in that they denied us the social setting that people need.

Given the strong preference many African American homebuyers express for a suburban home, the events and processes that took place in Baltimore County must be appreciated for giving African Americans broader (if still illegally segregated) housing options than they had before. But this history has also expanded a suburban environment that is unsustainable.

Several years ago there was a court case on Long Island against the mostly white town of Garden City.[8] Employees in the town's park would ask Black visitors for ID. Residents of the adjoining (mostly Black) town of Hempstead were told the park was for Garden City residents only and kicked out of the park. After a lawsuit, the town's solution was to ask *everyone* for ID, so that whites and Blacks from outside of the town could be excluded. That hardly seemed to me like a satisfactory outcome. After years of being illegally and discriminatorily excluded from a park, the appropriate remedy for the African American plaintiffs would be access to the park on the same basis as that whites had enjoyed for so long—unquestioned access regardless of one's address.

The same principle applies to the environmental question. After being shut out of suburbs literally and in the popular imagination, this book seeks to establish a place in the suburbs for African Americans. To respond to the obstacles and difficulties African Americans have faced getting into the suburbs by pointing out that autocentric suburbs are environmentally irresponsible and thus no one, including African Americans, should be allowed in hardly seems like a productive response. Environmental issues are not a problem unique to African American suburbs, they are a concern of all suburbs—of all communities. As African Americans are integrated into the social fabric of the suburbs, they can and do participate in developing responses to the environmental challenges we face.

It would be nice to think that the growth of African American suburbs or the integration of African Americans into suburbs would revise the environmentally wasteful shape suburbs take. After all, suburbs built at low densities, with higher volumes of private space than public space, lacking public transportation and requiring expensive, resource-guzzling automobiles were to a large degree a product of earlier suburbanites' desires to racially segregate their surroundings. African American suburbanization alone will not reverse those tendencies. But it is certainly more possible to create more inclusive, less spatially segregated (and spatially wasteful) suburbs if one of the primary logics of suburbanization—racial segregation—is rendered moot.

In terms of those environmental concerns, this study provides some cautions about how race is likely to matter in the consideration of environmental issues that will shape the suburbs. The punctuated equilibrium model provides two insights. First, it is possible that communities that face threats may exist in relative stability for some time, only to be struck by acute crises. Second, to the extent that environmental challenges confront all suburbs equally (like the savings and loan crisis of the

1980s and 1990s), there is likely to be some national-level response. But to the extent that these changes affect African Americans singularly or more dramatically (as the foreclosure crisis did) the political response is likely to be inadequate. Looking nationwide, there are some indications of how climate change could affect African Americans more directly. In the wake of hurricanes like Katrina and Sandy, it was striking how, just as was the case historically, today higher income people are more likely to live on higher ground and low-income people are likely to live down in flood-prone areas. To the extent that African American suburbs in various localities may be relegated to less desirable real estate, they may be at higher risk for flooding. Likewise, since African Americans have considerably less savings, on average, than whites, crises (such as hurricanes) that require substantial outlays for repairs (or relocation) would be more difficult for African American households to face without an adequate public program of support. This issue is much more than a suburban topic. One key is for public policy to address the needs of the full range of affected people, not only those with more resources. The second urgent need is for government to take all crises seriously, rather than failing to respond adequately to crises in communities of color. For at-risk suburbs, it is better to think about improvements to sustainability before crises strike.

Integration—By Whom?

Time and again the problems that face the African American middle class are rendered more acute by residential racial segregation. Yet integration has fallen off the political map.

In the integrationist era of the civil rights movements, African Americans clearly stuck to their end of the bargain: they took the nation on its word and moved out into the suburbs. They embraced suburban culture, espoused suburban political views, and celebrated the successes of the hardworking people in their own communities while (true to the suburban perspective) looking with quiet concern at poorer people farther down the road.

In that period it was whites who fell down on the deal, and did so dramatically. These new African American suburbanites were not desperately poor. Their arrival in the suburbs attested to their thrift, determination, and ability to find work that provided some security, offering more counterevidence than was ever needed to dispel whites' notion that potential Black neighbors might embody the "culture of poverty." To their credit, whites in the period I studied did not flee. But African Americans gained a suburban foothold only in areas where few whites wanted to live. African Americans made few gains in places where whites still wanted homes. And whites stopped moving in entirely as the number of African Americans grew to around 20 percent.

In this sense it was not Blacks who had a problem, it was whites. Community studies in sociology tend to focus on areas that manifest the most dramatic social problems, but unfortunately problems are often caused by one group and manifest in another. A solution to segregation would inevitably engage with whites.

One must ask if white Americans really want to live segregated lives in segregated communities in a segregated nation. There is some evidence this is not the preferred arrangement of most whites.[9] I submit that segregation handicaps all Americans—whites included—far more than it may benefit some subset of them. Even if segregation is not the outcome that individual whites prefer, the decisions individuals make *in the present structural situation* ensure that segregation will be reproduced again and again. Change requires altering public policy and, to do that, acknowledgment of the problem.

It is worth pointing out here that the evidence is that African Americans don't feel an urgent desire to integrate for its own sake, merely that it may be advantageous to them and the communities in which they already live. As the story of Liberty Road shows, for most people integration has been a strategic goal, not an end in itself. But in addition to being a means by which African Americans can access resources that segregation otherwise restricts, there are important and irreplaceable values to desegregation in its own right.

Any such change needs to happen with dialogue among African Americans about what they need. Critically, residential segregation began to reach extremely high levels in the United States around the 1920s, for reasons of safety for African Americans, who were threatened by anti-Black riots and vulnerable in more isolated or integrated areas. A valuable starting point in a dialogue would be understanding what African Americans would need to feel comfortable moving into neighborhoods that are largely white and are not now "spillover" suburbs next to larger Black communities. Is there a critical threshold of fellow African Americans that is necessary, or public actions to demonstrate that African Americans would actually be welcome, would be safe, and could be at ease in formerly white suburban neighborhoods? While research (and legislation) addressing segregation has appropriately examined the discriminatory practices of real estate agents, lenders, and others, less attention has been given to why most African Americans find an all-white neighborhood unappealing. That side of the equation has less to do with in-group loyalty or the anodyne notion that people like to "be with their own kind" than with the reality that all-white areas today still strike African Americans as unsafe, unpleasant, difficult places to try to live.

Would African Americans be welcome? Perhaps white reactions need, here, to be framed once again in terms of Negrophobia: whites need to stop being afraid. In this framing, avoiding resegregation can even have a conservative framing for whites. People should have a commitment to their property that dictates they stay as newcomers arrive. As Randallstown demonstrated, larger numbers of white residents stayed as the neighborhood transitioned than had in the city in decades past. But those homeowners' children abandoned the communities of their childhood to move elsewhere as adults. Once again, though it is consonant with liberal values of integration, preventing resegregation is also consistent with conservative "traditional" values of community and a connection to place.

Such a reframing would indeed represent a historic political shift. But with the demographic shifts making the Republicans' Southern Strategy less effective, the benefits to sounding an alarm of racial hysteria at the first sign of integration may be diminishing. And the benefits, even to whites, of segregating the nation's neighborhoods by race are hard to identify. Surely we would be better off if all schools were properly supported and all students well educated. Surely we would be better off if predatory mortgages had not borne down on Black and Latino communities and caused a collapse in housing prices. I advocate integration not because Blacks or whites are clamoring for it but because it will lead to better lives for all concerned.

While African Americans have found better housing options in suburbs like Randallstown, the current strategy of gaining access to the suburbs while experiencing continued segregation beyond the boundaries of those neighborhoods is not adequate. Home values don't appreciate sufficiently, schools continue to be plagued by unequal outcomes because of segregation, quality-of-life markers (like retail options) lag in African American suburbs, financial predation and other crises are left unaddressed as long as there are predominantly Black neighborhoods in which to focus their ill effects. The suburbs have been a step up for residents, but they are not a solution. It would be admirable to make changes in how we organize our communities that demonstrate that in the United States meritocracy works, for the middle class and for others. The African American middle class is larger than it has ever been. It has political power, organizational savvy, and determination. If people in the African American middle class are unconvinced the suburban strategy will work for them, what can they adopt in its place?

As I finished this book, I returned on another trip to the Randallstown suburbs. The summer heat has a peculiar effect on suburbs; it silences them, moving people inside, making the outdoor rhythms slow and quiet. On a hot day Black and white residents disappear into air-conditioned homes. What happens to a dream in the suburban sun?

African Americans have begun to achieve the suburban dream. The suburban dream, pursued by whites as well as Blacks, is a modest one: a decent home with green space around it, a life that may require careful budgeting but that is economically stable and provides an opportunity to raise children who can grow up to live lives with similar qualities.

Despite its modesty, the suburban dream has also been, undeniably, an exclusive dream, one in which residents' success, status, and security come by means of excluding others, others who have most often been defined racially and economically. African American suburbanites are simultaneously exploring how fully they will be able to realize the suburban dream in the larger, predominantly white suburbs, and whether they can achieve a suburban dream that is not as exclusive as the earlier, white-flight version. The determination and compassion of the residents I came to know in my research put them in a particularly strong position to redefine what it means to achieve the suburban dream in a more inclusive way for everyone. It is urgent to all of us that this new vision not be a dream deferred.

ACKNOWLEDGMENTS

Returning to the suburbs to write about them has been an intensely personal experience, but this work came into being only with the help of many other people. I grew up near Randallstown, and my parents first raised me in the suburbs and then spent days with my own children while I was conducting research for this project, while also looking out for news articles of interest and keeping me up to date on events in the area. The residents of Randallstown and its surroundings have been immensely generous with their time, opening up to me and providing me insight into their community that only they have. People who work in the county, in local institutions, and beyond opened their doors as well. Barbara Kellner at the archives of Columbia, Maryland, generously let me in on a holiday (Martin Luther King Day) to read up on the efforts of James Rouse to cross the color line. In the archives in Chicago, Kevin Loughran and Caroline Graham helped me obtain copies of Mark Satter's *Chicago Defender* columns.

There were invaluable contributors to this project and this community who died while I was working on it. Among them are Patricia Ferguson, Ella White Campbell, Emily Wolfson, John Michener, Mal Sherman, and Jeannette Cadwallader. I wish they could have seen the final product, and I hope they would find that I rendered accurately the work they did during their lives. My father, C. Donald Smith, also died midway through this project, from long-term complications of diabetes and high blood pressure. I had already been researching diabetes for several years when he died, and earlier drafts of this book had a substantial chapter on the effects of social stress on such diseases. There wasn't room for it in the final text, but it was one example of a powerful interrelationship I experienced between my personal life, my research priorities, and the endemic strains on the suburb I was studying,

I benefited immensely from the colleagues and friends who read over my work from its earliest moments. A writing group in New York, including John Krinsky, Rich Ocejo, and Debbie Becher, patiently read through many drafts of chapters. At Brooklyn College, a second writing group of Carolina Bank Muñoz and Tamara Mose were invaluable readers. My dissertation adviser and mentor, Sudhir Venkatesh, read multiple versions of the manuscript and always offered incisive, useful comments—a rare skill and a substantial commitment of time. Whatever inevitable shortcomings there are in the book are the result of me not following their advice farther than I was able.

I was lucky enough to have colleagues nearby who were fellow Baltimoreans. George Cunningham, Prudence Cumberbach, Robert Shapiro, and Robert Scott all happened to work on my floor on campus and know Baltimore well, each through their own professional and personal lenses. I benefited immensely. Kimberly Johnson, who was working on her own project, gave thoughtful feedback on early drafts.

In analyzing the ungainly collection of data a project like this digs up, my thanks to my colleague Diana Pan for introducing me to the wonders of the qualitative data analysis software Atlas.ti, and to former students Red Samaniego for collecting data on foreclosure soon after the housing crash and Tess Brustein for mapping foreclosure data.

My colleagues at Brooklyn College and the Graduate Center of the City University of New York are unparalleled, and I'm proud that my book came about side by side with the work they do. A writing boot camp organized by the dean's office at Brooklyn College was valuable for completing the book. Support for this project was provided by a PSC-CUNY Award, jointly funded by my union, the Professional Staff Congress, and The City University of New York.

As always, I thank my kids. They have shaped who I am, and thus what the book is. As city kids, they marvel at parts of the suburbs I took for granted. When they were little they thought a suburban house with stairs in it—unlike an apartment building where the stairs were out in the corridor—was luxurious. A mostly white suburban high school looked inherently weird to them, whereas it looked natural when I went to one. I want something more for their generation than the suburbs I grew up in. But I hope I can explain a part of the suburbs to them as well.

NOTES

INTRODUCTION

1   In some cases whites smeared black tar on the white marble steps. Homeowners scrubbed their marble stoop to keep it gleaming white, so the tar was a particularly pointed attack given the local culture. See W. Ashbie Hawkins, "A Year of Segregation in Baltimore," *Crisis*, November 1911, 27.

2   Carl Husemoller Nightingale, "The Transnational Contexts of Early Twentieth-Century American Urban Segregation," *Journal of Social History* 39, no. 3 (Spring 2006): 673. "Eutaw" is pronounced like "Utah."

3   I capitalize Black but not white. Touré, like others, argues that Black is a cultural identity, akin to Latino or Irish, and merits capitalization on that basis, but white does not hold a cultural meaning to people who are white. See the opening pages of Touré, *Who's Afraid of Post-Blackness? What It Means to Be Black Now* (New York: Free Press, 2011). Annette Lareau does so simply out of deference to her audience, "recognizing that some readers have strong views that Black should be capitalized." Lareau, *Unequal Childhoods: Class, Race, and Family Life* (Berkeley: University of California Press, 2003), 289n1. As W. E. B. Du Bois wrote regarding the decades-long campaign to capitalize "Negro," "I believe that 8 million Americans are entitled to a capital letter."

4   Garrett Power, "Apartheid Baltimore Style: The Residential Segregation Ordinances of 1910–1913," *Maryland Law Review* 42 (1982): 289–328.

5   Antero Pietila, *Not in My Neighborhood: How Bigotry Shaped a Great American City* (Chicago: Ivan R. Dee / Rowman & Littlefield, 2010), 24.

6   W. Ashbie Hawkins is often said to have been the first treasurer of the Niagara Movement, a predecessor of the NAACP, apparently after NAACP cofounder Mary White Ovington said so in a widely reprinted speech (Mary White Ovington, "How the NAACP Began," in *NAACP: Celebrating a Century: 100 Years in Pictures* [Layton, UT: Gibbs Smith, 2009], 16). A letter from Du Bois to the newly nominated treasurer makes it clear the treasurer was Mason A. Hawkins, a Harvard graduate, also of Baltimore, principal of Colored High School (later called Douglass High) (Letter from Du Bois to Mason A. Hawkins, September 3, 1908, W. E. B. Du Bois Collection, University of Massachusetts Library; *The First Colored Professional, Clerical and Business Directory of Baltimore City*, 1st annual ed., vol. 494 [1913–1914], 2). Mason Hawkins was not related to Ashbie: Frank Lincoln Mather, *Who's Who of the Colored Race: A General Biographical Dictionary of Men*

and Women of African Descent, vol. 1 (1915). Ashbie Hawkins's formal membership in civil rights organizations predates the attack on the home he owned.

7 Gretchen Boger, "The Meaning of Neighborhood in the Modern City: Baltimore's Residential Segregation Ordinances, 1910–1913," *Journal of Urban History* 35 (2009): 236–258, 242.

8 Pietila, *Not in My Neighborhood*, 25.

9 Hawkins was also the first African American to run for the US Senate in Maryland. Jason Torrs, "The Plot Sickens," *Baltimore City Paper*, May 30, 2007. First issue of *The Crisis*: Boger, "Meaning of Neighborhood," 242.

10 Hawkins was third president of the Baltimore branch: Hassan Giordano, "From Past to Present: An Overview of the NAACP-Baltimore Branch Presidents," *Baltimore Independent Examiner*, November 29, 2010.

11 "Ashbie Hawkins, Attorney for 50 Years, Dies at 78," *Baltimore Afro-American*, April 12, 1941.

12 Michael C. Dawson, *Behind the Mule: Race and Class in African-American Politics* (Princeton, NJ: Princeton University Press, 1994).

13 In 2000, median incomes for Randallstown: $53,753, Baltimore County: $50,667, Maryland: $52,868, United States: $41,994.

14 In addition to the fifty interviews in Baltimore, I made use of sixteen interviews on financial precarity and another dozen on chronic health problems for earlier versions of this project.

15 William H. Frey, *State of Metropolitan America: On the Front Lines of Demographic Transformation* (Washington, DC: Brookings Institute, 2010), 60. Doubling in size: Dawson, *Behind the Mule*, 9.

16 Power, "Apartheid Baltimore Style," 326.

17 US Census Bureau, "American Community Survey 5-Year Estimates" (2017), http://socialexplorer.com.

18 By 2018, median incomes for Randallstown: $70,331, Randallstown African Americans: $70,864, Baltimore County: $74,127, Maryland: $81,868, United States: $63,179. US Census Bureau, "American Community Survey 2013–2018" (2018), http://socialexplorer.com.

19 On immigrant and ethnic African American neighborhoods, see Orly Clerge, *The New Noir: Race, Identity and Diaspora in Black Suburbia* (Oakland: University of California Press, 2019). Other work has looked insightfully at race and identity outside the United States. See Jean Beaman, *Citizen Outsider: Children of North African Immigrants in France* (Oakland: University of California Press, 2017), and Ernesto Castañeda, *A Place to Call Home: Immigrant Exclusion and Urban Belonging in New York, Paris, and Barcelona* (Stanford, CA: Stanford University Press, 2018).

20 Kevin Fox Gotham, for instance, writes, "The crucial question regarding the suburbanization of African Americans is whether this racial movement represents neighborhood integration or resegregation and the growth of suburban African

American ghettoes." "Beyond Invasion and Succession: School Segregation, Real State Blockbusting, and the Political Economy of Neighborhood Racial Transition," *City and Community* 1, no. 1 (March 2002): 106.

21 William Julius Wilson, *The Truly Disadvantaged: The Inner City, the Underclass, and Public Policy* (Chicago: University of Chicago Press, 1987).

22 For examples of how urban sociology is defined by an interest in space, see the debate among Herbert Gans, Thomas F. Gieryn, and Sharon Zukin in "The Sociology of Space: A Use-Centered View," *City and Community* 1, no. 4 (December 2002): 329–348.

23 Kenneth T. Jackson, *Crabgrass Frontier: The Suburbanization of the United States* (New York: Oxford University Press, 1985), 287.

24 Jackson once said in a graduate seminar I took that if he had it to do over again, he would emphasize more the role of race in the formation of the suburbs.

25 Roasalyn Baxandall and Elizabeth Ewen, *Picture Windows: How the Suburbs Happened* (New York: Basic Books, 2001).

26 Herbert J. Gans, *The Levittowners: Ways of Life and Politics in a New Suburban Community* (New York: Vintage, 1967).

27 Richard Rothstein, *Color of Law: A Forgotten History of How Our Government Segregated America* (New York: Liveright, 2017).

28 Setha Low, *Behind the Gates: Life, Security, and the Pursuit of Happiness in Fortress America* (New York: Routledge, 2004).

29 David Harvey, *A Brief History of Neoliberalism* (New York: Oxford University Press, 2005).

30 Gérard Duménil and Dominique Lévy, *Capital Resurgent: Roots of the Neoliberal Revolution* (Cambridge, MA: Harvard University Press, 2004).

31 Judith Stein, *Pivotal Decade: How the United States Traded Factories for Finance in the Seventies* (New Haven, CT: Yale University Press, 2010); Neil Brenner, "Neoliberalism and the Urban Condition," *City* 9, no. 1 (April 2005): 101–107.

32 Harvey, *Brief History of Neoliberalism*, 151.

33 James Baldwin, *The Fire Next Time* (New York: Dial Press, 1963), 33.

34 Cedric J. Robinson, *Black Marxism: The Making of the Black Radical Tradition* (London: Zed Press, 1983).

35 If neoliberalism describes midcentury backlash politics, then it also includes attacks against women, from efforts to criminalize abortion to attempts to defund women's health clinics like Planned Parenthood. The neocolonial policies pursued in foreign affairs by those who are domestic neoliberals are certainly consistent with neoliberalism as well, but are hardly new developments.

36 Michael Omi and Howard Winant, *Racial Formation in the United Sates from the 1960s to the 1990s* (New York: Routledge, 1994), 56.

37 Loïc Wacquant, "Crafting the Neoliberal State: Workfare, Prisonfare, and Social Insecurity," *Sociological Forum* 25, no. 5 (June 2010): 197–220, 213.

38 Wacquant, "Crafting the Neoliberal State," 213–214.

39 Wacquant, "Crafting the Neoliberal State," 207.

40 Melvin L. Oliver and Thomas M. Shapiro, *Black Wealth / White Wealth: A New Perspective on Racial Inequality* (New York: Routledge, 2006).

41 Lisa Duggan, *Twilight of Equality? Neoliberalism, Cultural Politics, and the Attack on Democracy* (Boston: Beacon, 2003), xii.

42 Duggan, *Twilight of Equality?*, 14–15.

43 Kevin P. Phillips, *The Emerging Republican Majority* (New Rochelle, NY: Arlington House, 1969). Phillips's book is an interesting strategic document of racialization, though it is hamstrung by his reluctance to fully admit to the racial component of the strategy. His dissection of white ethnic voting patterns substitutes for discussing white racism.

44 My thanks to my colleague Naomi Braine for her observation that race and Black political representation are the best indicators of regressive welfare policies.

45 Christopher Niedt, "Gentrification and the Grassroots: Popular Support in the Revanchist Suburb," *Journal of Urban Affairs* 28, no. 2 (2006): 99–120.

46 David Theo Goldberg, *The Threat of Race: Reflections on Racial Neoliberalism* (Malden, MA: Wiley-Blackwell, 2009), 338.

47 Ayanna Alexander, Andrew Kreighbaum, and Paige Smith, "Biden's Racial Equity Challenge: Act Solo to Reverse Trump Moves," *Bloomberg Law*, December 29, 2020.

48 For instance, while working-class wages have stagnated or fallen for all groups, African Americans have been particularly hard hit. Unlike white households, African American families experienced absolute income declines between 1973 and 1993. Lynn A. Karoly, "The Trend in Inequality among Families, Individuals and Workers in the United States: A Twenty-Five Year Perspective," in *Uneven Tides: Rising Inequality in America*, ed. Sheldon Danziger and Peter Gottschalk (New York: Russell Sage Foundation, 1993); David R. Williams and Chiquita Collins, "US Socioeconomic and Racial Differences in Health: Patterns and Explanations," *Annual Review of Sociology* 21 (1995): 349–386. The recession that began in 2008 not only had a more serious effect on Blacks than on whites, imposing a higher unemployment rate on Blacks, but also increased the wage gap between whites and Blacks. Mark Roth, "Recession Has Taken Hidden Toll on Black Families," *Pittsburgh Post-Gazette*, June 7, 2011; Rakesh Kochhar, Richard Fry, and Paul Taylor, "Wealth Gaps Rise to Record Highs between Whites, Blacks, Hispanics: Twenty-to-One" (Washington, DC: Pew Research Center, July 26, 2011). While median white wealth dropped from $134,992 to $113,149 between 2005 and 2009, African American wealth was more than cut in half, from $12,124 to $5,677.

49 Paul Taylor, Rakesh Kochhar, Richard Fry, Gabriel Velasco, and Seth Motel, "Twenty-to-One: Wealth Gaps to Rise to Record High between Whites, Blacks and Hispanics" (Washington, DC: Pew Research Center, 2011).

50 Quoted in Michael Zweig, *The Working Class Majority: America's Best Kept Secret* (Ithaca, NY: ILR Press, 2011), 20.

51 The American dream is a "dream of a land in which life should be better and richer and fuller for everyone, with opportunity for each according to ability or

achievement. It is a difficult dream for the European upper classes to interpret adequately, and too many of us ourselves have grown weary and mistrustful of it. It is not a dream of motor cars and high wages merely, but a dream of social order in which each man and each woman shall be able to attain to the fullest stature of which they are innately capable, and be recognized by others for what they are, regardless of the fortuitous circumstances of birth or position." James Truslow Adams, *The Epic of America* (1931; repr., New York: Routledge, 2017).

52 Richard Lacayo, "Suburban Legend William Levitt: His Answer to a Postwar Housing Crisis Created a New Kind of Home Life and Culture: Suburbia," *Time*, December 7, 1998.

53 Michael Zweig, "Six Points on Class," *Monthly Review*, July 1, 2006.

54 The fact that the public imagines the middle class is larger than it really is and imagines the African American middle class is smaller than it really is poses a conundrum for research on the African American middle class. It's hard to correct the misimpressions in both directions.

55 Karyn Lacy, *Blue Chip Black: Race, Class, and Status in the New Black Middle Class* (Berkeley: University of California Press, 2007), 33–32; Editors of the *New York Times, Class Matters* (New York: Holt, 2005).

56 "United States Home Prices and Values," Zillow, January 17, 2019, http://zillow.com.

57 US Census Bureau, "Current Population Survey, 2014 Annual Social and Economic Supplement" (2014), www.census.gov. By this measure, among white households 29.8 percent are middle class.

58 Aldon Morris, *The Origins of the Civil Rights Movement* (New York: Free Press, 1984).

59 Malcolm X as told to Alex Haley, *The Autobiography of Malcolm X* (New York: Ballantine Books, 1964), 282, 315, 312, 320.

60 Malcolm X, *Autobiography*, 317.

61 Malcolm X, *Autobiography*, 314.

62 Malcolm's rhetoric may have been hyperbolic: his ambivalence toward integration was more broadly shared. Even participants in integration were far from "integration mad," more often seeing it as a strategic means to an end—access to better housing, schools, or jobs—rather than an end in itself.

63 E. Franklin Frazier, *Black Bourgeoisie: The Book That Brought the Shock of Self-Revelation to Middle-Class Blacks in America* (1957; repr., New York: Free Press, 1997).

64 Bart Landry, "A Reinterpretation of the Writings of Frazier on the Black Middle Class," *Social Problems* 26, no. 2 (December 1978): 211–222.

65 Kimberly Phillips, *AlabamaNorth: African-American Migrants, Community, and Working-Class Activism in Cleveland, 1915–1945* (Champaign: University of Illinois Press, 1999). Among working-class groups, Phillips discusses the Future Outlook League in Cincinnati.

66 Karen Miller, "Managing Inequality: Northern Racial Liberalism, African-American Activism, and Urban Politics in Interwar Detroit" (manuscript, 2012), introduction, 10–11; chap. 5, 210.

67 Darlene Clark Hine, "Black Professionals and Race Consciousness: Origins of the Civil Rights Movement, 1890–1050," *Journal of American History* 89 (2003): 1279–1294.

68 Wilson, *Truly Disadvantaged*, 56.

69 Dawson, *Behind the Mule*, 204.

70 Thomas F. Gieryn, "A Space for Place in Sociology," *Annual Review of Sociology* 26 (2000): 463–496; Gregory Smithsimon, *September 12: Community and Neighborhood Recovery at Ground Zero* (New York: New York University Press, 2011).

71 For one of the strongest uses of space by the Chicago school, see Gerald D. Suttles, *The Social Order of the Slum: Ethnicity and Territory in the Inner City* (Chicago: University of Chicago Press, 1968). One of the most mechanistic uses of space is Burgess's concentric rings.

72 Gieryn, "Space for Place."

73 Gieryn, "Space for Place."

74 Henri Lefebvre, *The Production of Space*, trans. Donald Nicholson-Smith (1974; Cambridge, MA: Blackwell, 1991); David Harvey, *The Condition of Postmodernity: An Enquiry into the Origins of Cultural Change* (Cambridge, MA: Basil Blackwell, 1980); Edward W. Soja, *Thirdspace: Journeys to Los Angeles and Other Real-and-Imagined Places* (Cambridge, MA: Blackwell, 1996).

75 Mike Davis, *City of Quartz: Excavating the Future in Los Angeles* (New York: Verso, 1990).

76 Peter Dreier, John Mollenkopf, and Todd Swanstrom, *Place Matters: Metropolitics for the Twenty-First Century*, 2nd ed. (Lawrence: University Press of Kansas, 2004).

77 See a history of suburbanization that was innovative for its Marxist analysis but did not discuss race: Patrick J. Ashton, "Urbanization and the Dynamics of Suburban Development under Capitalism," in *Marxism and the Metropolis: New Perspectives in Urban Political Economy*, 2nd ed., ed. William K. Tabb and Larry Sawers (New York: Oxford University Press, 1984), 54–81.

78 Andrew Wiese, *Places of Their Own: African American Suburbanization in the Twentieth Century* (Chicago: University of Chicago Press, 2004); see also Kevin M. Kruse and Thomas Sugrue, eds., *The New Suburban History* (Chicago: University of Chicago Press, 2006).

79 Alexandra Murphy, "'Litterers': How Objects of Physical Disorder Are Used to Construct Subjects of Social Disorder in a Suburb," *Annals of the American Academy of Political and Social Science* 642 (2012): 210–227.

80 Mary Pattillo, *Black Picket Fences: Privilege and Peril among the Black Middle Class*, 2nd ed. (Chicago: University of Chicago Press, 2013).

81 Steven Gregory, *Black Corona: Race and the Politics of Place in an Urban Community* (Princeton, NJ: Princeton University Press, 1998); Bruce D. Haynes, *Red Lines, Black Space: The Politics of Race and Space in a Black Middle-Class Suburb* (New Haven, CT: Yale University Press, 2001); Shirley Ann Wilson Moore, *To Place Our Deeds: The African American Community in Richmond, California, 1910–1963* (Berkeley: University of California Press, 2000).

82 Lacy, *Blue Chip Black*.

83 John Langston Gwaltney, *Drylongso: A Self-Portrait of Black America* (New York: Vintage, 1980); Lawrence Otis Graham, *Our Kind of People: Inside America's Black Upper Class* (New York: HarperCollins, 1999).

84 Robin D. G. Kelley, *Yo' Mama's Disfunktional! Fighting the Culture Wars in Urban America* (Boston: Beacon, 1998), 18.

85 "Punctuated equilibrium" comes from evolutionary biology. The process I observed does not mimic the process of punctuated equilibrium in evolution. I use the term, however, because it aptly describes the process in a way that is easy to understand, and because Gould (and his colleague Niles Eldredge) used the term to present an alternative model of large-scale change. Borrowing models helps give us new ways of understanding change. Stephen Jay Gould and Niles Eldredge, "Punctuated Equilibria: The Tempo and Mode of Evolution Reconsidered," *Paleontology* 3, no. 2 (1977): 115–151; Niles Eldredge and Stephen Jay Gould, "Punctuated Equilibria: An Alternative to Phyletic Gradualism," in *Models in Paleobiology*, ed. T. J. M. Schopf (San Francisco: Freeman Cooper, 1972), 82–115.

1. BEYOND BLOCKBUSTING

1 Michael L. Mark, *But Not Next Door, Baltimore Neighborhoods, Inc.: The First Forty Years* (Baltimore: Baltimore Neighborhoods, Inc., 2003).

2 Sherman's account comes from my interview with him. He tells a similar version of the story in Mark, *But Not Next Door*.

3 Quote excerpted in Manning Marable, *Malcolm X: A Life of Reinvention* (New York: Viking, 2011), 336.

4 Fortuitously, Sherman's timing was good. James Rouse was building the planned community of Columbia, Maryland, and was determined to make it a racially integrated community. Rouse hired Sherman to sell homes in Columbia. Other business innovations Sherman later developed allowed him to reestablish a very successful career in the field.

5 As Sherman tells the story, when Robinson moved from LA to Baltimore, he met Sherman and said that he had lived in all-white Brentwood, next to Beverley Hills, and wanted to live in a similar neighborhood in Baltimore. Sherman told him that was impossible because of the state of segregation in Baltimore. Robinson and Sherman continued to see each other socially, and at the end of the season when the Orioles had won the World Series (and Robinson had been named the Series' most valuable player), Robinson said to Sherman, "Look, I'm not going to spring training in Florida unless you get me a house in an all-white neighborhood." Sherman's telling of the story had many of the same obstacles Mackey's family experienced around the same time: "So spring training comes around, I haven't found anything for him. I get a call, some guy in Florida. He's yelling at me and he says to me, 'Sherman, what the fuck's wrong with you?' I say, 'Who am I talking to?' He says, 'This is Frank Cashen of the Orioles.' He says Frank [Robinson] won't

come to spring training and he says 'It's your fault because he won't find him a house in an all-white neighborhood.'"

Sherman could not find a house for Robinson to buy, so he proposed that the Orioles buy a house and rent it to Robinson. Eventually he found a woman willing to rent her house—but at a 66 percent premium, and she needed to know that most of the neighbors would be willing to have a Black baseball star living on the block. Sherman started knocking on doors: "The first person said no. So I said, 'Well, you accept him in the ballpark, you accept Blacks on the stage but you don't want him next door?' The next person I went to was hesitant and I said, 'Look, Frank Robinson will sign baseballs for your kids, give them bats,' Sherman laughed. 'I said, "The guy's a hero."' So I got three of the five people to OK it. She okayed the deal, Frank and Barbara moved in. He came to spring training, then he came up and moved in."

Fame is not a satisfactory antidote to white prejudice. But it is noteworthy that as with John Mackey, Frank Robinson's fame was not enough to overcome residents' opposition to having a Black neighbor.

6 Kevin Fox Gotham, *Race, Real Estate and Uneven Development: The Kansas City Experience, 1900–2000* (Albany: State University of New York Press, 2002), 25.

7 US District Court, Northern District of Indiana, Hammond Division, *Barrick Realty, Inc. v. City of Gary* (491 F.2d 161, 1974).

8 The court's definition of blockbusting borrows directly from the Federal Fair Housing Act, 42 USC § 3604 e, which states that it shall be unlawful "to induce . . . any person to sell or rent any dwelling by representations regarding the entry or prospective entry into the neighborhood of a person or persons of a particular race, color, religion, sex, handicap, familial status, or national origin."

9 "This process—buying the first property for a reasonable sum, then making successively lower and lower offers to those white property owners who remained and charging African Americans a premium—constituted the busting of a block." Amanda Seligman, *Block by Block: Neighborhoods and Public Policy on Chicago's West Side Chicago* (Chicago: University of Chicago Press, 2005), 158.

10 Seligman, *Block by Block*, 151.

11 The term "African American pioneers" is used by W. Edward Orser, *Blockbusting in Baltimore: The Edmondson Village Story* (Lexington: University Press of Kentucky, 1994).

12 Jonathan Rieder, *Canarsie: The Jews and Italians of Brooklyn Against Liberalism* (Cambridge, Ma: Harvard Press, 1985); Seligman, *Block by Block*; Maria Kefalas, *Working-Class Heroes: Protecting Home, Community, and Nation in a Chicago Neighborhood* (Berkeley: University of California Press, 2003); Orser, *Blockbusting in Baltimore*; Thomas S. Sugrue, *The Origins of the Urban Crisis: Race and Inequality in Postwar Detroit* (Princeton: Princeton University Press, 1996).

13 David Roediger, *The Wages of Whiteness: Race and the Making of the American Working Class* (New York: Verso, 1991).

14 Rieder, *Canarsie*, 201.

15 Though this doesn't moderate as much as clarify the comment, from the context in the book the speaker seemed to be saying not that an atom bomb should be dropped on Black Chicagoans but that the result of dropping a bomb on an area and letting Blacks move in was the same.

16 Kefalas, *Working-Class Heroes*, 43, 51, 53.

17 Sugrue, *Origins of the Urban Crisis*, 324, 241. Sugrue's grim assessment of the latitude of responses by whites to new Black neighbors is reminiscent of Dave Barry's satirical description of the impact of Reconstruction after the Civil War. The war brought transformation "from a totally segregated region where blacks had no rights into a totally segregated region where blacks were supposed to have rights but did not." Barry, *Dave Barry Slept Here: A Sort of History of the United States* (New York: Random House, 1989), 74.

18 Seligman, *Block by Block*, 150.

19 Seligman, *Block by Block*, 151.

20 Rieder, *Canarsie*, 3, 26.

21 Gotham, "Beyond Invasion and Succession"; Gotham, *Race, Real Estate and Uneven Development*.

22 Though it is perceived as a recent revision to the historical and popular conception of the suburbs, such revisionism was initiated over thirty years ago. Harold M. Rose, *Black Suburbanization: Access to Improved Quality of Life or Maintenance of the Status Quo?* (Cambridge, MA: Ballinger, 1976); Wiese, *Places of Their Own*; Becky M. Nicolaides and Andrew Wiese, eds., *The Suburb Reader* (New York: Routledge, 2005).

23 Lacy, *Blue Chip Black*.

24 Orser, *Blockbusting in Baltimore*, 5.

25 Attitudes and violence: Sugrue, *Origins of the Urban Crisis*; Rieder, *Canarsie*. School districts: Gotham, *Race, Real Estate and Uneven Development*; Gotham, "Beyond Invasion and Succession"; Rieder, *Canarsie*.

26 Thomas C. Schelling, "Dynamic Models of Segregation," *Journal of Mathematical Sociology* 1 (1971): 143–186; David Card, Alexandre Mas, and Jesse Rothstein, "Tipping and the Dynamics of Segregation," *Quarterly Journal of Economics* 123, no. 1 (February 2008): 177–218.

27 Gregory, *Black Corona*, 63.

28 Rieder, *Canarsie*, 79–91.

29 By this definition, the opposite of blockbusting (a transition from white to Black) is gentrification (a transition from Black to white). While gentrification can occur in non-Black neighborhoods as well, the definition clearly has a racial component, such that wealthier Blacks moving into poorer Black neighborhoods is not described as gentrification by residents or observers, nor is the appreciation of home values in a white suburban neighborhood that results in wealthier home buyers moving in. For a taste of the racial requirements of gentrification, see Lance Freeman, *There Goes the 'Hood: Views of Gentrification from the Ground Up* (Philadelphia: Temple University Press, 2007).

30 Seligman, *Block by Block*, 153.

31 Gregory, *Black Corona*, 62–63.

32 Young recalled that when they moved to Baltimore the team was owned by the Millers. The Black players were instructed to tell anyone in authority that "you're John Miller's niggers." Young explained, "That was very humiliating. You had to say . . . say to the cop. I made this illegal turn downtown by the bank because I was trying to get home by the time I had to pick up the oldest boy from second grade, and this cop stopped me, and of course [said] 'What the hell are you doing wrong blah blah blah.' Talking so nasty. When I said that about the Millers, [the cop said] 'Oh, honey why didn't you say that in the first place? Do you want an escort so you can get your little boy on time?' And I just thought, how insane. And how belittling: all of a sudden I become a different individual simply because of my employer—my husband's employer." Regarding the use of the word "nigger," Young recalled, "Of course that word was used at parties, at the house after the few home games . . . and these judges, lawyers, everybody [would say] 'Buddy, what was that nigger's name that worked for UCLA?' and oh, that's all you heard, it was very natural for them to refer to people like that. Although our neighbors who used to bring me fish and wild game never used those terms."

33 On norms: Rose Helper, *Racial Policies and Practices of Real Estate Brokers* (Minneapolis: University of Minnesota Press, 1969). On NAREB policy: Marylee C. Taylor, "Social Contextual Strategies for Reducing Racial Discrimination," in *Reducing Prejudice and Discrimination*, ed. Stuart Oskamp (New York: Psychology Press, 2013), 72.

34 Orser, *Blockbusting in Baltimore*, 91.

35 For detailed accounts of broker manipulation, price inflation, and the courts' complicity, see Beryl Satter's *Family Properties: Race, Real Estate, and the Exploitation of Black Urban America* (New York: Metropolitan Books, 2009).

36 Christopher Niedt, "The Politics of Prosperity and Crisis in an Industrial Suburb: Dundalk, Maryland, 1920–2005" (PhD diss., University of California, Berkeley, 2007), chap. 6. Niedt cites Paul Jarlow, "Liberty Road Area," *Sun*, August 15, 1971, in Envelope: Housing—Baltimore County, Maryland Room Vertical File of the Enoch Pratt Free Library; "Ban on Real Estate Pressure," *Evening Sun*, April 26, 1967; Douglas Connah, "Blockbusting in Baltimore," *Sun*, January 26, 1969; Ray Gill, "Housing Bill Will Bar," *News-American*, February 3, 1969; "Suburban Serenity Fading," *Evening Sun*, April 28, 1969; "FBI Blockbusting Inquiry," *Towson Times*, March 6, 1969.

37 Seligman, *Block by Block*, 150; Rieder, *Canarsie*, 169.

38 Wiese, *Places of Their Own*; Nicolaides and Wiese, *Suburb Reader*; Kruse and Sugrue, *New Suburban History*; Sugrue, *Origins of the Urban Crisis*; Gotham, "Beyond Invasion and Succession."

39 Louis S. Diggs, *From the Meadows to the Point: The Histories of the African American Community of Turner Station and What Was the African American Community in Sparrows Point* (Baltimore, 2003); Kimberly R. Abe, "Mapping a Paradox:

The African American Cultural Landscape in Antebellum Baltimore County Maryland" (master's thesis, Goucher College, 2005). Diggs's collection of archival documents, photos, and video and audio interviews of thousands of residents—many of them born at the turn of the past century—of small, historic, once-rural African American communities in Baltimore is a peerless resource and a national treasure. At present the archive has no institutional home, and I urge readers to consider the value to any library with which they are familiar to offer Mr. Diggs an archival institutional home that can share his resources.

40 The participants and organizers of the Baltimore '68 conference (University of Baltimore, April 3–4, 2008) have produced invaluable resources about Baltimore. See also Robert Gioielli, "Remaking the City: Urban Renewal in Baltimore" (paper, Baltimore '68: Riots and Rebirth, University of Baltimore, April 2008); Hayward Farrar, "Our Way or the Highway!!: How Baltimore's Botched Expressway Planning Blighted the City" (paper, Baltimore '68: Riots and Rebirth, University of Baltimore, April 2008).

41 Orser, *Blockbusting in Baltimore*, 4–5.

42 Dmitri Mehlhorn, "A Requiem for Blockbusting," *Fordham Law Review* 67, no. 3 (1998): 1153.

43 See also Susan Spiegel Glassberg, "Legal Control of Blockbusting," *Urban Law Annual* 1972 (1972): 145–179.

44 "Confessions of a Blockbuster," *Metropolitan Real Estate Journal*, May 1987, 14.

45 Raymond repeated as true Vitchek's claims that blockbusters hired Blacks to act disruptively in white neighborhoods, though she found in her own research that "although there is, from time to time, rumor of panic-peddling in southeast Oak Park, no documentation has yet been provided." Roberta Raymond, "The Challenge to Oak Park: A Suburban Community Faces Racial Change" (master's thesis, Roosevelt University, January 1972), 80. In the days before the Internet, finding the original article was challenging, especially when the publication date wasn't provided, so many researchers had little choice but to cite it secondhand.

46 In his discussion of Vitchek, Rothstein cites Colby.

47 Vitchek is also cited in Talcott Parsons and Kenneth Bancroft Clark, *The Negro American* (Boston: Beacon, 1969) and in Arnold Hirsch, *Making the Second Ghetto: Race and Housing in Chicago, 1940–1960* (Chicago: University of Chicago Press, 1998).

48 Cited in Wiese, *Places of Their Own*, 245, who found it in Baxandall and Ewen, *Picture Windows*, 80, who found it in Lawrence Harmon and Hillel Levine, *The Death of an American Jewish Community: A Tragedy of Good Intentions* (New York: Free Press, 1992), 195–196, who cite Anonymous, "Confessions of a Blockbuster," *Metropolitan Real Estate Journal*, May 1987, 14.

49 Personal communication to the author from Hillel Levine (after checking with Lawrence Harmon), October 5, 2013. According to Roger Draper, the second "Confessions" was an anonymous letter to the editor, not even an actual article. Roger Draper, "The Death of an American Jewish Community: A Tragedy of Good Intentions," *New Leader*, December 30, 1991.

50 Seligman, *Block by Block*, 152.

51 Mark Satter's son David later wrote a piece that sought to defend his father and gave the landlord the pseudonym "Norris" too. Satter, *Family Properties*, 223.

52 Seligman, *Block by Block*, 228 n13.

53 The quotes are of an email from Beryl Satter to the author, March 3, 2011.

54 Norris Vitchek (pseudonym) as told to Alfred Balk, "Confessions of a Block-Buster," *Saturday Evening Post*, July 14–21, 1962.

55 Satter, *Family Properties*, 73nn29–30.

56 See Bern interview in Satter, *Family Properties*, 75n37.

57 Seligman points out that letters to the *Garfieldian* generally opposed integration, but that there were some letter writers who supported integration. *Block by Block*, 1–2.

58 "'I Wrote Post Article, but I'm No Blockbuster,' Declares Satter," *Garfieldian*, August 1, 1962, courtesy of Beryl Satter. Seligman says locals considered the *Garfieldian* conservative. Amanda Irene Seligman, "With Apologies to Dracula, Werewolf, Frankenstein: White Homeowners and Blockbusters in Postwar Chicago," *Journal of the Illinois State Historical Society* 94, no. 1 (Spring 2001): 70–95.

59 Orser, *Blockbusting in Baltimore*, 136.

60 James Dilts, "Landlord's Lament: Don't Blame Goldseker," *Baltimore Sun*, March 9, 1971, quoted in Orser, *Blockbusting in Baltimore*, 136.

61 Helper, *Racial Policies and Practices*.

62 Raymond, "Challenge to Oak Park."

63 Helper, *Racial Policies and Practices*, 69, emphasis added.

64 Arsonists' methods were not obscure trade secrets, given the rash of arsons and their publicity in New York in the 1970s. See Joe Flood, *The Fires: How a Computer Formula Burned Down New York City—and Determined the Future of American Cities* (New York: Riverhead Books, 2011).

65 Helper, *Racial Policies and Practices*, 128.

66 Helper, *Racial Policies and Practices*, 128.

67 Helper, *Racial Policies and Practices*, 163.

68 Most opposed integration: Helper, *Racial Policies and Practices*, 130.

69 Helper, *Racial Policies and Practices*, 75.

70 Orser, *Blockbusting in Baltimore*, 90.

71 Seligman, *Block by Block* (153) suggested that Realtors (members of the National Association of Realtors) did not act as blockbusters because of the rules of their organization. From Crockett's account, Maryland Realtors were blockbusters. The Real Estate Board of Maryland (today the Maryland Association of Realtors) admitted its first African American member in 1960; Crockett joined in 1961 but did not gain access to the valuable multiple listings until 1963 or 1964 (interview with James Crockett, April 3, 2008).

72 When asked who benefited from selling across the color line, Crocket said, "Everybody except the homeowner." White homeowners sold their existing house, and the white realtor sold them a newer, more expensive house, a step up, farther out in the suburbs.

73 Gotham, "Beyond Invasion and Succession," 99.

74 Seligman, *Block by Block*, 136.

75 Quoted in Jason Policastro, "New Book on Segregation and Bigotry Holds Up a Harsh Mirror to Baltimore," *Baltimore Brew*, February 24, 2010, emphasis added.

76 Gotham, "Beyond Invasion and Succession," 94.

77 New York City Commission on Human Rights, "Blockbusting: A Report on an Unethical Practice" (1963).

78 New York City Commission on Human Rights, "Blockbusting."

79 Pietila, *Not in My Neighborhood*, 2010.

80 Satter, *Family Properties*.

81 Gotham, "Beyond Invasion and Succession," 106, emphasis added.

82 Mickey Lauria, "A New Model of Neighborhood Change: Reconsidering the Role of White Flight," *Housing Policy Debate* 9, no. 2 (1998): 395–424.

83 Robert H. Thomas, "Black Suburbanization and Housing Quality in Atlanta," *Journal of Urban Affairs* 6, no. 1 (1984): 17–27.

84 Obtaining better housing, not integration, has been the goal of African American moves to white neighborhoods for at least one hundred years. See George McMechen's 1910 explanation for moving (Power, "Apartheid Baltimore Style"; also see "Baltimore Tries Drastic Plan of Race Segregation; Strange Situation Which Led the Oriole City to Adopt the Most Pronounced 'Jim Crow' Measure on Record: Baltimore Tries Drastic Plan of Race Segregation," *New York Times*, December 25, 1910, magazine section SM2).

85 Douglas Massey and Nancy Denton, *American Apartheid: Segregation and the Making of the Underclass* (Cambridge, MA: Harvard University Press, 1993), 1.

86 W. E. B. Du Bois, *The Souls of Black Folk* (1903; repr., New York: Oxford University Press, 2007); John R. Logan and Harvey L. Molotch, *Urban Fortunes: The Political Economy of Place* (Berkeley: University of California Press, 1987).

87 And a problem that Moynihan imagined as a perversion of gender roles, no less: "A fundamental fact of Negro American family life is the often reversed roles of husband and wife." Daniel P. Moynihan, "The Negro Family: The Case for National Action" (Washington, DC: U.S. Department of Labor, 1965).

2. BUILDING A BLACK COMMUNITY

1 Friends of the Ellicott City Colored School Restored, "About the Ellicott City Colored School" (2008), www.ellicottcitycoloredschool.net.

2 In arguing that suburbanization should not be reduced to mechanistic processes, I appreciate Isabel Wilkerson's masterful *The Warmth of Other Suns: The Epic Story of America's Great Migration* (New York: Random House, 2010). Her rich accounts identify motives and opportunities among African Americans in the Great Migration (not the boll weevil or mechanized harvests). "People coming out of slums" comes from a history of neighborhood change in New York: Battery Park City Authority, "Master Plan" (2004), www.batteryparkcity.org.

3 The oral history of Lillian Rogers Dorsey and other members of her family, as well as other African Americans in historic Randallstown African American communities, is found in Louis S. Diggs, *Surviving in America: Histories of 7 Black Communities in Baltimore County Maryland* (Baltimore: Uptown Press, 2002).

4 Diggs, *Surviving in America*, 31.

5 Diggs, *Surviving in America*, 14–15.

6 Union Bethel AME Church, "Our Heritage" (2021), https://unionbethelamec.org.

7 Diggs, *Surviving in America*, 20. Diggs writes that church records show a donation from "W. Ashbee Hawkines."

8 Lenwood Johnson, introduction to Diggs, *From the Meadows to the Point*, 5.

9 Diggs, *From the Meadows to the Point*, 5.

10 Robert W. Lake and Susan Caris Cutter, "A Typology of Black Suburbanization in New Jersey since 1970," *Geographical Review* 70, no. 2 (April 1980): 167–181; Wiese, *Places of Their Own*, 244.

11 Pietila, *Not in My Neighborhood*, 211–237.

12 Pietila, *Not in My Neighborhood*, referencing the *Evening Sun*, September 19, 1972. Anderson canceled the order a month and a half later.

13 Johnson points out there was already a chapter in the historically Black industrial suburb of Turner Station, on the other side of the county. Johnson sought a chapter that would address issues in the rest of the county.

14 An account of the developer, Henry Knott, is supplied by James Crockett, interview, March 17, 2008. Former Social Security assistant commissioner Jack S. Futterman concurred that developers with large tracts of land, eager to profit from the ancillary development, were eager to "give it away for nothing, or give it to us for a very low price." According to John Michener, former Social Security administrator, at the time the headquarters were consolidated, the federal government required all agencies to locate in the suburbs to reduce their vulnerability to Soviet nuclear strikes against urban centers.

15 The developer James Rouse observed the significance of Social Security's move from Baltimore City in a speech in 1957, long before the hazards of suburbanization were well understood: "Baltimore will soon have a new million square foot Social Security Building on the far outlying edge of the City, poorly located with respect to highways and transportation lines and of doubtful convenience to the clerical force which it will employ. Its new State Office Building is now under construction nine blocks from downtown. Think what these two buildings might have meant as a logical and obvious core to a new central city plan." Speech to the National Retail Dry Goods Association, Statler Hotel, New York, January 8, 1957, Panel on Reversing the Down Trend of "Downtown," James Rouse Archives, Columbia, MD, series v.1, folder 11 "Speeches.").

16 James Loewen, *Lies My Teacher Told Me* (New York: New Press, 1995), which also describes President Woodrow Wilson's role in taking those posts from African Americans.

17 Memo to Elisabeth Mulholland from Lou Zawatsky (n.d., ca. 1968), from the collection of John Michener, in possession of the author.

18 "Fair Housing and the Social Security Administration," enclosure 3 (December 16, 1968), Michener collection.

19 The account of the multiple listing service comes from my interview with Michener.

20 Michener's account of getting rides to activist meetings in official government vehicles is also told in Antero Pietila's *Not in My Neighborhood*. I am indebted to Pietila for introducing me to Michener.

21 Memo from Howard Nickelson to John Michener (1968–1969).

22 Memo from Howard Nickelson to John Michener (1968–1969), emphasis original.

23 Letter from John Michener, October 10, 2011.

24 At the time although there were many Black employees, the leadership and policy office remained all white.

25 Hawkins, "Year of Segregation in Baltimore," 27.

26 Robert Gioielli, "'We Must Destroy You to Save You': Highway Construction and the City as a Modern Commons," *Radical History Review* 109 (Winter 2011): 62–82. Gioielli cites James Dilts, "Spreading or Ending Slums? Poor Shoved Out to Make Room for Rich, Foes Charge," *Baltimore Sun*, April 24, 1966. My thanks to Gioielli for directing me to the original report, Baltimore Urban Renewal and Housing Agency, "Displacement and Relocation, Past and Future" (March 1965).

27 Pietila, *Not in My Neighborhood*, 219.

28 Gans, *Levittowners*.

29 Orser, *Blockbusting in Baltimore*.

30 Satter, *Family Properties*.

31 "Fair Housing—A Job Not Done 56 Years Later," *Baltimore Sun*, May 27, 2015.

32 Peter Marx, *Jim Rouse: Capitalist/Idealist* (Lanham, MD: University Press of America, 2007).

33 "We thought it would be fun to try another 'excursion trip' for the company outing this year." James W. Rouse, "Internal Memorandum, Re: Company Outing," May 11, 1959, James Rouse Archives, Columbia, MD, box 404, folder JWR Co. Outing to Harper's Ferry 1959.

34 Joseph Rocco Mitchell and David L. Stebenne, *New City Upon a Hill: A History of Columbia, Maryland* (London: History Press, 2007), 35.

35 Letter to R. Steward Rauch from W. A. Clarke of MBA, March 29, 1954, James W. Rouse Collection of the Columbia Archives, record group 1, series 2, box 38, folder: "Committee on Financing Minority Housing, January—July 1954."

36 James Rouse, "Committee on Financing Minority Housing, James Rouse, Chairman" (handwritten address on legal paper, September 26, 1954), Rouse Collection.

37 Letter to Frank J. McCabe Jr. from Dean Richmond Hill, July 2, 1954, Rouse Collection.

38 Interview with Malcolm Sherman, January 2009, re: survey, Rouse Collection.

39 Letter to the Mortgage Bankers Association of America from C. William Fleming Co., July 7, 1954, Rouse Collection.

40 Letter from Miles Colean to James Rouse, March 31, 1954, Rouse Collection. Letter from W. A. Clarke (MBA) to Reginald A. Johnson (National Urban League), February 8, 1954, Rouse Collection. Clarke wrote that "our Mortgage Bankers Association committee on this subject is now almost formed." Letters inviting members to join Rouse's committee went out seven weeks later.

41 Letter to James Rouse from Jane C. Reinheimer, Philadelphia Housing Opportunities Program, June 1954, Rouse Collection.

42 Miles L. Colean, "Comment on the Anti-Segregation Decision," Memo to Members of the Committee on Financing Minority Housing, May 27, 1954, Rouse Collection.

43 Citizens Planning and Housing Association, "Special Report—Home Mortgage Monitoring," (n.d. ca. June 1974), Rouse Collection. Rouse made loans for average suburban homes: the average Rouse VA/FHA loan in the county was for $24,053 in 1974, and the average value of a vacant home for sale (typically a new home in the county) in 1970 was $24,977. US Census Bureau, "Housing Tenure, Value and Cost 1970" (2012), http://socialexplorer.com.

44 Kimbriell Kelly, "Costly Choices," *Chicago Reporter*, September 26, 2007.

45 In his interview with me, Ross said the other source for mortgages for African Americans at the time was Baltimore Federal Savings and Loan.

46 Nicholas Dagen Bloom, *Merchant of Illusion: James Rouse, America's Salesman of the Businessman's Utopia* (Columbus: Ohio State University Press, 2004).

47 Pietila, *Not in My Neighborhood*.

48 Rieder, *Canarsie*.

49 Massey and Denton, *American Apartheid*.

50 Pietila, *Not in My Neighborhood*, 15.

51 Pietila, *Not in My Neighborhood*.

52 Text of speech by Antero Pietila to the Baltimore City Historical Society, May 9, 2008, in possession of the author.

53 The Census Bureau is prohibited from collecting religious information about Americans. For this discussion, I follow Stephen Steinberg's practice of using census identification as "Russian" as a substitute for "Jewish." See Steinberg, *Ethnic Myth: Race, Ethnicity, and Class in America* (Boston: Beacon, 1989).

54 In 2000 the Census Bureau found over ten thousand Russian speakers in the Baltimore area. Kelly Brewington, "'I Feel Myself at Home Here': The Region's Thousands of Russian Immigrants Are Thriving," *Baltimore Sun*, August 23, 2005.

55 Diggs, *From the Meadows to the Point*.

56 Alana Semuels, "No, Most Black People Don't Live in Poverty—or Inner Cities," *Atlantic*, October 12, 2016.

3. DESEGREGATION

1 The two activists had known each other from years of work in the same community. They had apparently not worked together after a disagreement on an issue

in the past but, as "politicians at heart," avoided having any public disagreement, which would have seemed counterproductive.

2 An incomplete list would include Massey and Denton, *American Apartheid*; Oliver and Shapiro, *Black Wealth / White Wealth*; Rothstein, *Color of Law*; Joe R. Feagin and Melvin P. Sikes, *Living with Racism: The Black Middle-Class Experience* (Boston: Beacon, 1995).

3 Liz Atwood, "'Sold' Signs to Rise Again: Ban Was Remnant of Blockbusting Panics in 1970s: Realtors Lobby for Repeal. Baltimore's Ban Ends May 1. Balto. County Expected to Act Soon," *Baltimore Sun*, April 13, 1997. For reasons no one could explain, though the "for sale" sign ban was ruled unconstitutional as a result of Crockett's efforts, bans on "sold" signs remained on the books at least until the late 1990s.

4 Karl Taeuber and Alma Taeuber, *Negroes in Cities: Residential Segregation and Neighborhood Change* (New York: Atheneum, 1969), 106.

5 Taeuber and Taeuber, *Negroes in Cities*, 107.

6 Orser, *Blockbusting in Baltimore*; Gotham, *Race, Real Estate and Uneven Development*; Wiese, *Places of Their Own*, 216.

7 Lest the reader think that those two wildly disproportionate numbers are a typographical error, I will repeat that the ratio of white to Black was 16,000 to 31. Accounting for the 28 people listed as something other than white or Black, by that measure the five tracts were 99.996 percent white.

8 Note that the preference for new homes over older ones is contrary to urban gentrifiers' preference for "historic" houses. I would argue that aesthetics have a material dimension, since gentrifiers are financially more able to take on the greater risk (and potential payoff) of investing in an old, urban house in a transitioning neighborhood, compared to middle-class suburbanites who seek the greater financial predictability of new construction in more homogenous suburbs.

9 Orser, *Blockbusting in Baltimore*.

10 Wiese, *Places of Their Own*, 216.

11 Seligman, *Block by Block*, 213; Rachael Woldoff, "'Little Tel Aviv' No More: Elderly White Stayers and Neighborhood Racial Change" (paper, American Sociological Association, 2006).

12 Gotham, "Beyond Invasion and Succession," 90.

4. GROWTH

1 That the subway station is so far from the mall is distinctly reminiscent of the *transit racism* identified in the 1996 death of seventeen-year-old Cynthia Wiggins, killed trying to cross a highway to get from a bus stop to her job at a shopping mall that had prohibited public bus lines from making stops there. Shopping malls want transit lines to bring low-cost workers from low-income urban neighborhoods but try to make them inconvenient enough that only people affluent enough to have cars will be likely to shop there. Robert Doyle Bullard, Glenn S. Johnson, and Angel O. Torres, *Sprawl City: Race, Politics, and Planning in Atlanta*

(Washington, DC: Island Press, 2000); David W. Chen, "Suit Accusing Shopping Mall of Racism over Bus Policy Settled," *New York Times*, November 18, 1999.

2 Leticia Martin is a pseudonym.

3 Under the theory of regulation, liquor licenses are used to control an industry with the potential for social harm. Under the revenue theory, they are regulated to generate license and tax revenue for the government. On theories of liquor control, see Malcolm M. Gaynor, "Indirect Control of Organized Crime through Liquor License Procedure," *Journal of Criminal Law, Criminology and Police Science* 49 (1958): 65.

4 Richard L. Block and Carolyn Rebecca Block, "Space, Place and Crime: Hot Spot Areas and Hot Places of Liquor-Related Crime," *Crime Prevention Studies* 4, no. 7 (1995): 151, 145–183.

5 Urbana, Illinois, is one example. Kevin Dollear, "Second Liquor Licensing Restriction Ordinance to Come to a Vote," *Daily Illini*, June 16, 2011.

6 Paul Czapkowicz, "Chicago Heights Reduces Number of Liquor Licenses," *Times of Northwest Indiana*, June 22, 2011.

7 Sharon Zukin, *Point of Purchase: How Shopping Changed American Culture* (New York: Routledge, 2004), 64.

8 Walmart is the world's largest corporation in terms of sales, if not market valuation. Dan Burrows, "Planet Walmart: Five Big Facts about the World's Largest Company," *Daily Finance*, October 13, 2010.

9 *The Messenger* (Kings Park Association newsletter), July 2010.

10 Josh Kellermann and Stephanie Luce, "The Walmartization of New York" (ALIGN: The Alliance for a Greater New York, September 21, 2011). On precarious work: Arne L. Kalleberg, "Precarious Work, Insecure Workers: Employment Relations in Transition," *American Sociological Review* 74 (February 2009): 1–22.

11 For a compelling account of battles with Walmart in an urban setting (and the role of race in the urban as opposed to suburban case), see Dorian Warren, "Walmart Surrounded Community Alliances and Labor Politics in Chicago," *New Labor Forum* 14, no. 3 (Fall 2005): 16–23.

12 Kenneth N. Oliver, "Reports on Community News & Views," Fall 2011.

13 "Assembly Passes Bill Affecting Only Walmart," *Washington Post*, April 10, 2005, C05.

14 "A Big Box of Hope on Liberty Road," *Baltimore Sun*, February 16, 2011; "Say Bye-Bye to One Tough Year," *Community Times*, December 27, 2001.

15 "Another Walmart Bill," *Baltimore Sun*, May 4, 2010.

16 Cindy Mumby, "Whither Walmart? Retailer Reactivates Traffic Study on Possible Bel Air Store, Local Residents Plan to Fight," *The Dagger*, May 7, 2012; Cindy Mumby, "Walmart Schedules Community Meeting; Plans to Build Bel Air Store May Be Moving Ahead," *The Dagger*, July 1, 2012.

17 Larry Perlu, "No Love for Walmart after Developer's Presentation: Public Meeting Being Arranged with Representatives of Big Box Chain," *Baltimore Messenger*, March 25, 2010.

18 Janet Metzner, "Gifts for Randallstown: Library Renovations, New Walmart, Hundreds of New Jobs," *Pikesville Patch*, February 11, 2011.

19 Susan C. Ingram, "Liberty Road Biz Group Hears Corridor Update," *Carroll County Times*, March 23, 2010.

20 "Another Walmart Bill," *Baltimore Sun*, May 4, 2010.

21 Among many others, see Warren, "Walmart Surrounded Community Alliances."

22 Michael Dresser, "State Unveils Bus Route Changes Less Sweeping Than Prior Proposal," *Baltimore Sun*, July 29, 2005.

23 Maryland Department of Transportation, "Greater Baltimore Bus Initiative & Public Hearings for Proposed Bus Service Changes" (May 2005), brochure in possession of the author.

24 Robin Liggett, Anastasia Loukaitou-Sideris, and Hiroyukl Iseki, "Journeys to Crime: Assessing the Effects of a Light Rail Line on Crime in the Neighborhoods," *Journal of Public Transportation* 6, no. 3 (2003): 85–115.

25 Here residents are adopting the "decent" attitude toward "street" behavior identified by Elijah Anderson in *Code of the Street: Decency, Violence, and the Moral Life of the Inner City* (New York: Norton, 1999).

26 As a city dweller who has lived with bus lines on my street, I understand that one purpose of buses is to increase serenity by reducing car traffic. African American residents never explicitly assigned a race to the poor people without cars who were expected to ride buses out from the city and commit crimes. But the stereotype so neatly matched the racialized images of crime used by whites in opposition to mass transit that it is hard to imagine that there was a separate American stereotype that associated "urban" with "criminal" without reference to African Americans.

27 Virginia Terhune, "But Some Routes Will Be Added, Ended or Changed," *Owings Mills Times*, August 4, 2005.

28 Wolfson objected to this logic: "But I say that if we had waited for everyone to agree, we wouldn't have had a civil rights bill!"

5. BARRIERS

1 Henri Lefebvre, "The Right to the City," in *Writings on Cities*, trans. Eleonore Kofman and Elizabeth Lebas (New York: Blackwell, 1996), 147–159.

2 Don Mitchell, *The Right to the City: Social Justice and the Fight for Public Space* (New York: Guilford, 2003), 220.

3 The right to public space and the right to the city were taken for granted by a growing number of the gentrifying upper middle class moving into cities, who had been effectively pacified by cappuccino, to turn Sharon Zukin's apt phrase. Zukin, *The Cultures of Cities* (New York: Blackwell, 1996), 28.

4 David Harvey, "The Right to the City," *New Left Review* 53 (September–October 2008. Also in Harvey, *Rebel Cities: From the Right to the City to the Urban Revolution* (New York: Verso, 2012), 3–27.

5 Gareth Millington, *"Race," Culture and the Right to the City* (London: Palgrave Macmillan, 2011), 10–11.

6 On the right to the city, see Mark Purcell, "Citizenship and the Right to the Global City: Reimagining the Capitalist World Order," *International Journal of Urban and Regional Research* 27, no. 3 (September 2003), cited in Anna Plyushteva, "The Right to the City and the Struggles over Public Citizenship: Exploring the Links" (Urban Reinventors Paper Series, 2005–2009).

7 Harvey, "Right to the City."

8 Purcell, "Citizenship and the Right to the Global City," 565.

9 Alex Haley, *Autobiography of Malcolm X* (1964; repr., New York: Ballantine, 1973), 419.

10 Eduardo Bonilla-Silva, *Racism without Racists: Color-Blind Racism and the Persistence of Racial Inequality in the United States* (Lanham, MD: Rowman & Littlefield, 2003).

11 Massey and Denton, *American Apartheid*, 33.

12 Massey and Denton, *American Apartheid*, 90.

13 Massey and Denton, *American Apartheid*, 90–91.

14 Massey and Denton, *American Apartheid*.

15 Massey and Denton, *American Apartheid*, 225, emphasis original.

16 Neal A. Brooks and Eric G. Rockel, *A History of Baltimore County* (Towson, MD: Friends of the Towson Library, 1979). See also Abe, "Mapping a Paradox."

17 As historian Louis Diggs points out, whereas farther south the Baptist church has played a larger role in Black communities, African Methodist Episcopal (AME) churches have been far more common in Baltimore County. The fact that the AME church was founded in nearby Philadelphia may provide part of the explanation for the denomination's predominance over Baptist churches in the area.

18 Diggs, *From the Meadows to the Point*.

19 "Comments of Eastern Shore Newspapers on Lynching," *Baltimore Sun*, December 6, 1931, Maryland State Archives. See also a biography of George Armwood by the Maryland State Historical Society.

20 David Halle, Robert Gedeon, and Andrew A. Beveridge, "Residential Separation and Segregation, Racial and Latino Identity, and the Racial Composition of Each City," in *New York and Los Angeles: Politics, Society, and Culture—A Comparative View*, ed. David Halle (Chicago: University of Chicago Press, 2003), 170.

21 Despite the Dickensian name, the Orphans' Court exists today in Baltimore County, dealing with estates and guardianship involving minors.

22 Lawrence Jackson, "Slickheads," *n+1*, no. 15 (Winter 2013).

23 Lorraine Mirabella, "50 Years Later, Desegregation of Gwynn Oak Amusement Park Celebrated Former Protesters, and Child Who Broke Color Barrier by Riding Merry-Go-Round, Return," *Baltimore Sun*, July 7, 2013.

24 Darius James, *Negrophobia: An Urban Parable* (New York: St. Martin's, 1993).

25 *Zelig* is a 1983 film in which the main character unintentionally adopts characteristics of people around him.

26 Benjamin Heim Shepard and Gregory Smithsimon, *The Beach Beneath the Streets: Contesting New York City's Public Spaces* (New York: State University of New York Press, 2011).

6. FORECLOSURE

1 For the 1970–2010 census data I owe a great debt to the Longitudinal Tract Database compiled by John Logan and others as part of Brown University's initiative in Spatial Structures in Social Sciences: John R. Logan, Zengwang Xu, and Brian Stults, "Interpolating US Decennial Census Tract Data from as Early as 1970 to 2010: A Longitudinal Tract Database," *Professional Geographer* 66, no. 3 (2014): 412–420.

2 To resolve confusion: Belair Road (one word) leads to the area of Bel Air (two words). I discuss Belair Road in this chapter. It is often pronounced closer to "Blair" by locals.

3 Baltimore County planners quietly take pride in the Urban-Rural Demarcation Line (URDL), which was one of the first municipal efforts to constrain sprawl. By restricting access to county water and sewage lines to land within the URDL, large-scale development farther out in the county is prevented. Even its partisans concede the system is not perfect and can encourage lower density, septic-tank-based sprawl. Others argue the URDL was built to restrain the construction of more affordable housing in the county. Niedt, "Politics of Prosperity."

4 A caution: data in 1970 were generally calculated as averages, not medians, making comparisons difficult. Averages and medians are not interchangeable in census data.

5 Piet M. A. Eichholtz and David M. Geltner, "Four Centuries of Location Value: Implications for Real Estate Capital Gain in Central Places" (paper, March 2002). The British expression "safe as houses" reflects the expectation that an investment in housing provides modest but nearly risk-free returns. Race likely plays a role in the more volatile American cycles of disinvestment, redevelopment, and gentrification. The US pattern simultaneously imperils the modest investments of Black and white homeowners alike but provides opportunities for substantial profits from the gentrifiers and developers that Logan and Molotch, *Urban Fortunes*, call active entrepreneurs and structural speculators.

6 Thomas Piketty, *Capital in the Twenty-First Century* (Cambridge, MA: Belknap, 2014).

7 Commercial real estate plays an underappreciated role in racial school funding inequities: businesses pay more in taxes and demand less in services, and are more likely to locate in white municipalities. A white school district may therefore have more tax money while residents pay lower property taxes. To the extent offices, malls, and other businesses turn away from Black communities, those areas must burden their residents, already short-changed on disposable income from lower family wealth, more expensive mortgages, and racially unequal pay

in the labor market, with higher property taxes, yet still not have equal funding for schools.

8 Elijah Anderson, *Streetwise: Race, Class, and Change in an Urban Community* (Chicago: University of Chicago Press, 1990).

9 Rachael Woldoff, *White Flight / Black Flight :The Dynamics of Racial Change in an American Neighborhood* (Ithaca, NY: Cornell University Press, 2011).

10 Susan Saegert, Desiree Fields, and Kimberly Libman, "Deflating the Dream: Radical Risk and the Neoliberalization of Homeownership," *Journal of Urban Affairs* 31, no. 3 (2009): 297–317.

11 Home price data from the National Association of Realtors and the Federal Housing Finance Agency. Compiled by JP's, "Real Estate Charts: Baltimore, Maryland" (n.d.), http://www.jparsons.net/housingbubble/baltimore.html.

12 The map shows one dot for every five households earning $40,000 or more in 2000, equivalent to $50,700 in 2010 dollars. A map of households making $75,000 or more in 2000 (equivalent to $95,000 or more in 2010 dollars) showed a virtually identical geographic distribution of dots but, of course, fewer dots. Data from US Census Bureau 2000, mapped by Tess Brustein.

13 Mapping similar data, researchers found furthermore that African American neighborhoods in the Baltimore-Washington area had higher levels of subprime loans than would be expected given economic conditions, and that white areas had lower than predicted levels of subprime lending. Elvin K. Wyly, Mona Atia, Holly Foxcroft, Daniel J. Hammel, and Kelly Phillips-Watts, "American Home: Predatory Mortgage Capital and Neighbourhood Spaces of Race and Class in the United States," *Geografiska Annaler* 88B (2006): 120–121.

14 Jacob S. Rugh and Douglas S. Massey, "Racial Segregation and the American Foreclosure Crisis," *American Sociological Review* 75, no. 5 (2010): 629–651.

15 Joyce Coleman is a pseudonym.

16 Debbie Gruenstein Bocian, "Foreclosures by Race and Ethnicity: The Demographics of a Crisis" (Center for Responsible Lending, May 20, 2011).

17 This is consistent with my findings on financial experiences of African Americans, who were more likely to experience dramatic reversals of their financial situation. Such events could be said to constitute punctuated equilibrium at a personal level.

18 The distinction between social "issues" and individual "troubles" is C. Wright Mills's. Regarding education as a solution to individualized social problems, one observer has written that "to the extent that [a financial education program] mystifies and depoliticizes the social relations of production and the capitalist economy by individualizing socially-related risk (and treating it as a technical rather than political problem), [such education] aids in disempowering the citizens, delegitimizes collective risk solutions and unjustly holds the individual consumers responsible for economic risks they cannot manage." Christopher Arthur, "Financial Literacy: Neoliberalism, the Consumer and the Citizen" (master's thesis, University of Toronto, 2011).

19 My interviews do not constitute a random sample. Two of the three organizations were reached through referrals from Black churches. There were also whites working on foreclosure issues, of course. But the resources directed at the foreclosure problem nationally reflect the racialization of neoliberalism, in which problems are addressed in racially unequal ways.

20 The post office residents described as notoriously corrupt was the Henry W. McGee Station, formerly the Hyde Park Station.

21 Correspondents of the *New York Times, How Race Is Lived in America: Pulling Together, Pulling Apart* (New York: Holt and Co/Times Books), 2001, 28.

22 Raghuram G. Rajan, *Fault Lines: How Hidden Fractures Still Threaten the World Economy* (Princeton, NJ: Princeton University Press, 2010).

7. CONSERVATIVE POLITICS

1 Evers Burns played professional basketball for the Sacramento Kings.

2 William Bradford Huie, "Killers' Confession," *Look*, January 1956.

3 David T. Beito and Linda Royster Beito, *Black Maverick: T. R. M. Howard's Fight for Civil Rights and Economic Power* (Champaign: University of Illinois Press, 1999), 130.

4 Marshall once responded to suggestions that he should present himself as an inspiration to Black children by saying that "Negro kids are not fools. They know when you tell them there is a possibility that someday you'll have a chance to be the *only* Negro on the Supreme Court, those odds aren't too good."

5 On Reagan as an enemy of civil rights: Bob Herbert, "Righting Reagan's Wrongs?," *New York Times*, November 13, 2007; Pedro A. Noguera and Robert Cohen, "Remembering Reagan's Record on Civil Rights and the South African Freedom Struggle," *The Nation*, February 11, 2011.

6 Adam Himmelsbach, "Standing Up at an Early Age: Views on Gay Rights of Ravens' Ayanbadejo Are Rooted in Upbringing," *New York Times*, September 14, 2012; "Burns Backs Off Bid to Silence Ravens Player," *Baltimore Sun*, September 9, 2012.

7 Himmelsbach, "Standing Up at an Early Age," 2012.

8 *The New Black* (dir. Yoruba Richen, 2013). Exit polls found 46 percent of Black Marylanders voted in favor of the gay marriage proposal, 6 percent less than the overall electorate. "African Americans and Latinos Spur Gay Marriage Revolution," *Washington Post*, November 12, 2012.

9 For instance, white evangelist Jim Wallis, founder and editor of *Sojourners Magazine* and an adviser to President Obama, describes himself as politically "progressive . . . or even radical on issues like poverty and racial justice," but conservative on gender and sexuality. Jim Wallis, "The Bible Is Neither Conservative or Liberal," *Sojourners*, June 12, 2008.

10 Bonilla-Silva, *Racism without Racists*.

11 "Politics in Baltimore: McMechen in Race for City Councilman in the Fourteenth Ward," *Indianapolis Recorder*, May 1, 1915, 1.

12 Pietila, *Not in My Neighborhood*, 228. Pietila also writes that the Republican Agnew supported early gun control legislation, automobile emission controls, and reduction of industrial pollution, all far from contemporary Republican Party priorities.

13 John Hope Franklin and Alfred A. Moss, *From Slavery to Freedom: A History of African Americans*, 7th ed. (1947; New York: McGraw-Hill, 1994), 387.

14 Phillips, *Emerging Republican Majority*, 106. Phillips's data, from the Republican National Committee 1964 Election Analysis, are measured by precinct and wards, so the votes of whites who lived in predominantly Black districts are included.

15 Kim Phillips Fein, *Invisible Hands: The Making of the Conservative Movement from the New Deal to Reagan* (New York: Norton, 2009), 143.

16 Alexander P. Lomis, *Southern Politics in the 1990s* (Baton Rouge: Louisiana State University Press, 1999), 8.

17 Matthew D. Lassiter, *The Silent Majority: Suburban Politics in the Sunbelt South* (Princeton, NJ: Princeton University Press, 2006), 274.

18 On class and party affiliation: Pew Research Center, "Wide Gender Gap, Growing Educational Divide in Voters' Party Identification: Trends in Party Affiliation among Demographic Groups" (March 20, 2018).

19 Eric D. Knowles, Brian S. Lowery, Elizabeth P. Shulman, and Rebecca L. Schaumberg, "Race, Ideology, and the Tea Party: A Longitudinal Study," *PLOS ONE* 8, no. 6 (2013); Christopher S. Parker, "2010 Multi-State Survey of Race & Politics" (Seattle: University of Washington, Institute for the Study of Ethnicity, Race, and Sexuality, 2010), https://depts.washington.edu.

20 Louis Menand, *The Metaphysical Club: A Story of Ideas in America* (New York: Farrar, Straus and Giroux, 2002).

21 Maryland State Board of Elections, "Eligible Active Voters on Precinct Register: 2012 Presidential Primary Election" (March 20, 2012).

22 Micah Cohen, "In North Carolina, Obama's 2008 Victory Was Ahead of Schedule," *FiveThirtyEight*, September 4, 2012.

23 Philip F. Rubio, *A History of Affirmative Action 1619–2000* (Jackson: University Press of Mississippi, 2001); Terry H. Anderson, *The Pursuit of Fairness: A History of Affirmative Action* (New York: Oxford University Press, 2004).

24 Dawson, *Behind the Mule*, 208–211.

25 Dawson, *Behind the Mule*, 208–211.

CONCLUSION

1 Piketty, *Capital in the Twenty-First Century*.

2 US Census Bureau, "Quarterly Residential Vacancies and Homeownership, Third Quarter 2018" (CB18-161, October 30, 2017); US Census Bureau, "Residential Vacancies and Homeownership in the Fourth Quarter 2013" (CB14-09, January 31, 2014), 9.

3 John Cassidy, "Janet Yellen: A Keynesian Woman at the Fed," *New Yorker*, April 3, 2013.

4 Ta-Nehisi Coates, *We Were Eight Years in Power: An American Tragedy* (New York: One World, 2017), 343.

5 US Census Bureau, "QuickFacts: Randallstown CDP, Maryland," www.census.gov.

6 Gregory Smithsimon, *Cause: And How It Doesn't Always Equal Effect* (New York: Melville House, 2018).

7 Low, *Behind the Gates.*

8 My thanks to a former student for information on this case: Ian Mactavish, "The Discriminatory Practice of Exclusionary Policies in the Public Parks of Garden City: Can an Old Dog Be Taught a New Trick?" (paper, April 28, 2006), collection of the author.

9 Massey and Denton, *American Apartheid.* But see also Bonilla-Silva, *Racism without Racists.*

INDEX

Page numbers in *italics* indicate Figures, Tables, and Photos

ABOUT THE AUTHOR

GREGORY SMITHSIMON is Professor of Sociology at Brooklyn College, City University of New York, and the Graduate Center of the City of New York. He is the author of *September 12: Community and Neighborhood Recovery at Ground Zero*, *The Beach Beneath the Streets: Contesting New York City's Public Spaces*, and *Cause: . . . And How It Doesn't Always Equal Effect*.

www.ingramcontent.com/pod-product-compliance
Lightning Source LLC
Chambersburg PA
CBHW032101040426
42336CB00040B/639